# 中国当代书画名家作品收藏指南（第三辑）

孟云飞 主编
封莎 翻译

中央编译出版社

# 《中国当代书画名家作品收藏指南》编辑委员会

名 誉 主 任：高占祥
名誉副主任：王 琦　沈 鹏　刘 艺
执 行 主 任：田爱生
副 主 任：吕立新　刘金富
艺 术 顾 问：廖静文　赵长青　李 铎　姚治华　米景扬　张旭光
　　　　　　邹德忠　田伯平　梅墨生　李洪海　李 涵　史希光
　　　　　　董辰生　石晓玲
编 委：张铜彦　张瑞祥　张金卫　夏国珠　顾 莹　鲁 闽
　　　　韩振刚　李家骝　吴守峰　缪法宝　荆利斌　易 如
　　　　何学斌　郭利杰　杨 军　张天文　高 菲　周佳洁
　　　　王雪玉　袁 睿　朱 清　程 宇　周 钊　阴秀芳
主 编：孟云飞
副 主 编：杨文国
摄 影：薛立强
特 约 编 辑：谷 嫚
责 任 校 对：许文瑞

# 序 言

中华民族文明的历程，于今已达数千年之久了。中国书画作为民族文化艺术的重要部分，为促进人类文明和社会进步发挥了巨大的历史作用。独特的中国书画艺术，造就了许许多多伟大的艺术巨匠，他们为我们留下了极其丰富的艺术瑰宝。

胡锦涛总书记在中国文联第八次全国代表大会、中国作协第七次全国代表大会上指出："全面建设小康社会、开创中国特色社会主义新局面的历史进程必将推动我国文艺事业全面发展繁荣，中华民族的伟大复兴必将伴随着中华文化的伟大复兴。" 建国后，尤其是改革开放30年来，社会稳定，国民经济飞速发展，党和政府对文化建设的高度重视，促使了文化艺术产业的大力发展。人民群众生活水平随着经济的发展，得到了很大的提高，收藏书画艺术作品已经成为很多人尤其是企业家、收藏家重要的文化生活内容。艺术品市场已经成为不可或缺的投资市场之一。

为了让广大书画爱好者及企业家、收藏家更好、更准确地了解把握书画艺术品市场，了解书画家的艺术风格、特点、市场认知度及收藏价值，提高书画收藏的水平，我们特邀请了全国著名书画艺术家、文化部文化艺术评估委员会的专家以及拍卖行业的专家，组织编撰了《当代中国书画名家作品收藏指南》一书，供社会广大书画艺术品投资者、企业家、收藏家参考。

# Preface

Chinese civilization has a history of thousands of years, and being an indispensible part of national culture and art, Chinese painting and calligraphy have been playing an important role in the promotion of human civilization and social progress in history. Numerous great art masters have contributed to the unique art of Chinese painting and calligraphy, leaving later generations with art treasures of extremely abundance.

President Hu Jintao, General Secretary of CPC, said in the Eighth National Congress of China Federation of Literary and Art Circles and the Seventh National Congress of the China Writers Association, "The historical process of building well-off society in an all-round way and creating a new situation in building socialism with Chinese characteristics is bound to promote the overall development and prosperity of our literature and art, and the great rejuvenation of the Chinese nation will be accompanied by the same great rejuvenation of the Chinese culture." Since the People's Republic of China was founded, especially the three decades after China's reform and opening up, China has been enjoying a long-term social stability and rapid development of national economy; meanwhile, our Party and governments have attached great importance to the cultural construction, which has vastly promoted the development of arts and culture industry. With the great improvement of people's living standard benefited from the economic development, it has become the primary culture life for people, especially for entrepreneurs and collectors, to collect calligraphy and painting works; consequently, the art market has also turned to be indispensable for investment.

With the aim of benefiting all the painting and calligraphy enthusiasts, entrepreneurs and collectors and providing with professional information on painting and calligraphy art market, the artistic style, characteristics and market awareness of the artists and the collection value of their works to ensure high-level painting and calligraphy collections, national renowned artists and experts from Arts Assessment Committee of Ministry of Culture and from the auction industry as well are invited to compile Collection Guide to Contemporary Chinese Painting and Calligraphy Works for the reference of art investors, entrepreneurs and collectors.

*Zhanxiang Gao*

|  |  |
|---|---|
| 紫荷 | 九七 |
| 张源太 | 九八 |
| 陈锡安 | 九九 |
| 李安儒 | 一〇〇 |
| 朱淑玉 | 一〇一 |
| 江太生 | 一〇二 |
| 李修举 | 一〇三 |
| 张本堂 | 一〇四 |
| 余斯清 | 一〇五 |
| 卢振先 | 一〇六 |
| 佘汉武 | 一〇七 |
| 袁康年 | 一〇八 |
| 史文青 | 一〇九 |
| 吴继海 | 一一〇 |
| 何悦丰 | 一一一 |
| 陈品睿 | 一一二 |
| 李爱民 | 一一三 |
| 张春生 | 一一四 |
| 陈书文 | 一一五 |
| 郝振新 | 一一六 |
| 陈飞云 | 一一七 |
| 李玉清 | 一一八 |
| 萧辉 | 一一九 |
| 洪国林 | 一二〇 |
| 邱天章 | 一二一 |
| 张汉 | 一二二 |
| 陈肇新 | 一二三 |
| 贺伟国 | 一二四 |
| 赵元华 | 一二五 |
| 辛德翔 | 一二六 |
| 许振华 | 一二七 |
| 刘永志 | 一二八 |
| 张建中 | 一二九 |
| 王根顺 | 一三〇 |
| 刘希舜 | 一三一 |
| 陈鸿娟 | 一三二 |
| 翟鸿藻 | 一三三 |
| 王天成 | 一三四 |
| 刘世铮 | 一三五 |
| 潘振德 | 一三六 |
| 吴庆瑞 | 一三七 |
| 王敬 | 一三八 |
| 何海生 | 一三九 |
| 杨启运 | 一四〇 |
| 张耀宗 | 一四一 |
| 谢明宗 | 一四二 |
| 赵明山 | 一四三 |
| 张明宇 | 一四四 |
| 王义 | 一四五 |
| 王烨 | 一四六 |
| 欧作兴 | 一四七 |
| 何松枝 | 一四八 |
| 韩伟 | 一四九 |
| 魏军民 | 一五〇 |
| 刘尧彬 | 一五一 |
| 段庆昌 | 一五二 |
| 孟凡荣 | 一五三 |
| 刘天鹏 | 一五四 |
| 张明康 | 一五五 |
| 杨柏林 | 一五六 |
| 张学范 | 一五七 |
| 胡甫英 | 一五八 |
| 邢顺华 | 一五九 |
| 蔡云飞 | 一六〇 |
| 郑吕荣 | 一六一 |
| 龚云江 | 一六二 |
| 江海滨 | 一六三 |
| 张昆 | 一六四 |
| 李永高 | 一六五 |
| 潘永文 | 一六六 |
| 李同军 | 一六七 |
| 叶泽洲 | 一六八 |
| 吴隆湜 | 一六九 |
| 李凤楼 | 一七〇 |
| 袁世煜 | 一七一 |
| 韩纪友 | 一七二 |
| 王仲彦 | 一七三 |
| 张玉明 | 一七四 |
| 杨恒春 | 一七五 |
| 赖建成 | 一七六 |
| 张合文 | 一七七 |
| 王乃献 | 一七八 |
| 张伯周 | 一七九 |
| 麻小五 | 一八〇 |
| 徐惠中 | 一八一 |
| 刘永林 | 一八二 |
| 吕渊明 | 一八三 |
| 赵亦兵 | 一八四 |
| 蒋光前 | 一八五 |
| 刘永林 | 一八六 |
| 张义俊 | 一八七 |
| 贺也频 | 一八八 |
| 李会妨 | 一八九 |
| 乔士华 | 一九〇 |
| 刘建新 | 一九一 |
| 罗少模 | 一九二 |
| 刘茂发 | 一九三 |
| 李焕然 | 一九四 |
| 吴长太 | 一九五 |
| 李宝春 | 一九六 |
| 彭牧童 | 一九七 |
| 韩公修 | 一九八 |
| 林桥 | 一九九 |
| 张汉杰 | 二〇〇 |
| 梁万宝 | 二〇一 |
| 杨万宝 | 二〇二 |
| 杨正温 | 二〇三 |

# 目 录

|  |  |
|---|---|
| 陈洪军 | 一 |
| 陈廷佑 | 二 |
| 赵兴发 | 三 |
| 张瑞祥 | 四 |
| 鲁 闽 | 五 |
| 陈 吉 | 六 |
| 郝志国 | 七 |
| 顾典章 | 八 |
| 荆利斌 | 九 |
| 高 菲 | 一〇 |
| 张天文 | 一一 |
| 柴振福 | 一二 |
| 赵玉林 | 一三 |
| 汤禄仕 | 一四 |
| 王德法 | 一五 |
| 赵达武 | 一六 |
| 易 如 | 一七 |
| 赵 君 | 一八 |
| 徐宝铭 | 一九 |
| 杨宪金 | 二〇 |
| 于建明 | 二一 |
| 崔永波 | 二二 |
| 彭 强 | 二三 |
| 任仲德 | 二四 |
| 田子昌 | 二五 |
| 方文士 | 二六 |
| 马福友 | 二七 |
| 刘保进 | 二八 |
| 骆 云 | 二九 |
| 李镇锐 | 三〇 |
| 王春生 | 三一 |
| 张文东 | 三二 |

|  |  |
|---|---|
| 张朝彬 | 三三 |
| 王春林 | 三四 |
| 李俊香 | 三五 |
| 贺振涛 | 三六 |
| 唐明芳 | 三七 |
| 吕 哲 | 三八 |
| 何玉超 | 三九 |
| 张文魁 | 四〇 |
| 彭 列 | 四一 |
| 邓新江 | 四二 |
| 葛凤兰 | 四三 |
| 金 鸣 | 四四 |
| 贾宝山 | 四五 |
| 崔长才 | 四六 |
| 李 玲 | 四七 |
| 刘如意 | 四八 |
| 史国霖 | 四九 |
| 谢光辉 | 五〇 |
| 王立文 | 五一 |
| 张邦文 | 五二 |
| 王勇智 | 五三 |
| 王文学 | 五四 |
| 于福岭 | 五五 |
| 于振莲 | 五六 |
| 桑吉仁谦 | 五七 |
| 周 彬 | 五八 |
| 张晓民 | 五九 |
| 涂正康 | 六〇 |
| 甄德贤 | 六一 |
| 艾创奇 | 六二 |
| 贾建国 | 六三 |
| 冯尚信 | 六四 |

|  |  |
|---|---|
| 张渤涛 | 六五 |
| 王国卿 | 六六 |
| 何学芬 | 六七 |
| 贺振涛 | 六八 |
| 唐明芳 | 六九 |
| 吕 哲 | 七〇 |
| 何玉超 | 七一 |
| 张文魁 | 七二 |
| 邓新江 | 七三 |
| 彭 列 | 七四 |
| 葛凤兰 | 七五 |
| 金 鸣 | 七六 |
| 贾宝山 | 七七 |
| 崔长才 | 七八 |
| 李 玲 | 七九 |
| 刘如意 | 八〇 |
| 史国霖 | 八一 |
| 谢光辉 | 八二 |
| 王立文 | 八三 |
| 张邦文 | 八四 |
| 王勇智 | 八五 |
| 王文学 | 八六 |
| 于福岭 | 八七 |
| 桑吉仁谦 | 八八 |
| 于振莲 | 八九 |
| 周 彬 | 九〇 |
| 张晓民 | 九一 |
| 涂正康 | 九二 |
| 甄德贤 | 九三 |
| 艾创奇 | 九四 |
| 贾建国 | 九五 |
| 冯尚信 | 九六 |

| 姓名 | 编号 |
|---|---|
| 张弓强 | 一〇二 |
| 赵汉忠 | 一〇三 |
| 沈志昂 | 一〇四 |
| 张友新 | 一〇五 |
| 马海元 | 一〇六 |
| 冯萍 | 一〇七 |
| 林坚 | 一〇八 |
| 马贵生 | 一〇九 |
| 赵润英 | 一一〇 |
| 谭连华 | 一一一 |
| 杨道顺 | 一一二 |
| 刘光政 | 一一三 |
| 朱钢 | 一一四 |
| 马秀亮 | 一一五 |
| 槐芳 | 一一六 |
| 陈志春 | 一一七 |
| 吉师 | 一一八 |
| 万若愚 | 一一九 |
| 顾建华 | 一二〇 |
| 王志刚 | 一二一 |
| 贺祖荣 | 一二二 |
| 徐如彬 | 一二三 |
| 张春水 | 一二四 |
| 罗孟基 | 一二五 |
| 叶升夫 | 一二六 |
| 尹晓彦 | 一二七 |
| 周建华 | 一二八 |
| 陈艳 | 一二九 |
| 贺勤江 | 一三〇 |
| 李羿 | 一三一 |
| 张怡 | 一三二 |
| 赵志金 | 一三三 |
| 王立民 | 一三四 |
| 佟起来 | 一三五 |
| 王绍文 | 一三六 |
| 徐声才 | 一三七 |
| 曾繁堪 | 一三八 |
| 苏望秦 | 一三九 |
| 侯培强 | 一四〇 |
| 张洪彬 | 一四一 |
| 吴广华 | 一四二 |
| 樊长金 | 一四三 |
| 张茂华 | 一四四 |
| 罗士捷　袁人秋 | 一四五 |
| 谭克成 | 一四六 |
| 张志远 | 一四七 |
| 郜士贞 | 一四八 |
| 陈秀兰 | 一四九 |
| 常厚仁 | 一五〇 |
| 刘西秦 | 一五一 |
| 王自强 | 一五二 |
| 段惠娟 | 一五三 |
| 党正 | 一五四 |
| 梁伟仪 | 一五五 |
| 唐永葆 | 一五六 |
| 陈福圣 | 一五七 |
| 万长发 | 一五八 |
| 魏习武 | 一五九 |
| 季佩芳 | 一六〇 |
| 曾光艺 | 一六一 |
| 李文志 | 一六二 |
| 韩凤山 | 一六三 |
| 刘士毅 | 一六四 |
| 钱飞龙 | 一六五 |
| 孙振山 | 一六六 |
| 于春雨 | 一六七 |
| 梁青山 | 一六八 |
| 赵锡武 | 一六九 |
| 古建雄 | 一七〇 |
| 方东霖 | 一七一 |
| 王忠民 | 一七二 |
| 谢从荣 | 一七三 |
| 蔡喜明 | 一七四 |
| 赵志祥 | 一七五 |
| 方永柏 | 一七六 |
| 梁冠英 | 一七七 |
| 裴敦安 | 一七八 |
| 孙其彬 | 一七九 |
| 王文其 | 一八〇 |
| 潘星儒 | 一八一 |
| 释宏正 | 一八二 |
| 高志水 | 一八三 |
| 江金明 | 一八四 |
| 刘桓麟 | 一八五 |
| 吕慧泉 | 一八六 |
| 肖志敏 | 一八七 |
| 谢庆会 | 一八八 |
| 安震 | 一八九 |
| 张福增 | 一九〇 |
| 任国政 | 一九一 |
| 孙法先 | 一九二 |
| 权万通 | 一九三 |
| 吴晓懿 | 一九四 |
| 刘萍 | 一九五 |
| 袁展泉 | 一九六 |
| 陶光辉 | 一九七 |
| 刘德生 | 一九八 |
| 王世元 | 一九九 |
| 苏世忠 | 三〇〇 |

# 陈洪军　　Chen Hongjun

陈洪军，1957年8月生，北京人，现任北京山水画会理事、白雪石艺术研究会副会长、北京水墨画研究会副秘书长、中国人民对外友好协会艺术创作院副秘书长。

润笔价格：50,000元/平尺

Chen Hongjun, born in August 1957, is from Beijing. He is currently the director of the Beijing Landscape Painting Association, vice president of the Snow Stone Art Research Association, deputy secretary-general of the Beijing Ink Painting Research Association and deputy secretary-general of the Art Institute of the Chinese People's Association for Friendship with Foreign Countries.
*Reference price: 50,000 yuan / square foot*

《漓江一曲千峰秀》　　96cm×178cm　　"Mountains Become Beautiful Because of a Lijiang Song"

## 陈廷佑　*Chen Tingyou*

陈廷佑，男，1954年，河北省深州人，历任国务院参事室、中央文史研究馆处长、办公室副主任、巡视员、中华书画家杂志副总编。中华诗词学会常务理事、中国书法家协会会员、中国作家协会会员。

润笔价格：8,000元/平尺

Chen Tingyou, male, born in 1954, is from Shenzhou, Hebei. He served as the director of the Central Research Institute of culture and history, deputy director of the Office, inspector, deputy editor of the Chinese painting and calligraphy magazine, executive director of the Institute of Chinese poetry, member of Chinese Calligraphers Association, and member of Chinese Writers Association.
*Reference price: 8,000 yuan / square foot*

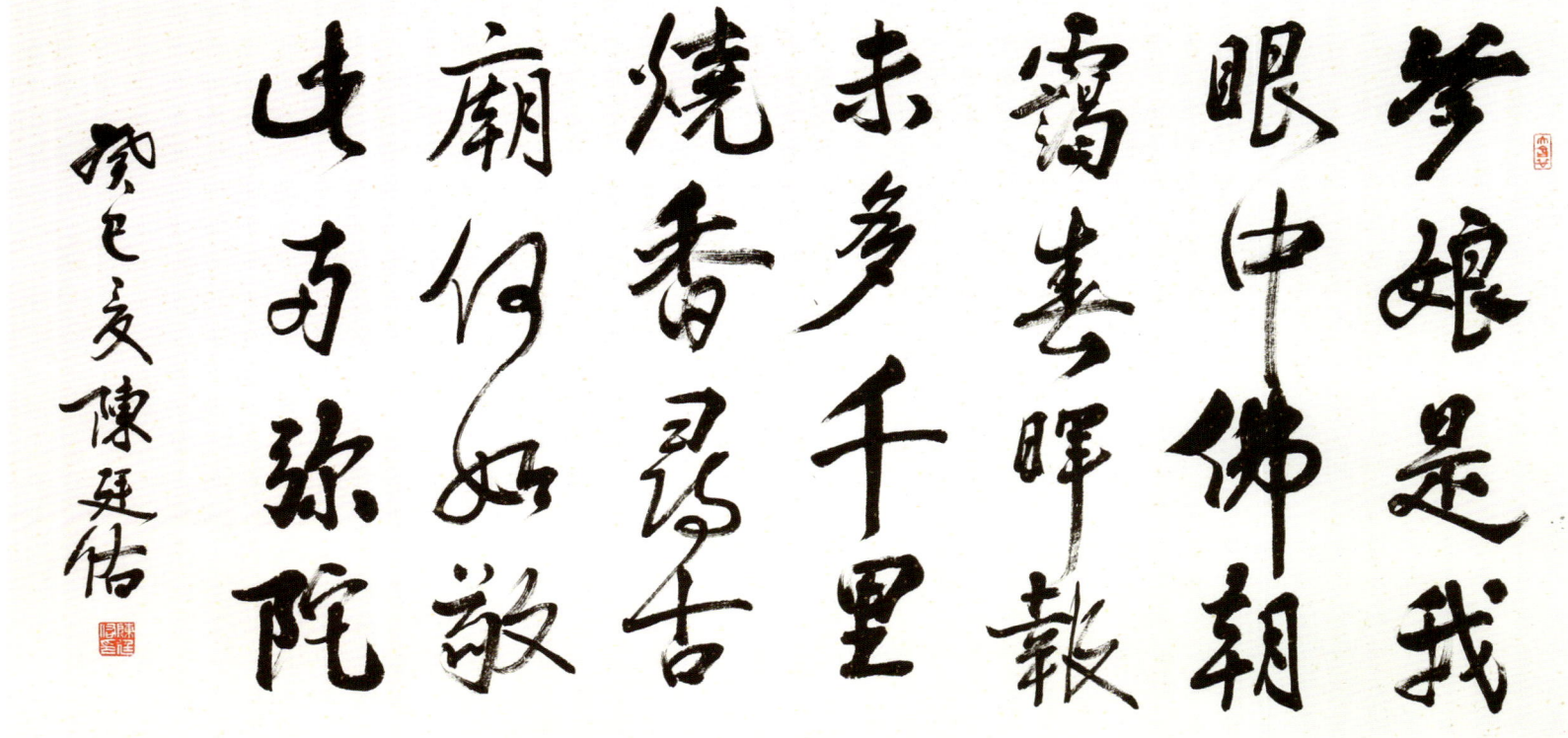

自作诗《爹娘是我眼中佛》　68cm×138cm　*"Original Poetry "Father and Mother are Buddha in My Eyes "*

# 赵兴发　*Zhao Xingfa*

赵兴发，男，1945年生，中将，曾任海军副司令员，现为第十一届全国政协委员，中国将军书画研究院名誉院长，中国美术家协会会员，中国书法家协会会员。

润笔价格：14,000元/平尺

Zhao Xingfa, male, was born in 1945. He has the title of Lieutenant, served as deputy commander of the Navy. He is currently the member of the Eleventh CPPCC National Committee, honorary president of the Chinese general painting and calligraphy Institute, member of Chinese artists Association, and member of Chinese Calligraphers Association.

*Reference price: 14,000 yuan / square foot*

《八骏雄风》　137cm×69cm　"the Power of Eight Stallions"

# 张瑞祥 *Zhang Ruixiang*

张瑞祥，字云白，1954年生于河北巨鹿。现为中共中央直属机关书画协会副主席，中共中央编译局书画协会常务副主席兼秘书长，中国人才研究会艺术家学部委员会副秘书长，中国职工书法家协会理事，北京市西城区文联理事，中国书法家协会会员。

润笔价格：16,000元/平尺

Zhang Ruixiang with a pen name as Yunbai, from Julu Heibei, was born in 1954. He is currently the vice president of Painting and Calligraphy Association directly under the CPC Central Committee, Executive vice president and Secretary-General of Painting and Calligraphy Association in The CPC Central Compilation and Translation Bureau, deputy Secretary-general of The artists Academy Committee in China Talent Research Association, director of China Calligraphers Association of workers, Director of Beijing Xicheng Federation of literary and Art Circles, and member of Chinese Calligraphers Association.

*Reference price: 16,000 yuan / square foot*

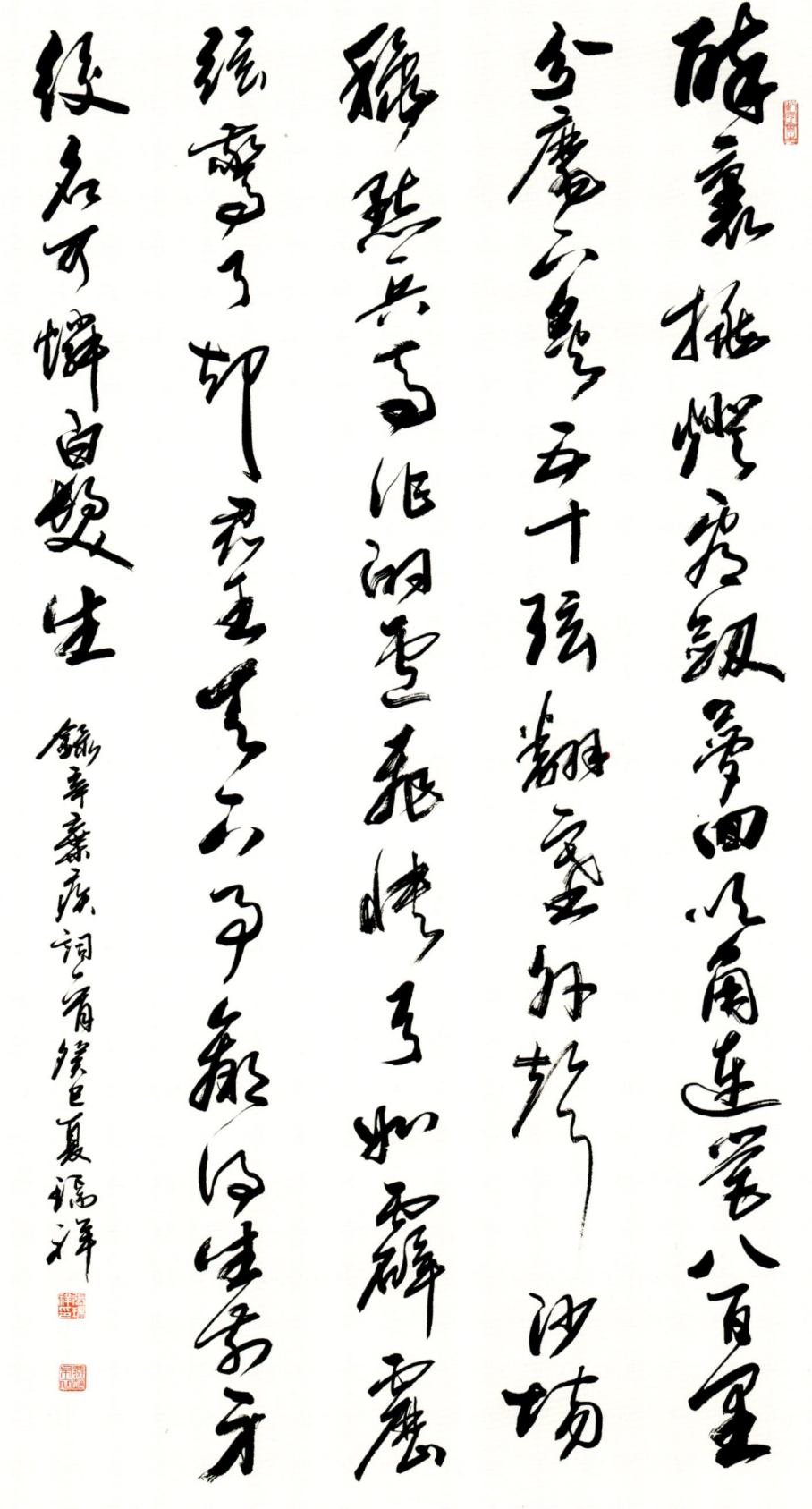

《录辛弃疾词》　　180cm×98cm　　"Collection of Xin Qiji's Poems"

# 鲁闽　　*Lu Min*

鲁闽，男，1959年10月生，祖籍山东，现为清华大学美术学院教授。
作品被美国、日本、瑞典、新加坡、韩国等国家和个人收藏。
润笔价格：16,000元/平尺

Lu Min, male, from Shandong, was born in October 1959. He is a professor in academy of fine art at Tsinghua University. His works have been kept by the United States, Japan, Sweden, Singapore, South Korea and other countries and individuals.
*Reference price: 16,000 yuan / square foot*

《观东岳山云寺海潮》　　69cm×138cm　　"View of the Tides of Cloud Temple in Dong Yue"

# 陈吉  *Chen Ji*

陈吉，1958年9月生，福建福州人，中国书法家协会会员，福建省书法家协会副主席，福建省海峡书画研究院副院长，福州市人大书画院院长，寿山印社名誉社长，第六次全国书法家代表大会代表。现任福建省文化厅副厅长。

润笔价格：8,000元/平尺

Chen Ji, from Fuzhou, was born in September 1958. He has been the member of Chinese Calligraphers Association, vice chairman of Fujian Calligrapher's Association, vice president of The painting and Calligraphy Institute of Fujian Province, vice president of Academy of painting and calligraphy in Municipal People's Congress of Fuzhou, honorary president of Shoushan Yin society, and representative of The Sixth National Calligrapher Congress. Now he is the deputy director of Fujian Provincial Department of culture.

*Reference price: 8,000 yuan / square foot*

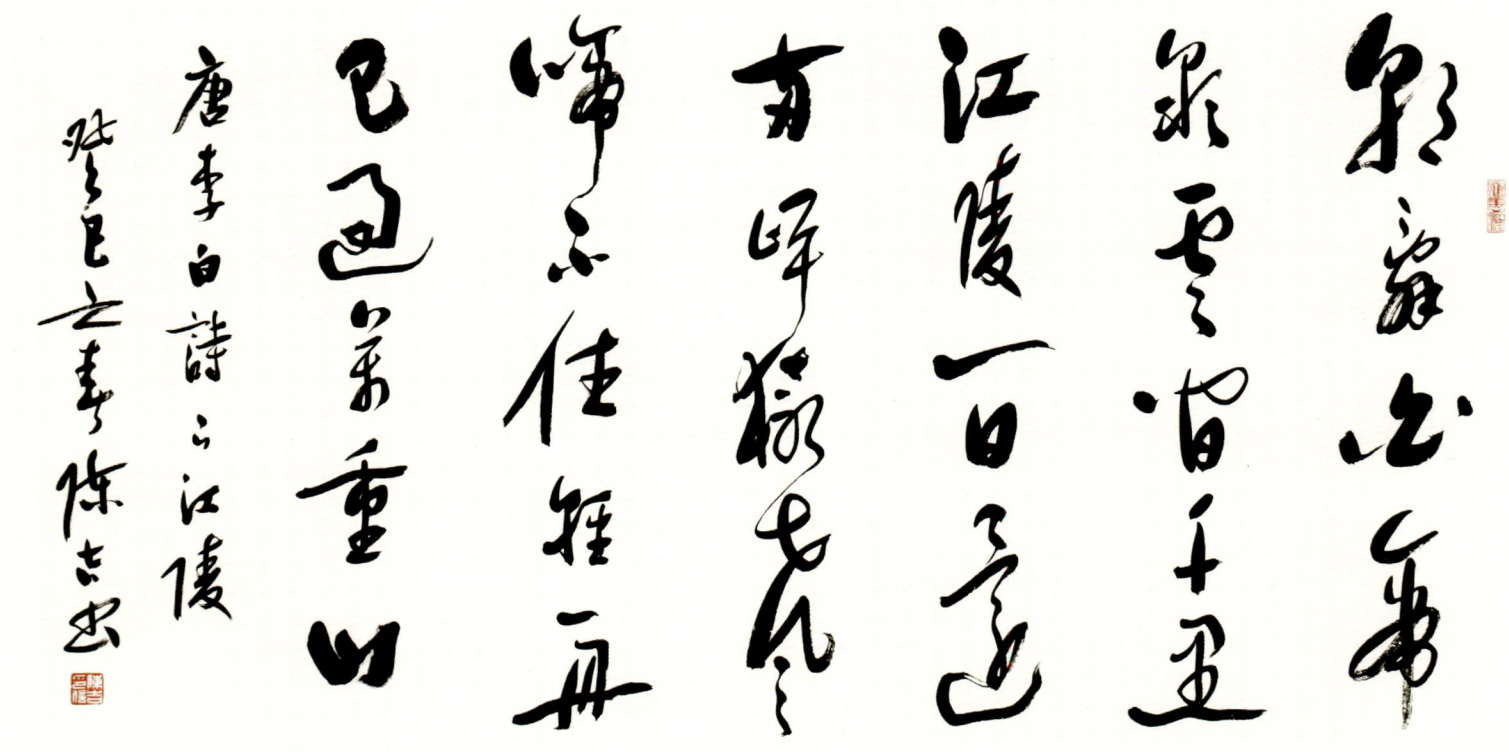

《江陵》　97cm×180cm　　"Jiang Ling"

# 郝志国 *Hao Zhiguo*

郝志国，中国美术家协会会员，中国版画家协会理事，大同大学美术教授，中国优秀版画家鲁迅奖获得者，作品参加全国及出国美术展。作品被深圳艺术馆、神州版画博物馆、青岛美术馆、宁夏博物馆、深圳博物馆等多家单位及个人收藏。

润笔价格：20,000元/平尺

Hao Zhiguo, member of Chinese artists Association, member of Chinese artists Association, professor of the fine art of Datong University, has wined the Lu Xun prize for Chinese Painters. His Works have participated in the national and overseas art exhibition and are kept by Shenzhen Art Museum, Shenzhou Museum, Qingdao Art Museum, Ningxia Museum Shenzhen Museum and a number of units and individuals.

*Reference price: 20,000 yuan / square foot*

《守望》　69cm×137cm　　"Keep Watching"

# 顾典章　*Gu Dianzhang*

顾典章，男，笔名：典璋。郡望武陵，别署武陵典璋、愚公。号怡心斋主。大学文化。任中国书画界联合会理事、副秘书长，国家一级美术师，世界东方北京书画院常务副院长，中国书法艺术研究院研究员，北京世纪名人国际书画院院士。

润笔价格：10,000元/平尺

Gu Dianzhang, male, possesses pen names as Dianzhang, Junwang Wuling, Wuling Dianzhang, Yugong and Moderator of Yixin building. He has a University degree. He is the director of Chinese painting and calligraphy circles federation and deputy secretary general, national A-level artist, Executive vice president of east of the World Beijing painting and Calligraphy Institute, researcher of The Calligraphy Art Research Institute of China and academician of Beijing century international celebrity calligraphy and painting Association.

*Reference price: 10,000 yuan / square foot*

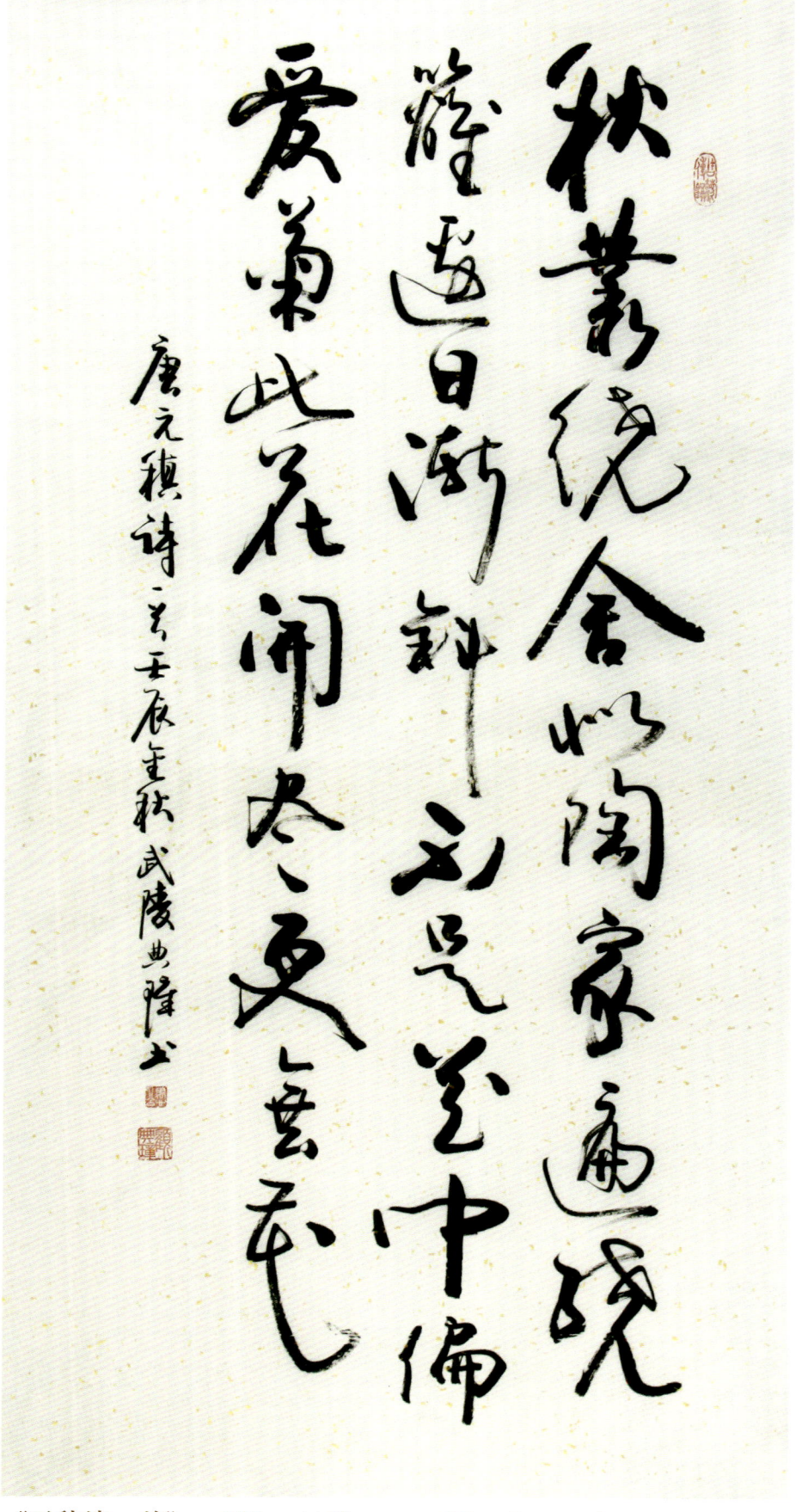

《元稹诗一首》　　138cm×69cm　　"One Poem of Yuan Zhen"

# 荆利斌 *Jing Libin*

荆利斌，1959年生，辽宁省葫芦岛市人，现为中国美术家协会会员，中国国画家协会常务理事，《中国美术》杂志副主编，毕业于中国艺术研究院研究生院第四届中国画名家班，作品多次参加全国性大型展览并获奖。

润笔价格：16,000元/平尺

Jing Libin, from Huludao City, Liaoning Province, was born in 1959. He is the member of Chinese Artists Association, Executive director of Chinese Painters Association, Associate editor of "Chinese art" magazine. He was Graduated from the fourth session of Chinese painting class in Graduate School of China Art Research Institute and his works have Participated in many large national exhibitions and wined awards.

*Reference price: 16,000 yuan / square foot*

《雾月探春晓》　　138cm×69cm　　"Moon after Rain in Spring"

# 高菲　　*Gao Fei*

高菲，男，山东烟台人，现居北京。现为中国文联艺术指导委员会艺术研究员、北京书法家协会会员、中国左笔书画家协会主席、中国扇子艺术协会理事、国际工商总会左笔书法委员会主席。

润笔价格：10,000元/平尺

Gao Fei, male, from Shandong Yantai, now lives in Beijing. He is the art researcher of China Federation of literary and art circles art Steering Committee, member of Beijing Calligraphers Association, chairman of China left-handed Calligraphers Association, Director of Chinese Fan Art Association and president of the left-handed calligraphy of the International Committee of the chamber of Commerce and industry.

*Reference price: 10,000 yuan / square foot*

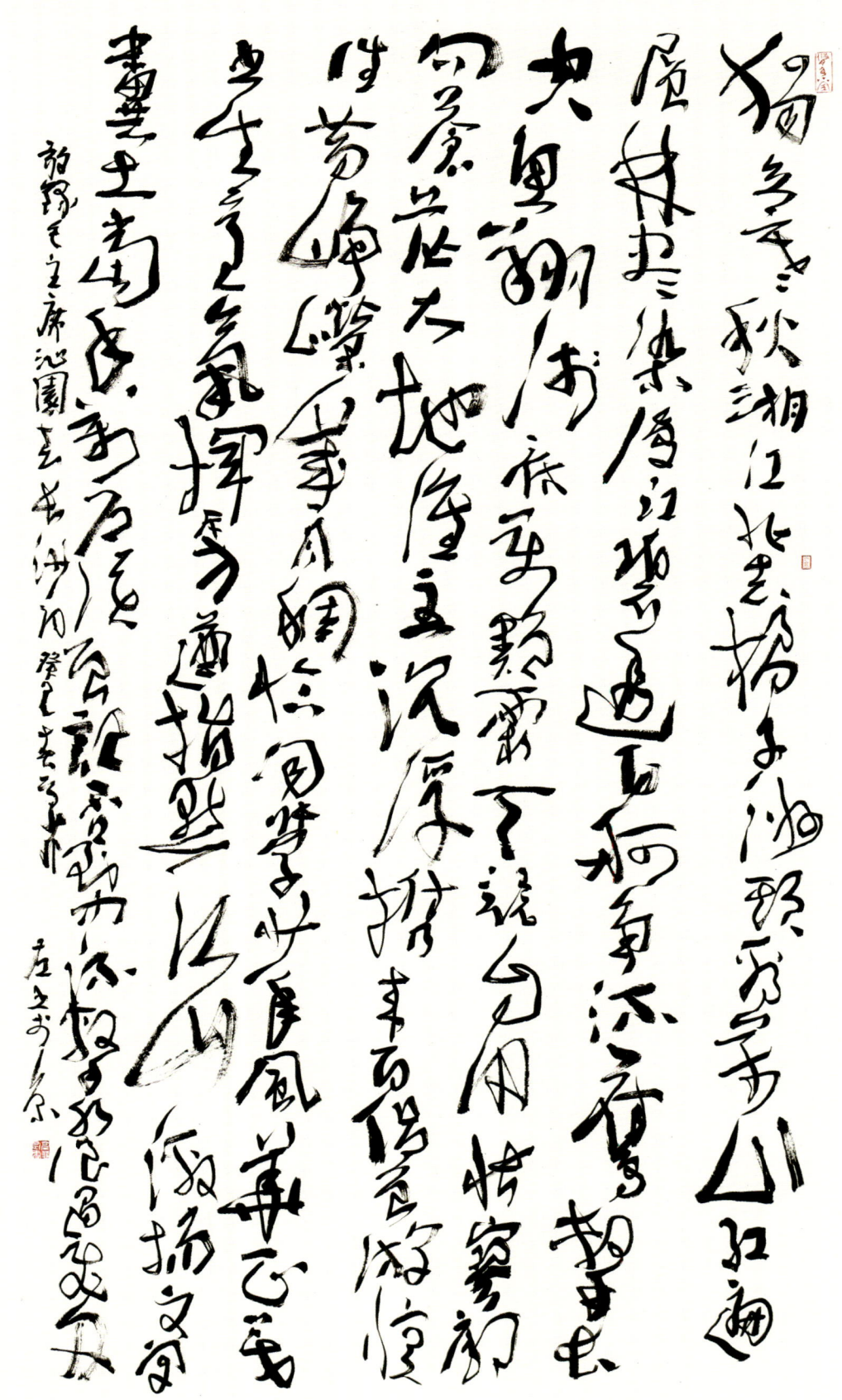

《沁园春·长沙》　　180cm×98cm　　"To the Tunes of Qin Yuan Chun- Changsha"

# 张天文 *Zhang Tianwen*

张天文，字瀚清，号熹微堂主人，1953年生。祖籍河南新安县，中国书法家协会会员，中国书画家协会常务理事，中国书法学会理事，北京长城书画院副院长，北京国防大学耕砚堂书画院艺术顾问。国画《国寿康宁》被人民大会堂收藏。

润笔价格：12,000元/平尺

Zhang Tianwen with a pan name as Han Qing and Holder of Xiwe Hall, from Xin'an County, Henan, was born in 1953. He is the member of Chinese Calligraphers Association, executive Director of Chinese Artists Association, Director of Chinese Calligraphy Association, vice president of The the Great Wall of Beijing painting and Calligraphy Institute, art consultant of Geng Yan Tang in Beijing National Defense University. His Traditional Chinese painting "May the country prosperous" is kept by the Great Hall of the people.

*Reference price: 12,000 yuan / square foot*

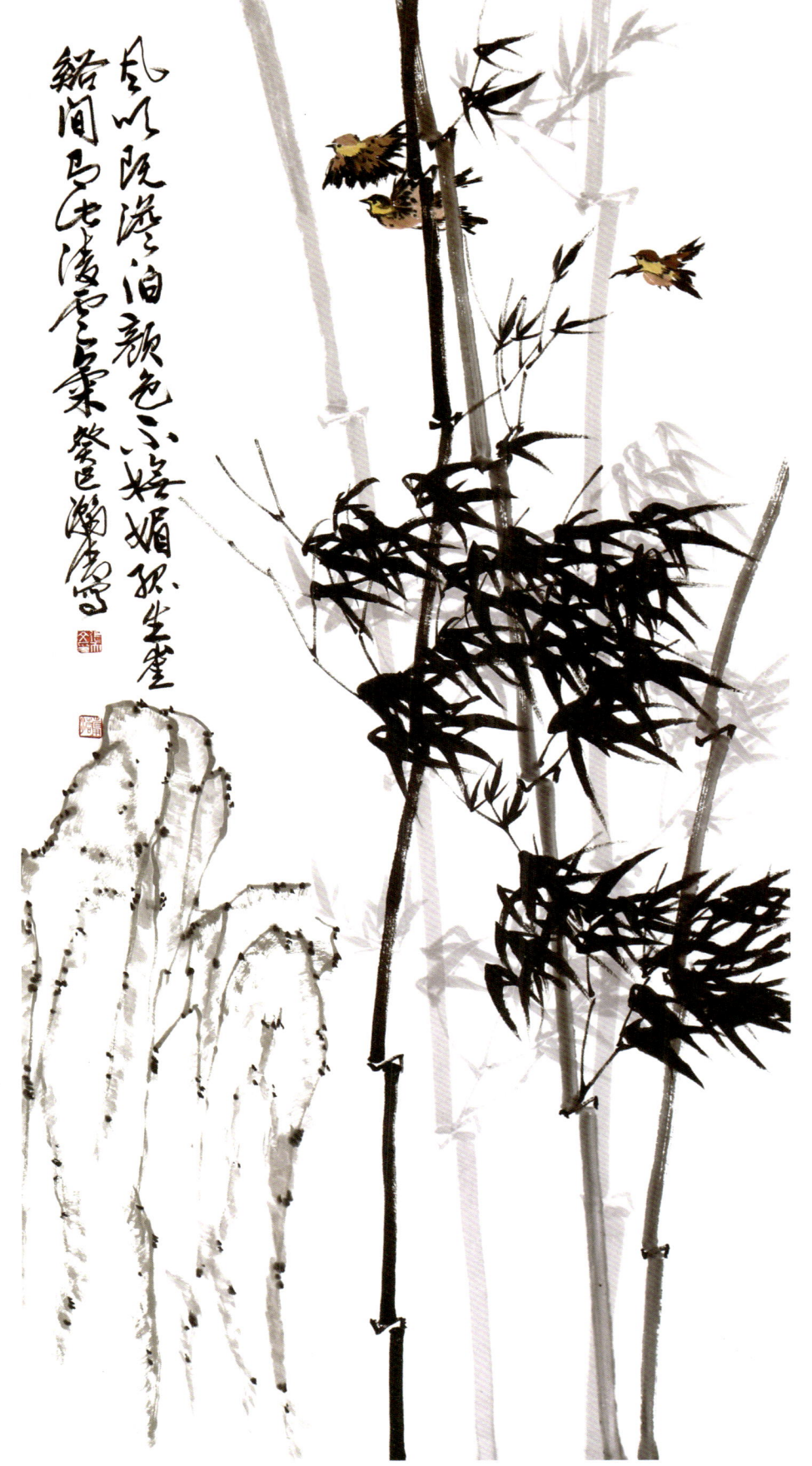

《风明既淡泊》　　137cm×69cm　　*"Indifferent Wind"*

## 柴振福  *Chai Zhenfu*

柴振福,男,字怡然,别署逸兴斋主。以"二王"为宗,遍习张旭、怀素、书谱等历代名家行草书,于右任草书用功最勤,专研行草书。出版有《柴振福书法集》。现为中国书法家协会会员,中国北京湖社书画院理事、中国中华东方杰书画院常务理事和书法研究会副主任研究员。

润笔价格:8,000元/平尺

Chai Zhenfu, male, possesses pen names as Yiran and Moderator of Yixing Building. Learning through the cursive of Zhang Xu, Huai Su, Shu Pu and other masters, his works inherited the style of the "Two Wangs". He is most diligent in right-handed cursive and specializes in that area. He has published " calligraphy sets of Chai Zhenfu" and holds the office of member of Chinese Calligraphers Association, director of Painting Academy in Beijing Lake Society, executive director of China Oriental Dongfang Jie Calligraphy and painting academy, and vice director researcher of the study of calligraphy.

*Reference price: 8,000 yuan / square foot*

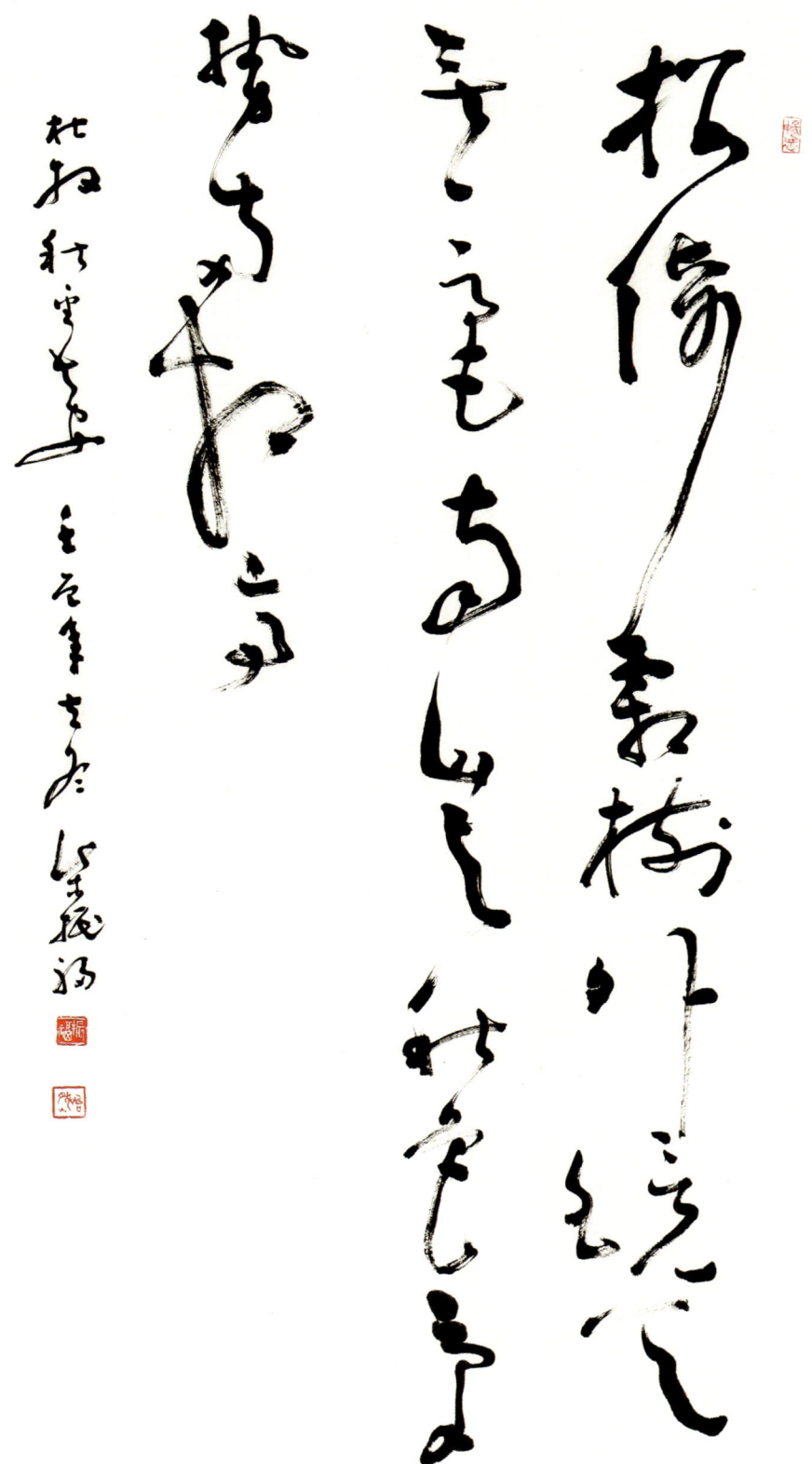

杜牧《长安秋望》　　137cm×69cm　　Du Mu "View of Changan in Autumn"

# 赵玉林  Zhao Yulin

赵玉林，男，笔名，三友，草原书画院院长，包头市美术家协会副主席，中国美协内蒙分会会员，台北故宫书画研究院名誉院长，泰山书画研究院客座教授，《画家》杂志社编委，国家历史博物馆特邀书画家，东方水墨签约书画家。

润笔价格：16,000元/平尺

Zhao Yulin, male, possesses a pen name as Sanyou. He is the president of Grassland Academy of painting and calligraphy, vice president of Baotou City Artists Association, member of Inner Mongolia branch of Chinese Artists Association, honorary president of The the Imperial Palace of Taipei painting and Calligraphy Institute, visiting professor of Taishan Mountain painting and Calligraphy Institute, editorial board member of "The artist" magazine, guest artists of The National Museum of history, Signing calligrapher of the Oriental ink painting.

*Reference price: 16,000 yuan / square foot*

《太行秋瀑》    89cm×180cm    *"Waterfall of Taihang Mountain in Autumn"*

# 汤禄仕　*Tang Lushi*

汤禄仕，1966年6月生于江苏扬州宝应，中国书法家协会会员，职业书法家，以"扬州八怪"金农"漆书"体笑傲书坛。书法作品多次入选国家级重大展览并被人民大会堂、中国国家博物馆等国家机构收藏。

润笔价格：8,000元／平尺

Tang Lushi, from Baoying, Yangzhou, Jiangsu, was born in June 1966.he is the member of Chinese Calligraphers Association, professional calligrapher. He is famous for the style of "Yangzhou Eight Eccentrics" and Jin Nong "Qi " . His works have been selected for the national exhibition and are kept by the Great Hall of the people, the National Museum of China and other national institutions.

*Reference price: 8,000 yuan / square foot*

《爱莲说》　220cm×48cm　　*"Essay to Express the Love for Lotus"*

# 王德法　Wang Defa

王德法，男，艺名德法，青花堂主。1968年生于河北衡水，现为河北省美术家协会会员，中国书画研究院艺委会委员，中国美术家花鸟研究协会理事，北京扇子协会会员，北京青花蓝艺术创作院院长。

润笔价格：16,000元/平尺

Wang Defa, male, with pan names as Defa and Holder of Qinghua Hall, was born in 1968 in Hengshui, Hebei. He is member of Hebei Province Artists Association, Commissary of Chinese painting and Calligraphy Institute, Director of Chinese artists painting Research Association, members of the Beijing fans Association, president of Beijing blue and white Blue Art Institute.

*Reference price: 16,000 yuan / square foot*

《四条屏》　138cm×34cm×4　"A Set of Four Paintings"

## 赵达武　*Zhao Dawu*

赵达武，男，1957年元月出生于书香门第之家，八旗后裔，中国美术书画院副院长，现当选为中国书画艺术促进会常务理事、清华艺术创作研究会常务理事、中国艺术家协会理事、中国艺术科学研究院院士。

润笔价格：10,000元/平尺

Zhao Dawu, male, offspring of The Eight Banners, was born in January 1957 in a family full of literary atmosphere. He is the vice president of Chinese art of calligraphy and painting academy and has been currently elected as the director of China Council for the promotion of painting and calligraphy art, executive director of Study of Art in Tsinghua University, director of the Chinese Artists Association, and the Academician of China Art Research Institute.
*Reference price: 10,000 yuan / square foot*

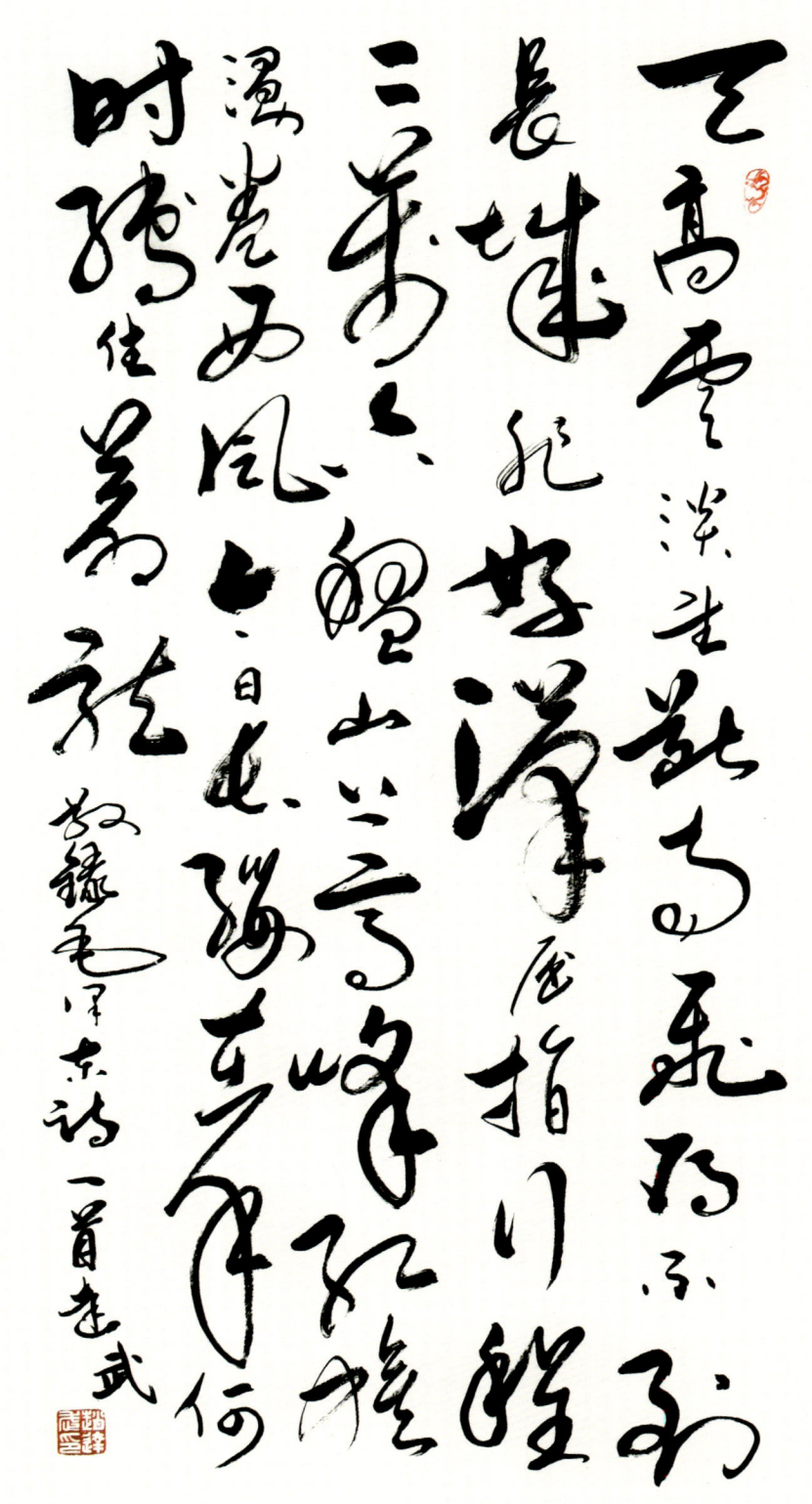

《天高云淡》　　137cm×69cm　　"High Sky, Pale Cloud"

# 易如  *Yi Ru*

易如，女，画家，教授。字：燕；笔名：意如。曾就读于西南师范大学美术学院，清华大学中央工艺美术学院高研班，中国艺术研究院研究生班，先后师承刘大为、朱理存、王雪岩、马振声、苏保祯、黄纯尧等老师。现任中国国际女艺术家协会主席、国际女艺术家协会理事。

润笔价格：12,000元/平尺

Yi Ru, female, with a pan name as Yi Ru, she is a painter and professor. She attended Academy of Fine Arts in Southwestern Normal University, central academy of Fine Arts research classes in Tsinghua University, graduated class of China Art research institude. She successively learnt from Liu Dawei, Zhu Licun, Wang Xueyan, Ma Zhensheng, Su Baozhen, Huang Chunyao, etc. She is currently the chairman of the China International Association of women artists and director of the International Association of women artists.
*Reference price: 12,000 yuan / square foot*

《山到秋色无限好》　　98cm×180cm　　"The Scenery of the Mountain in Autumn is Infinitely Good"

## 赵君 *Zhao Jun*

赵君，男，出生于沈阳。现任北大资源学院教授，北京东方大学传统文华学院副教授，中国传统书画艺术研究院院长。

润笔价格：7,000元/平尺

Zhao Jun, male, was born in Shenyang. He is the professor of Peking University Resource College, associate professor at Traditional Cultural Institute Burapha University in Beijing and the president of the Chinese traditional painting and calligraphy art research Institute.
*Reference price: 7,000 yuan / square foot*

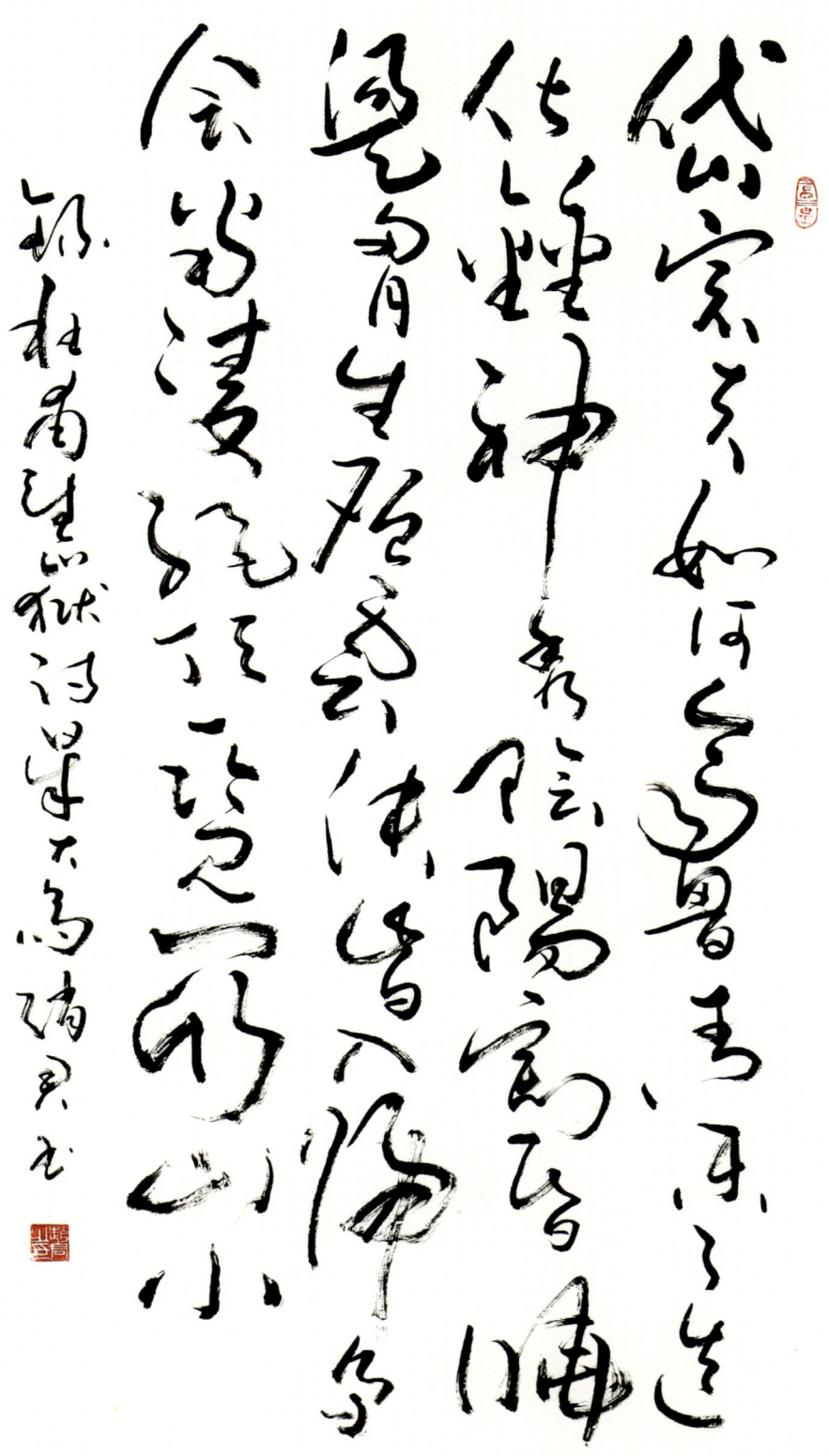

杜甫《望岳》　139cm×68cm　　*Du Fu "View of Mountain Tai"*

## 徐宝铭  Xu Baoming

徐宝铭，1944年生，黑龙江省美术家协会会员，中国书画研究院研究员，中国马文化博物馆艺术顾问，中央电视台网络频道书画名家联谊会副主席。

润笔价格：12,000元/平尺

Xu Baoming was born in 1944. he is the member of Heilongjiang Artists Association, researcher of Chinese painting and Calligraphy Institute, consultant of The Art Museum of China horse culture, vice president of the Calligraphers Association of CCTV network channel.

*Reference price: 12,000 yuan / square foot*

《三骏图》　　69cm×138cm　　*"Three Horses"*

# 杨宪金　YANG Xian Jin

杨宪金，山东省肥城市人，1947年生。1964年进入中南海警卫团，1980年被任命为中南海画册编辑委员会主任，1992年受命筹建西苑出版社，任社长兼总编。现为中国书法家协会会员、中国水墨研究院院长。

润笔价格：6,000元/平尺

YANG Xian Jin, from Fei City, Shandong, was born in 1947. He entered Into the Zhongnanhai guards regiment in 1964, and was appointed as head of Zhongnanhai Editorial Committee of the album In 1980. he was appointed to build the Xiyuan press in 1992 and to be the publisher and editor. He is currently the member of Chinese Calligraphers Association and the president of the Chinese painting research Institute.

*Reference price: 6,000 yuan / square foot*

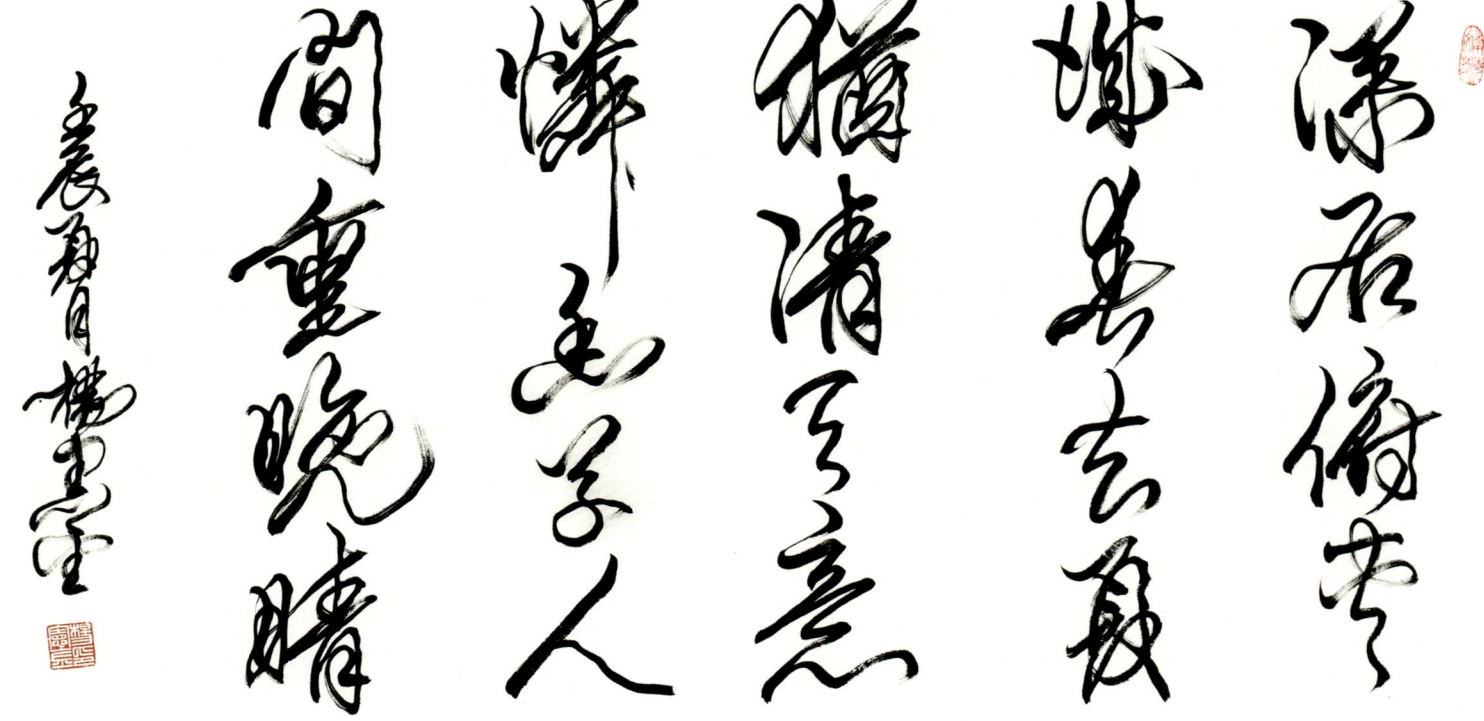

《李商隐诗一首》　69cm×138cm　　"One Poem of Li Shangyin"

# 于建明  *Yu Jianming*

于建明，1961年生，哈尔滨人，现为文化部艺术交流中心特聘画家，中国国画家协会理事，黑龙江画院特聘画家，先后进修于浙江美术学院和哈尔滨师范大学。

润笔价格：16,000元/平尺

Yu Jianming, from Harbin, was born in 1961, he is the invited painter of The Ministry of culture and art exchange center, director of Chinese Painters Association, invited painter of Heilongjiang Academy. He Studied at Academy of Fine Arts in Zhejiang and Harbin Normal University.

*Reference price: 16,000 yuan / square foot*

《江南胜揽图》　69cm×240cm　　*"Scenic Spots of Jiangnan"*

# 崔永波  *Cui Yongbo*

崔永波，山东省淄博市人，1991年入伍。现为空军北京某部干部、中校军衔。系中国书法家协会会员、北京书法家协会理事、中国收藏家协会会员、北京书法院研究员、北京市美术家协会会员、中央直属机关青联委员等。中国书法家协会第六次全国书代会代表。

润笔价格：7,000元/平尺

Cui Yongbo, from Zibo City, Shandong, joined the army in 1991. he is currently the cadres in one unit of The air force of the Beijing military and has the level of Lieutenant Colonel. He is the member of Chinese Calligraphers Association, director of Beijing Calligrapher's Association, member of China Association of collectors, researcher at the Beijing Academy of calligraphy, member of Beijing Artists Association, commissary of the All-China Youth Federation in Departments under the Party Central Committee and representative of the sixth book congress of the Chinese Calligraphers Association.

*Reference price: 7,000 yuan / square foot*

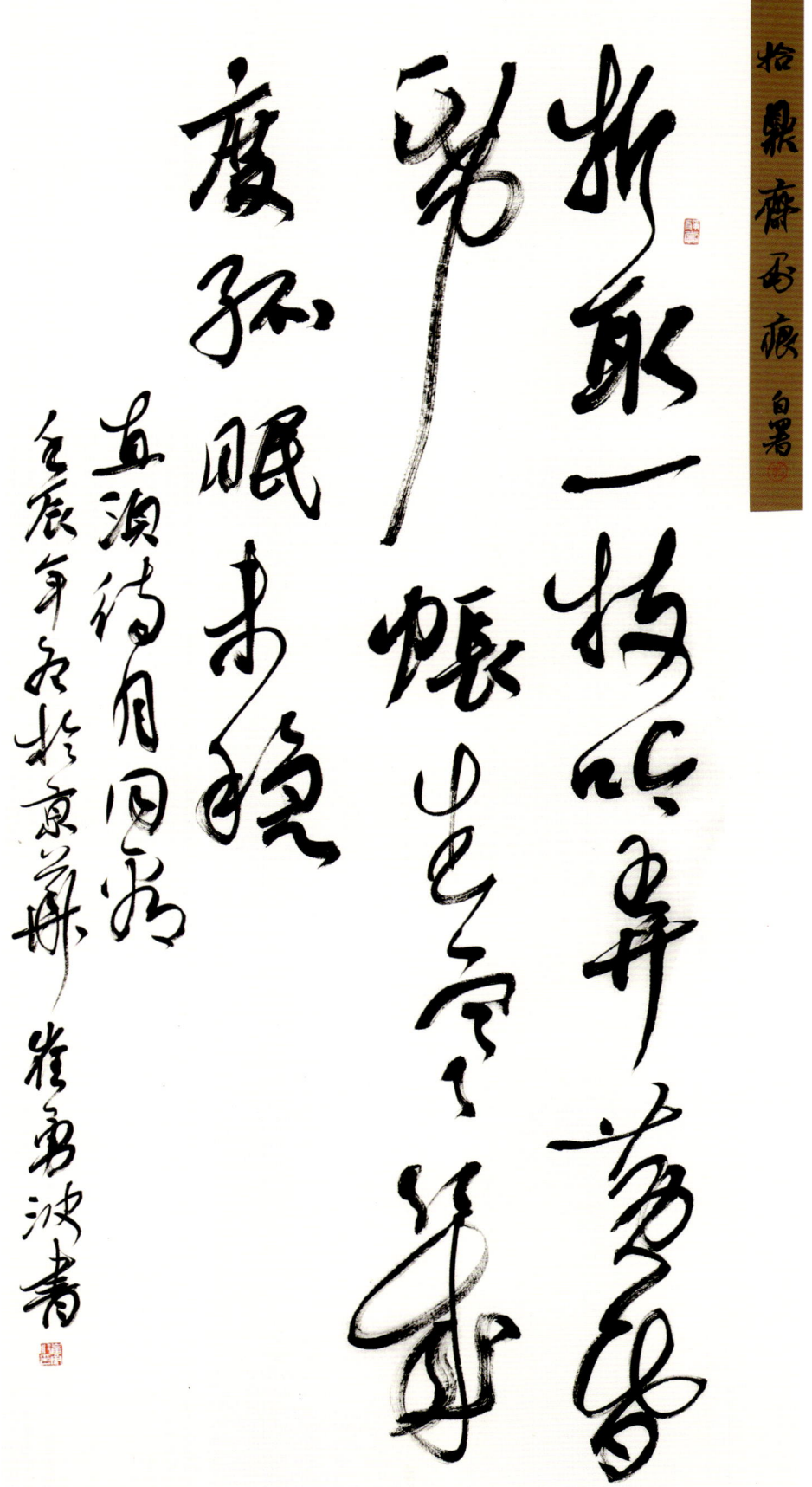

《行草一幅》　　137cm×68cm　　"A Cursive"

# 彭强  **Peng Qiang**

彭强，男，笔名：浩之，河北邢台市人，现居北京，系中国美术家协会河北会员、中国书画艺术家协会常务理事、北京名人翰墨书画院院长。

润笔价格：16,000元/平尺

Peng Qiang, male, with a pan name of Haozhi, is from Xingtai City, Heibei and now is living in Beijing. He is the member or the Chinese Artists Association in Heibei, executive director of China Artists Association and president of Beijing celebrity calligraphy Academy of painting and calligraphy.
*Reference price: 16,000 yuan / square foot*

《世事如意》　69cm×137cm　　*"May Everything be Fine"*

# 任仲德  *Ren Zhongde*

任仲德，男，汉族，字俊德，号云岗游子，1943年生于山西云岗，内蒙古包头人，内蒙古书法家协会会员，包头市青山区书法家协会主席，大漠书画院常务副院长。

润笔价格：6,000元/平尺

Ren Zhongde, male, Han nationality, possesses pan names of Junde and Wanderer of Yungang. Born in 1943 in Yungang, Shanxi, he is from Baotou, Inner Mongolia. He is the member of Inner Mongolia Calligraphers Association, The chairman of Baotou Qingshan District Calligraphers Association and the Executive vice president of Han painting Association.

*Reference price: 6,000 yuan / square foot*

《录篆刻联》　　136cm×69cm　　*"A Set of Seal Cutting"*

# 田子昌　*Tian Zichang*

田子昌，男，1955年生，国家一级美术师，中国艺术促进会理事，中国民间艺术协会会员，北京市美术家协会会员。

润笔价格：14,000元/平尺

Tian Zichang, male, was born in 1955. he is a National A-level artist, director of China Council for promotion of Art, member of the Chinese Folk Art Association, member of Beijing Artists Association.

*Reference price: 14,000 yuan / square foot*

《山川瑞雪飘》　　180cm×98cm　　*"Heavy Snow in Mountains"*

# 方文士  *Fang Wenshi*

方文士，男，笔名鹤山，1934年10月生，辽宁鞍山人，中国书法研究院艺术委员会会员，中国书画函授大学书法教授，辽宁省书法家协会会员，鞍山市书法家协会理事。

润笔价格：5,000元/平尺

Fang Wenshi with a pan name as Heshan, male, born in October 1934, is from Anshan, Liaoning. He is a member of Art Committee of China Calligraphy Research Institute, professor of China calligraphy and painting correspondence university, member of Liaoning Calligraphers Association, member of Anshan Calligraphers Association.
*Reference price: 5,000 yuan / square foot*

《学道篇》　46cm×137cm　"Chapter of Learning"

# 马福友　*Ma Fuyou*

马福友，男，1953年出生，祖籍北京，现为中国艺术家协会常务理事，中国艺术家协会书画家研究会秘书长，自幼酷爱音乐与绘画，近些年得到诸多绘画界名家悉心指点，潜心钻研，集音乐与绘画于一体，别具一格地把音乐之美融入了绘画之中。

润笔价格：16,000元/平尺

Ma Fuyou, male, born in 1953, is a native of Beijing. He is the Executive director of China Artists Association, Secretary-General of China Artists Association and calligraphy. He was very fond of music and painting At an early age. Under the careful guidance of many painting masters in recent years, he has set the beauty of music into painting and invented his own style.

*Reference price: 16,000 yuan / square foot*

《高风亮节》　　137cm×69cm　　"Ethical"

## 刘保进  *Liu Baojin*

刘保进，男，二炮某基地原副政委，正师职，大校军衔，现为中国文学艺术工作者联合会副主席，中国诗书画研究会副会长，中国书法家协会会员，昆明市书协副主席。

润笔价格：5,000元/平尺

Liu Baojin, male, he was the former deputy political commissar of The Second Artillery, has the level of division and Senior Colonel rank , he is the vice president of China workers federation of literary and art, vice president of Chinese poetry and painting research, member of Chinese Calligraphers Association, vice chairman of Kunming calligraphers Association.
*Reference price: 5,000 yuan / square foot*

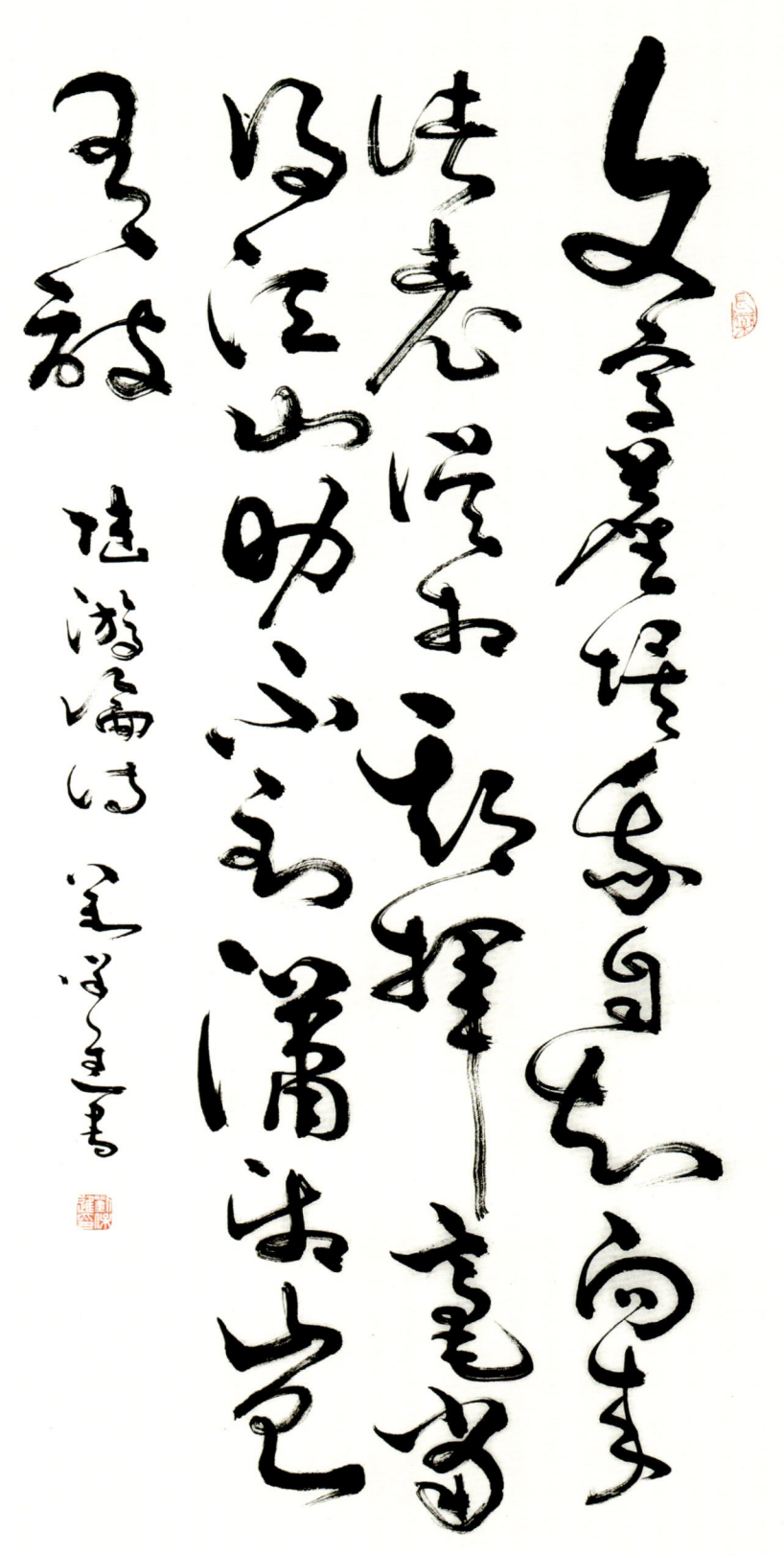

陆游《论诗》　　136cm×69cm　　*Lu "Poetry"*

# 骆云　*Luo Yun*

骆云，1960年11月生于河北衡水，中国美协河北分会会员，河北山水画研究理事，中国书画家协会理事。作品载入经典大型画册，国际奥林匹克书画大赛特聘画家。1998年受马来西亚新山中华文化总会之邀到马来西亚举办个人画展，获得成功。

润笔价格：16,000元/平尺

Luo Yun was born in November 1960 in Hengshui, Hebei. He is A member of Hebei branch of Chinese Artists Association, Director of the Hebei landscape painting, director of China Artists Association. His works was collected into the photo albums of classic works. He is the invited painter of The International Olympic painting and calligraphy competition. He held personal exhibitions in 1998 invited by the Association of Chinese culture in Malaysia Bahru in Malaysia and made a hit.

*Reference price: 16,000 yuan / square foot*

《清风明月》　70cm×140cm　　*"Cool Breeze and Bright Moon"*

## 李镇锐  *Li Zhenrui*

李镇锐，男，1955年7月生，广东潮州人，现供职于潮州市公安局，系中国书法家协会会员，中国书画艺术家协会副主席，中国工艺美术家协会会员，广东省文化学会理事，广东省书法家协会会员，潮州市书法协会常务理事。

润笔价格：5,000元/平尺

Li Zhenrui, male, frome Chaozhou, Guangdong, was born in July 1955. he is now working for Chaozhou Public Security Bureau. He is the member of Chinese Calligraphers Association, vice chairman of the Chinese Artists Association, member of Chinese Artists Association, director of Guangdong Province Culture Society, member of Guangdong Provincial Calligrapher Association, executive director of Chaozhou calligrapher Association.

*Reference price: 5,000 yuan / square foot*

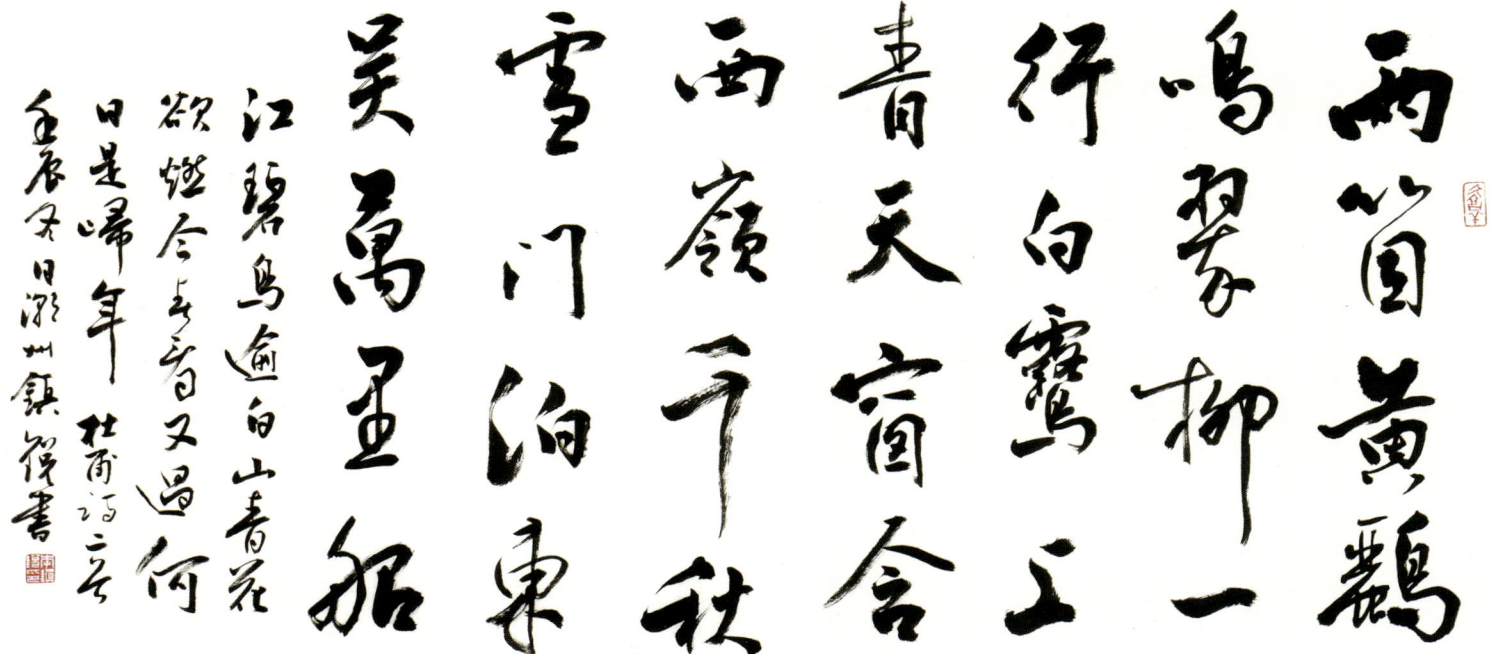

《杜甫诗两首》　　69cm×137cm　　*"Two Poems of Du Fu"*

# 王春生　Wang Chunsheng

王春生，男，河北人，中国著名书画家，1965年生，河北省雄县人。现任中国书法艺术研究院理事，中国画家协会理事，一级美术师，中国美术家协会河北分会会员，中国书法家协会河北分会会员，燕南书画院院长。

润笔价格：12,000元/平尺

Wang Chunsheng, male, from Xiong country, Hebei Province, was born in 1965. He is a famous painter and the member of China Calligraphy Art Research Institute, member of China Artists Association, artist of the first grade, member of Hebei branch of Chinese Artists Association, member of Hebei branch of China Calligraphers Association, president of Yan Nan Academy of painting and calligraphy.

*Reference price: 12,000 yuan / square foot*

《雅园赏香》　70cm×142cm　　"Sweet-smelling in Ya Garden"

### 张文东  Zhang Wendong

张文东，美籍华人，1956年出，毕业于厦门大学中文系，现任美国海峡两岸文化交流基金会董事会主席、美国福建同乡会副会长、美国福建书画家协会会长、清华美院驿站副会长、福建省商业高等专科学校客座教授。

润笔价格：7,000元/平尺

Zhang Wendong, Chinese-American, was born in 1956. He was graduated from Xiamen University Department of Chinese and he is currently the president of The United States of America cross-strait cultural exchange foundation, vice president of the Association of Fujian fellow provincials or townsmen in the United States of America, president of the Fujian Artists Association in United States, vice president of Tsinghua University Station, guest professor of Fujian Commercial College.

*Reference price: 7,000 yuan / square foot*

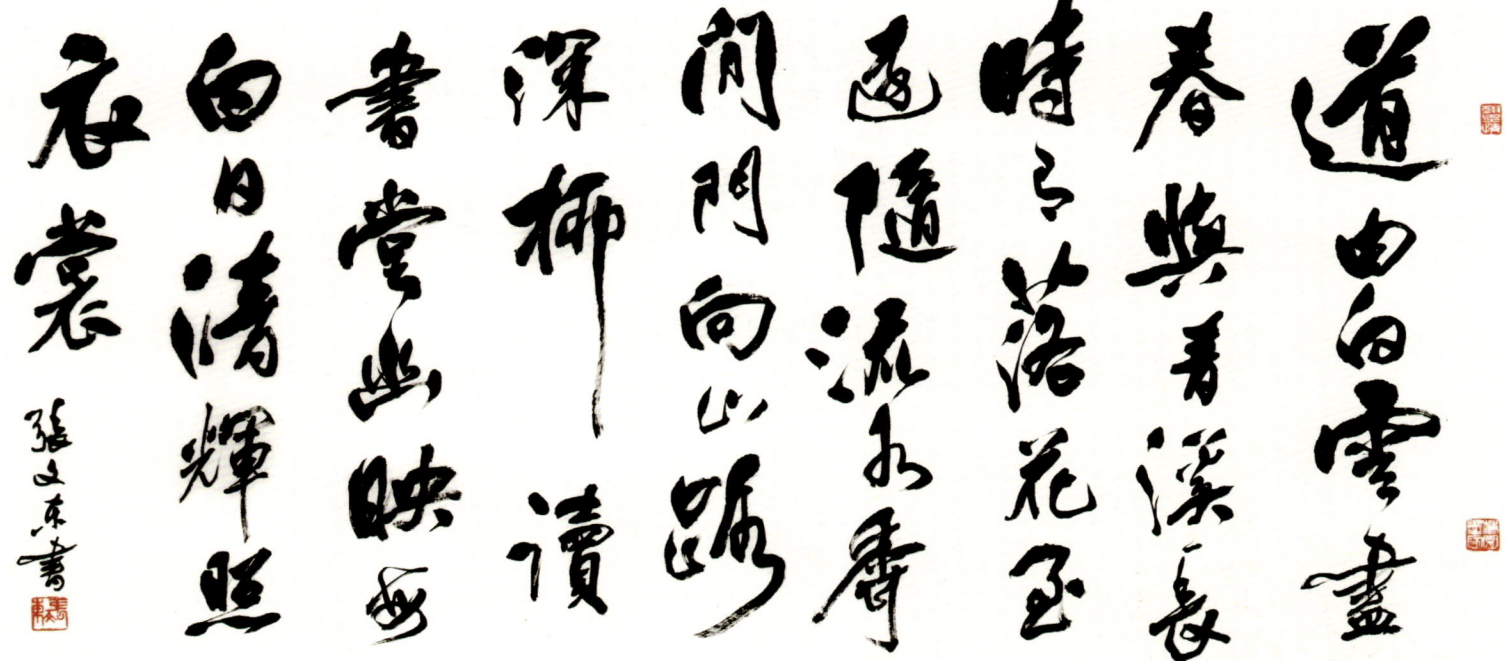

刘慎虚《阙题》　　138cm×68cm　　*Liu Shenxu "Nameless"*

# 张朝彬 *Zhang Chaobin*

张朝彬，号愚石公，1968年生，河北邯郸人，现居北京，现为中国美术家协会河北分会会员，中国书画研究院院士，中国美术家山水研究会理事，北京名人翰墨书画院院长。

润笔价格：12,000元/平尺

Zhang Chaobin with a pan name of Yushi, from Handan, Heibei, was born in 1968 and now is living in Beijing, he is A member of Hebei branch of Chinese Artists Association, academician of the Chinese Academy of painting and calligraphy, director of China Artists landscape research, president of Beijing celebrity calligraphy Academy of painting and calligraphy.

*Reference price: 12,000 yuan / square foot*

《富水长流时》   138cm×68cm   "Water Flows"

### 王春林　*Wang Chunlin*

王春林，男，1963年生，辽宁兴城人，辽宁省书法家协会会员，葫芦岛市书法家协会副主席，市青年书法家协会主席。

润笔价格：6,000元/平尺

Wang Chunlin, male, from Xing City, Liaoning, was born in 1963, he is a member of Liaoning Calligraphers Association, vice chairman of Huludao Calligrapher's Association, president of The youth Calligraphers Association.
*Reference price: 6,000 yuan / square foot*

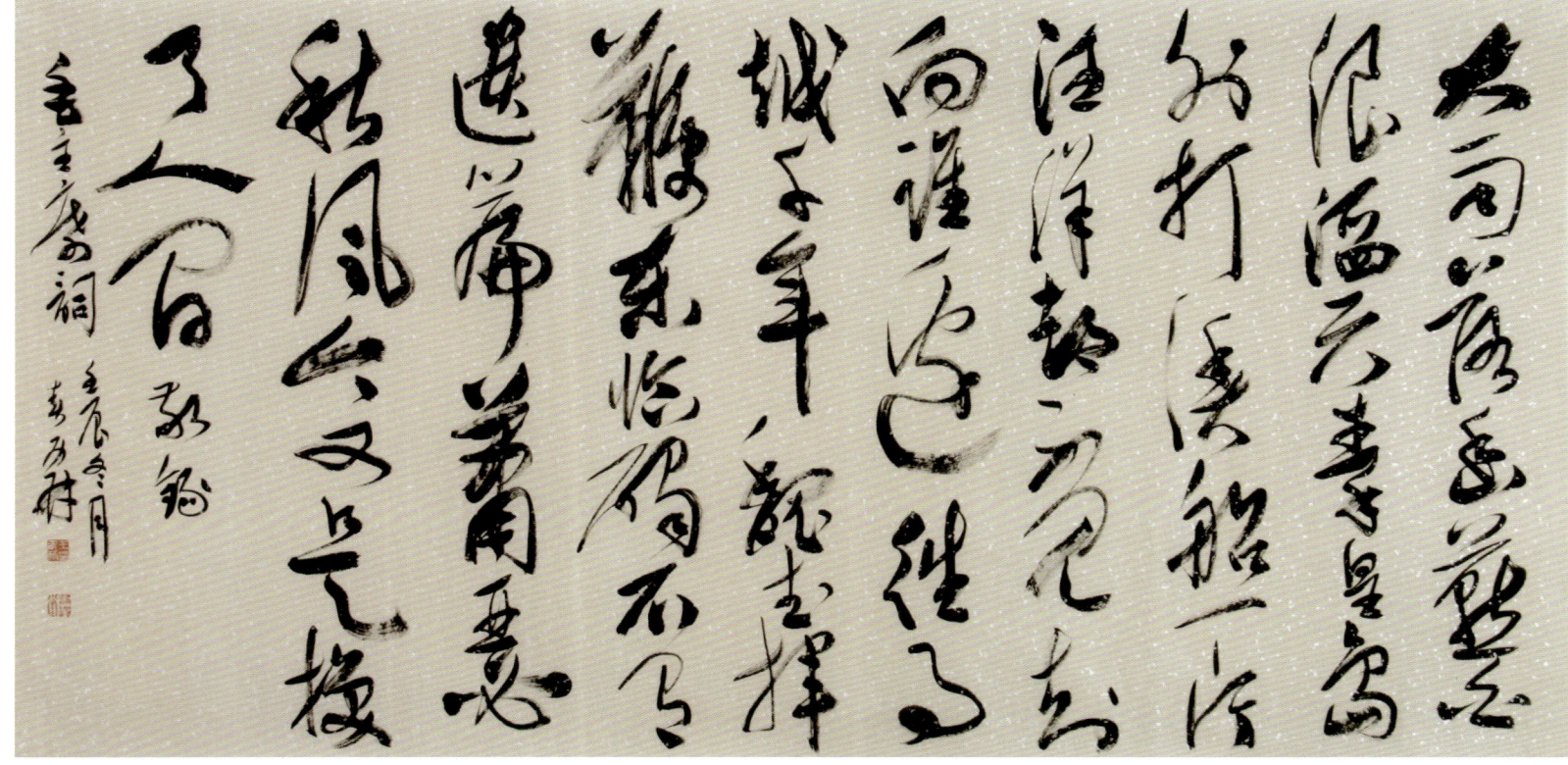

《毛泽东词一首》　　68cm×138cm　　*"One Poem of Mao Zedong"*

# 李俊香  *Li Junxiang*

李俊香，1957年生，安徽人，号梅影堂主、怡香斋主，现为中国北京国创书画院院士，安徽省美协会员，淮北市美协副主席，淮北国画院特聘画师。

润笔价格：10,000元/平尺

Li Junxiang, from Anhui, was born in 1957 and possesses pan names of Holder of Mei Ying Hall and Moderator of Yi Xiang Building. She is a Academician of Beijing Guo Chuang Shu academy of painting, member of Anhui Province Artists Association, vice chairman of Huaibei Artists Association, invited painter of Huaibei Chinese Painting academy.

*Reference price: 10,000 yuan / square foot*

《花鸟四条屏》　133cm×22cm×4　　"A Set of Four Paintings of Flowers and Birds"

## 孔繁祥  *Kong Fanxiang*

孔繁祥，男，现为山东省书协会员，曲阜市书协副主席，孔子故里书画院副院长兼秘书长，承孔书院曲阜孔府书画院院长。

润笔价格：7,000元/平尺

Kong Fanxiang, male. He Is the member of Shandong province book society, vice chairman of Qufu Calligraphers Association, vice president and Secretary-general of the hometown of Confucius calligraphy and painting academy, president of Qufu Academy of painting and calligraphy in Chengkong academy.

*Reference price: 7,000 yuan / square foot*

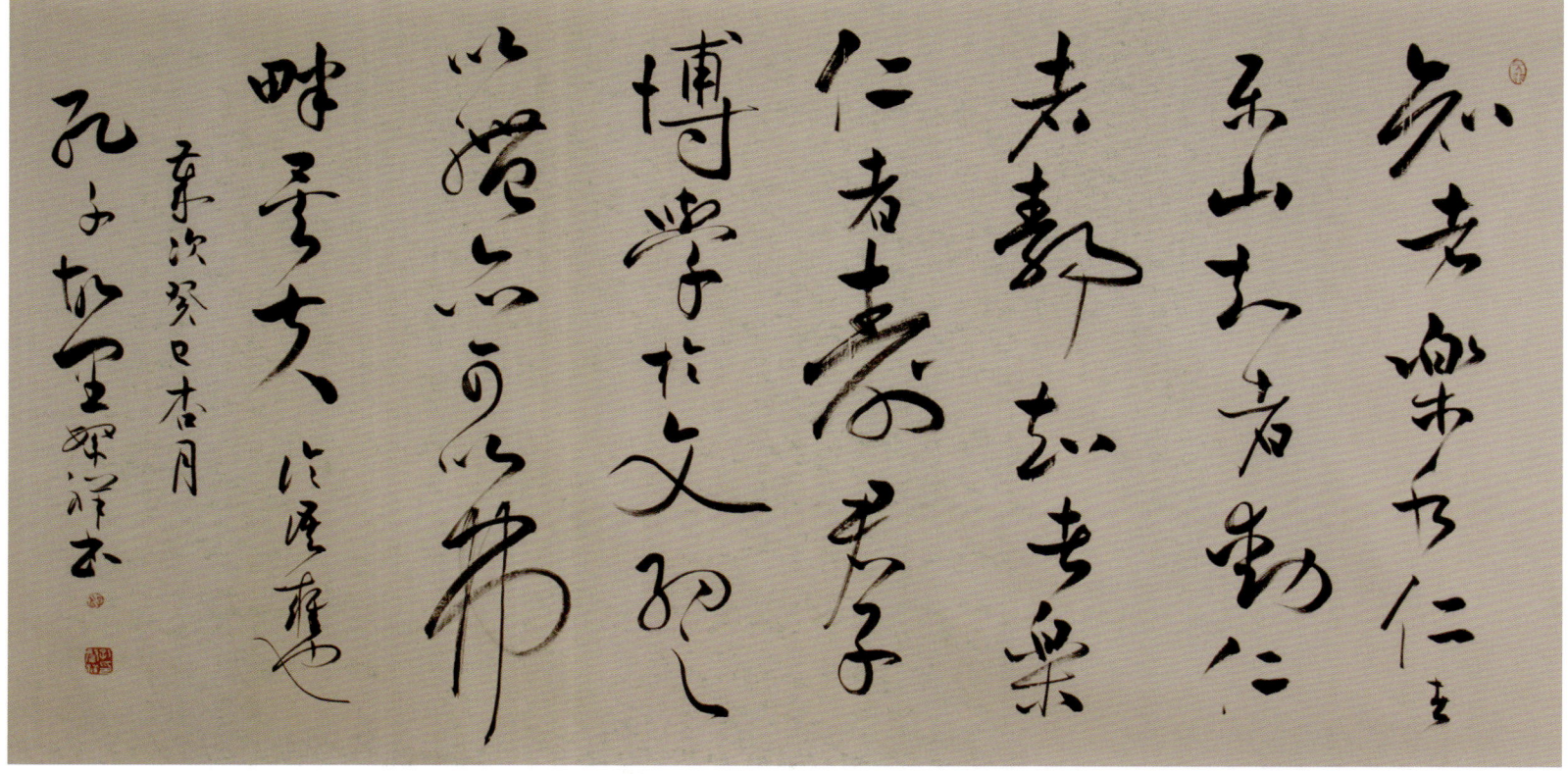

《论语》　68cm×138cm　　*"The Analects"*

# 冯纪新　*Feng Ji new*

冯纪新，男，1944年生，安徽金寨人，任中国书画艺术家协会副主席，安徽省美术家协会会员，六安市美术家协会艺术顾问；曾任市委宣传部副部长，兼任市文联主席、党组书记。

润笔价格：14,000元/平尺

Feng Ji new, male, from Jinzhai, Anhui, was born in 1944. He is the vice chairman of the Chinese Artists Association, member of Anhui Province Artists Association, art consultant of Liu'an City Artists Association. He served as Former deputy Minister of Municipal Propaganda Department, chairman and Party secretary of the Federation of literary and Art Circles.

*Reference price: 14,000 yuan / square foot*

《岩壑山居》　　69cm×139cm　　*"Living in Mountains with Gully and Rock"*

## 岳维瀚　*Yue Weihan*

岳维瀚，男，字浩之，号长人，别署老瀚，1950年生，天津人，现为河北省书法家协会会员，唐山市书法家协会理事，天津市书法家协会会员。
润笔价格：5,000元/平尺

Yue Weihan, male, from Tianjin, was born in 1950 and possesses pan names as Haozhi, Changren and Laohan, he is the member of Hebei Calligraphers Association, director of Tangshan City Calligrapher's Association, member of Tianjin city Calligraphers Association.
*Reference price: 5,000 yuan / square foot*

辛弃疾《清玉案》　　137cm×70cm　　*Xin Qiji "To the Tunes of Gray Jade Table"*

# 任承家 *Ren Chengjia*

任承家，1944年出生，四川乐山人，中国书法家协会会员，乐山书画院常务副院长，乐山市美术家协会副主席，乐山市书法家协会副主席，四川省美术家协会会员，曾任乐山市音乐家协会常务理事。

润笔价格：8,000元/平尺

Ren Chengjia, from Leshan, Sichuan, was born in 1944. he is the member of China Calligraphers Association, executive vice president of Leshan Painting and Calligraphy Institute, vice chairman of Leshan City Artists Association, vice president of Leshan City Calligraphers Association, member of Sichuan Artists Association, former executive director of Leshan City Musicians Association.

*Reference price: 8,000 yuan / square foot*

《醉春》　　137cm×68cm　　*"Drunk Spring"*

## 樊中尧　*Fan Zhongyao*

樊中尧，男，中国硬笔书法家协会会员，中国金融书协会员，平顶山市书协常务理事，王铎故宫书画院名誉院长。

润笔价格：5,000元/平尺

Fan Zhongyao, male. He is the member of the Chinese Pen Calligraphers Association, member of China's financial Calligraphers, executive director of Pingdingshan City Calligraphers Association, honorary president Wang Duo Forbidden Painting academy.
*Reference price: 5,000 yuan / square foot*

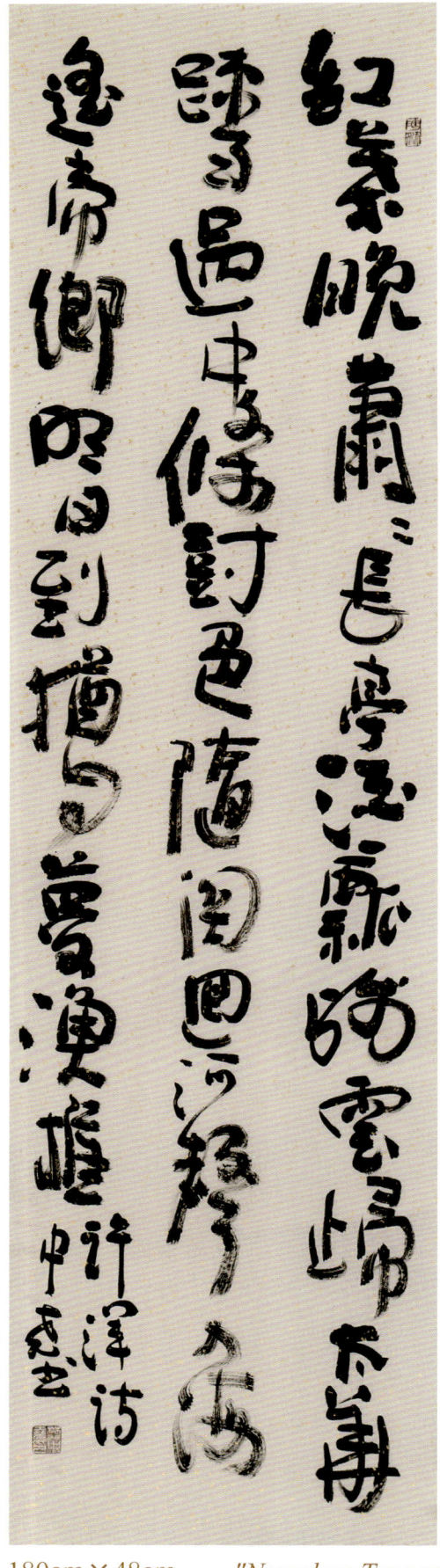

《秋日赴阙题潼关驿楼》　　180cm×48cm　　"Nameless Tongguan Station House in Autumn"

# 李晓天　*Li Xiaotian*

李晓天，男，1961年生于安徽省寿县。现任中国扇子艺术学会常务理事，美中文化教育经济基金会荣誉主席。

润笔价格：6,000元/平尺

Li Xiaotian, male, was born in 1961 in Shou country, Anhu. He is the executive director of the China Fan Art Society, honorary president of the United States and China Cultural Education Economics Foundation.
*Reference price: 6,000 yuan / square foot*

《曲涧流翠》　69cm×137cm　　*"Jade Green Flowing in Rivers"*

### 陈列  *Chen Lie*

陈列，男，1963年5月生于山东青岛，现任中央国家机关书画协会常务理事、外交部书画协会秘书长、外交部诗词协会副秘书长等职。

润笔价格：5,000元/平尺

Chen Lie, male, born in May 1963 in Qingdao, Shandong, is currently executive director of the Painting and Calligraphy Association in central state organs, Secretary-general of the Painting and Calligraphy Association in the ministry of foreign affairs, deputy Secretary-General of the Poetry Association in the ministry of foreign affairs.
*Reference price: 5,000 yuan / square foot*

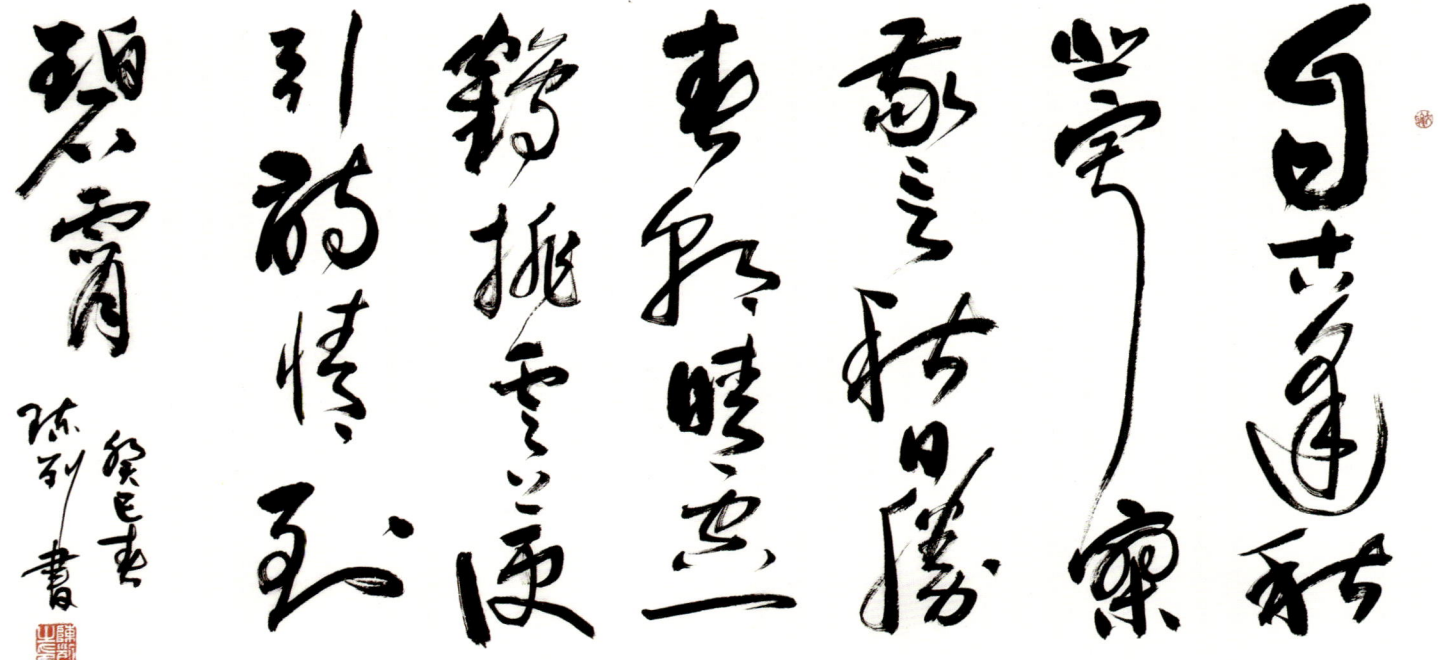

李白《客中作》　　137cm×67cm　　*Li Bai "Written as a Guest"*

# 杨国志  *Yang Guozhi*

杨国志，男，1947年生，国家一级美术师，黑龙江省美协会员，大庆市美协副主席，文化部国韵书画院特聘画家。

润笔价格：8,000元/平尺

Yang Guozhi, male, was born in 1947. He is a national A-level artist, member of the Heilongjiang Provincial artist Association, vice president of the Daqing City Artists Association, Distinguished painter of State Rhyming Painting academy of the Ministry of Culture.

*Reference price: 8,000 yuan / square foot*

《富贵大吉图》　138cm×70cm　"Painting of Wealth and Good Luck"

## 刘自力  *Liu Zili*

刘自力，男，字德令，1963年生，天津市人，现任中国书法家协会会员，中央国家机关书画协会常务理事，外交部书画协会副会长，中国书画协会理事，中国书画院副院长。

润笔价格：7,000元/平尺

Liu Zili, male, from Tianjin, with a pan name as De Ling, was born in 1963. He is currently a member of Chinese Calligraphers Association, executive director of the Calligraphy Association in the central state organs, vice president of the Painting and Calligraphy Association in the ministry of foreign affairs, of Chinese Painting and Calligraphy Association, director of the China Painting and Calligraphy Association , vice president of Chinese Painting and Calligraphy academy.

*Reference price: 7,000 yuan / square foot*

《铸魂》　137cm×68cm　　"Soul of Casting "

# 戴铁松  *Dai Tiesong*

戴铁松，男，1963年生，河北承德人，现为河北省美术家协会会员，承德美协理事，北京名人翰墨书画院副秘书长，国家二级美术师。

润笔价格：8,000元/平尺

Dai Tiesong, male, born in 1963, is from Chengde, Hebei. He is the member of Hebei Province Artists Association, director of Chengde Artists Association, deputy Secretary-General of Beijing calligraphy painting and calligraphy celebrity, national B-level artists.

*Reference price: 8,000 yuan / square foot*

《净土清音图》　66cm×133cm　　*"Painting of Pure Land and Buddhism Music"*

## 郝应辉　*Hao Yinghui*

郝应辉，男，1976年2月生于山东省宁阳县，山东省书协会员，东营市书协会员。
2001年7月作品入选《第四届当代青年书画展》并获青年组一等奖，2004年入编《中国当代书法家图鉴辞典》。
润笔价格：7,000元/平尺

Hao Yinghui, male, was born in February 1976 in Ningyang County, Shandon. He is the member of Shandong Province Calligraphers, member of Dongying City Calligraphers Association.
His work was Selected into "the fourth exhibition of contemporary youth arts " and won first prize in the young group in July 2001, and was edited into the "Illustration Dictionary of Chinese contemporary calligraphers."
*Reference price: 7,000 yuan / square foot*

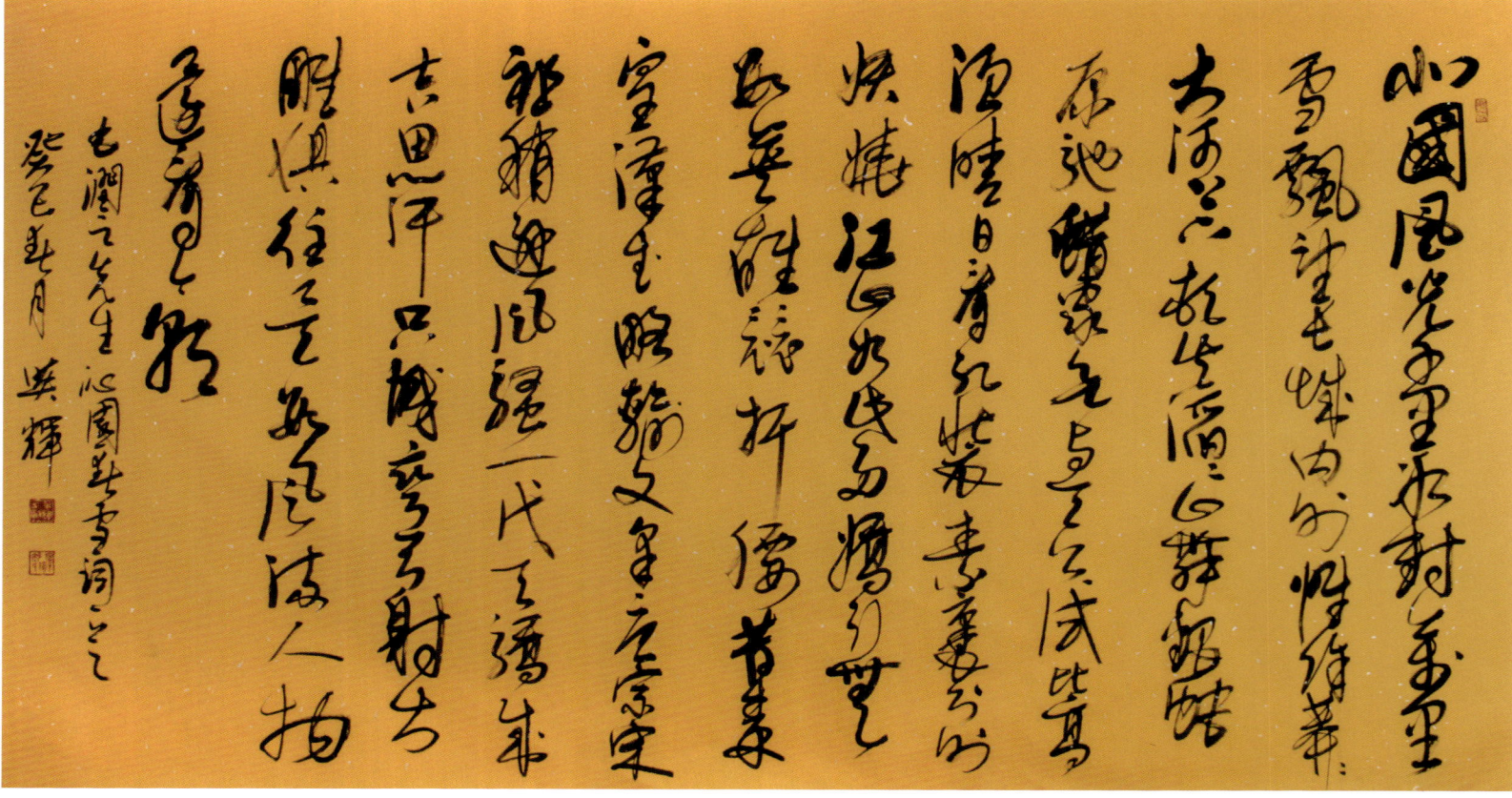

《沁园春·雪》　98cm×180cm　*"To the Tunes of Qin Yuan Chun - Snow"*

# 吕建文  *Lv Jianwen*

吕建文，男，字可风，汉族，1947年生，石家庄人，现为香港美术家协会副主席，中国画院画家，国家一级美术师，中国当代百杰画家，中国书画印研究院常务理事。

润笔价格：14,000元/平尺

Lv Jianwen, male, Han nationality, with a pan name as Kefeng, he was born in 1947 in Shijiazhuang. He is currently the vice chairman of the Hong Kong Artists Association, Chinese Painting artist, national A-level artist, one of the hundred outstanding contemporary Chinese painters, and executive director of Chinese Painting, Calligraphy and Seal Institute.

*Reference price: 14,000 yuan / square foot*

《无尽泉声》　90cm×90cm　　"Endless Sound of Spring"

## 马建智  *Ma Jianzhi*

马建智，男，1962年10月生于河北石家庄市，现就职总参谋部，大校军衔。中国长城书画院理事，中国榜书艺术研究会会员。

润笔价格：4,000元/平尺

Ma Jianzhi, male, was born in October 1962 in Shijiazhuang, Hebei. He is the Colonel rank in the General Staff, director of the China Great Wall Painting and Calligraphy Institute, member of the China Calligraphy Art Research Association.
*Reference price: 4,000 yuan / square foot*

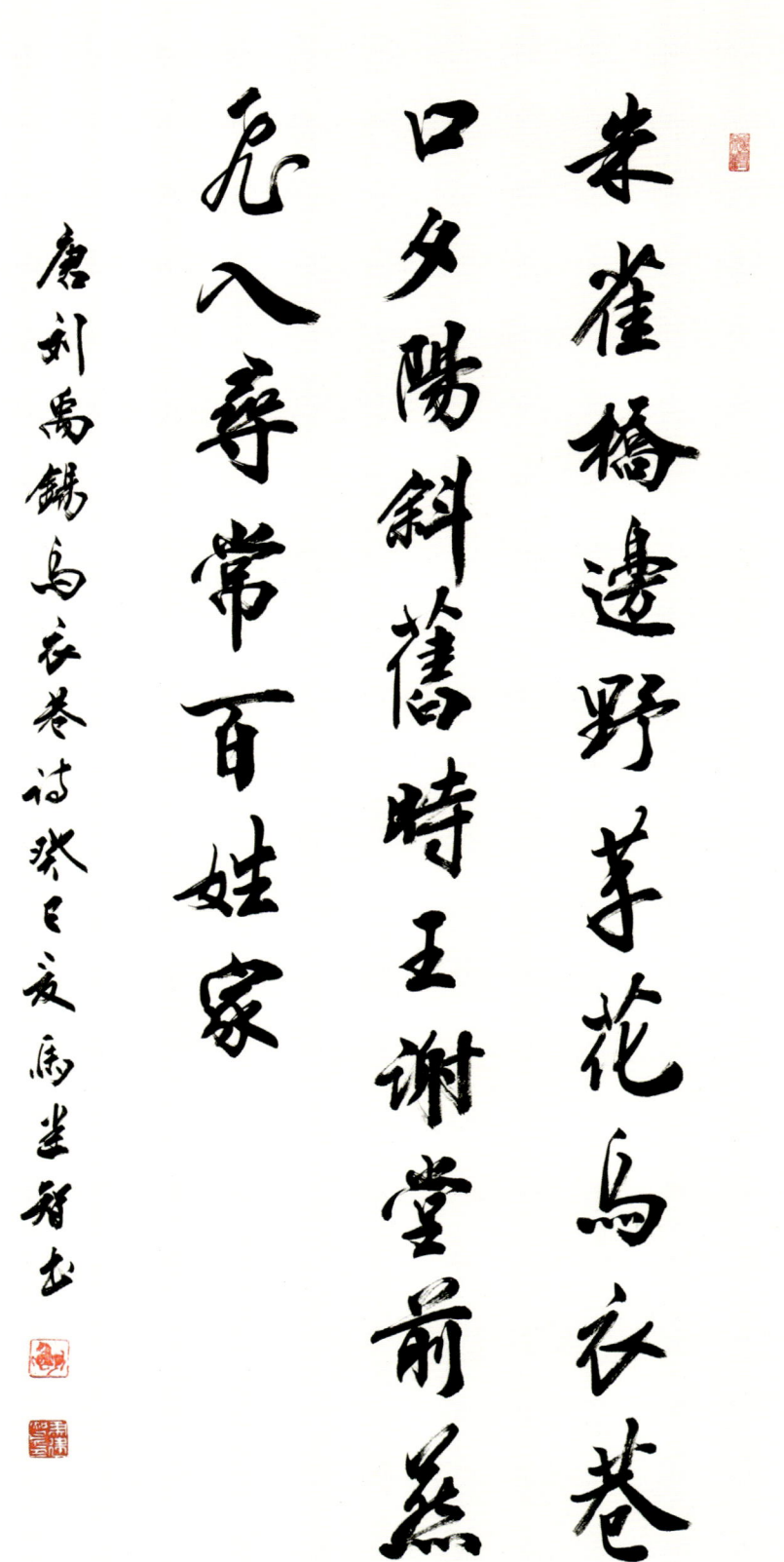

刘禹锡《乌衣巷》　　138cm×69cm　　*Liu Yuxi "Wu Yi Street"*

# 曾永松　*Zeng Yongsong*

曾永松，男，广东人，现为中国艺术家协会会员，广东省美术家协会会员，河源美术研究院副院长，河源市美术家协会副主席，中国画院特聘画家。

润笔价格：10,000元/平尺

Zeng Yongsong, male, is from Guangdong. He is now the member of the China Artists Association, member of the Guangdong Provincial Artists Association, vice president of the Heyuan Art Research Institute, vice chairman of the Heyuan City Artists Association, Distinguished painter of the Chinese Painting academy.
*Reference price: 10,000 yuan / square foot*

《东江美如画》　　98cm×180cm　　*"Beautiful Dongjiang"*

## 苏红云  *Su Hongyun*

苏红云，男，河北平乡县人，历任人民教师、解放军战士、公社党委书记、县人民政府办公室主任、县政协副主席等职，系河北省作协、书协会员。

润笔价格：4,000元/平尺

Su Hongyun, male, is from Pingxiang County, Hebei. He served as a teacher, a PLA soldiers, the party secretary of the commune, head of a office of the county government, vice chairman of the county CPPCC. He is now the member of the Provincial Writers Association and Calligraphers associaton.
*Reference price: 4,000 yuan / square foot*

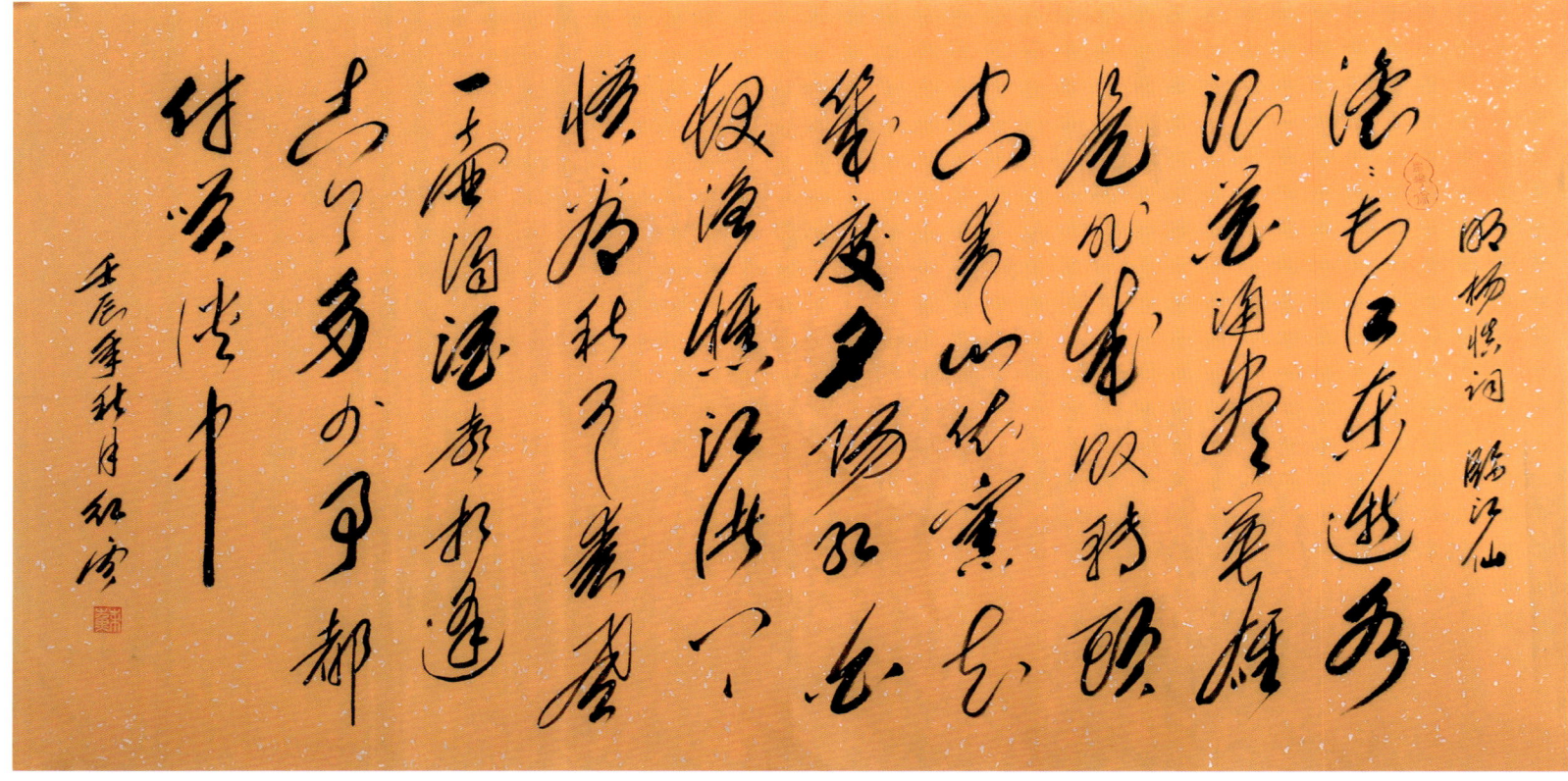

杨慎《临江仙》　　69cm×136cm　　*Yang Shen "Riverside Immortal"*

## 王广然  *Wang Guangran*

王广然，男，河北省大城县人，艺痴先生，黑龙港河居士。河北省美术家协会会员，白石门下弟子，会意水墨画创始人，中国国画艺术研究院副院长，中国国际书画研究院副院长，中国画院一级画师，中国画家协会理事，中国书画研究院院士。

润笔价格：8,000元/平尺

Wang Guangran, male, is from Dacheng County, Hebei. He is known as Mr. Arts Fanatic and Lay Buddhist of Heilonggang River. He is the disciple of Naishi, and is the fonder of the ink style known as Knowing. He is the member of Hebei Artists Association, vice president of Chinese Painting Art Research Institute, vice president of China International Painting and Calligraphy Research Institute, an A-level painter in Chinese Painting academy, director of Chinese artists Association, academician of Chinese Painting and Calligraphy Institute.

*Reference price: 8,000 yuan / square foot*

《连年有余》  69cm×137cm  *"Surplus Year after Year"*

## 查德元  *Zha Deyuan*

查德元，男，1934年生，大学文化，中共党员、主任编辑，原任湖北省老河口市文联主席，现为国际书画艺术研究院院士，湖北省书法协会会员，老河口市书画协会副主席。

润笔价格：5,000元/平尺

Zha Deyuan, male, born in 1934, possesses a university degree. He is Communist Party members and chief editor. He served as chairman of the Laohekou literary federation in Hubei, and currently holds the office as the academician of International Fine Art Academy, member of Hubei Calligraphy Association, vice chairman of Laohekou Painting and Calligraphy Association.
*Reference price: 5,000 yuan / square foot*

王维《过香积寺》　　178cm×60cm　　*Wang Wei, "Passing by the Xiangji Templey"*

# 任照彩 *Ren Zhaocai*

任照彩，男，1944年8月1日生，青岛人，现为中国书画家协会理事，中国国画院院士，北京京华兰亭书画院名誉院长，中国书画研究院研究员。

润笔价格：12,000元/平尺

Ren Zhaocai, male, born on August 1, 1944, is from Qingdao. He is the director of Chinese Calligraphers Association, academician of Chinese painting academy, honorary president of Beijing Jing Hua Lanting Calligraphy Institute, researcher of Chinese Painting and Calligraphy Institute.

*Reference price: 12,000 yuan / square foot*

《浩然群山》　　70cm×137cm　　*"Huge Mountains"*

# 孙理庆  *Sun Li Qing*

孙理庆，男，1939年出生，浙江省温岭市人，杭州大学中文系毕业，任温岭市人大常委会主任，温岭市文联名誉主席，系浙江省、台州市、温岭市书协会员，温岭市美协会员，浙江省诗词楹联学会会员。

润笔价格：7,000元/平尺

Sun Li Qing, male, born in 1939, from Wenling, Zhejiang, was graduated from Hangzhou University, majoring in Chinese. he served as director of the standing committees of Wenling, Honorary Chairman of Wenling Literary Federation, member of Calligraphers Association in Zhejiang Province, Taizhou City and Wenling City. He is also the member of Wenling artists Association, Zhejiang poetry and couplet Society.

*Reference price: 7,000 yuan / square foot*

王维《山居秋暝》　　137cm×68cm　　*Wang Wei, "Raining Mountains on Autumn Evening"*

# 田克军　*Tianke Jun*

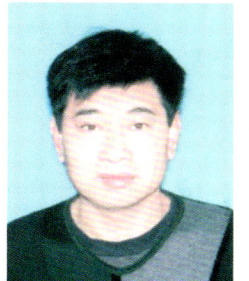

田克军，男，河北省人，霸州美协理事，中国书画联谊会燕南分会理事，中国书画家联谊会会员。
润笔价格：12,000元/平尺

Tianke Jun, male, is from Hebei. He is director of Bazhou Artists Association, director of Yannan branch of Chinese Calligraphy Association, member of Chinese Painting and Calligraphy Association.
*Reference price: 12,000 yuan / square foot*

《山水》　　137cm×70cm　　*"Landscape"*

## 刘国峰  *Liu Guofeng*

刘国峰，男，1974年7月10日生，河南省洛阳人，中国书法家协会会员，达州市青年书法家协会主席，达县书法家协会名誉主席，《纸墨有约》报副主编。

润笔价格：5,000元/平尺

Liu Guofeng, male, born on July 10, 1974, is from Luoyang, Henan. He is member of China Calligraphers Association, president of Dazhou Young Calligraphers Association, honorary chairman of Daxian Calligraphers Association, deputy editor of "Meeting paper and ink".

*Reference price: 5,000 yuan / square foot*

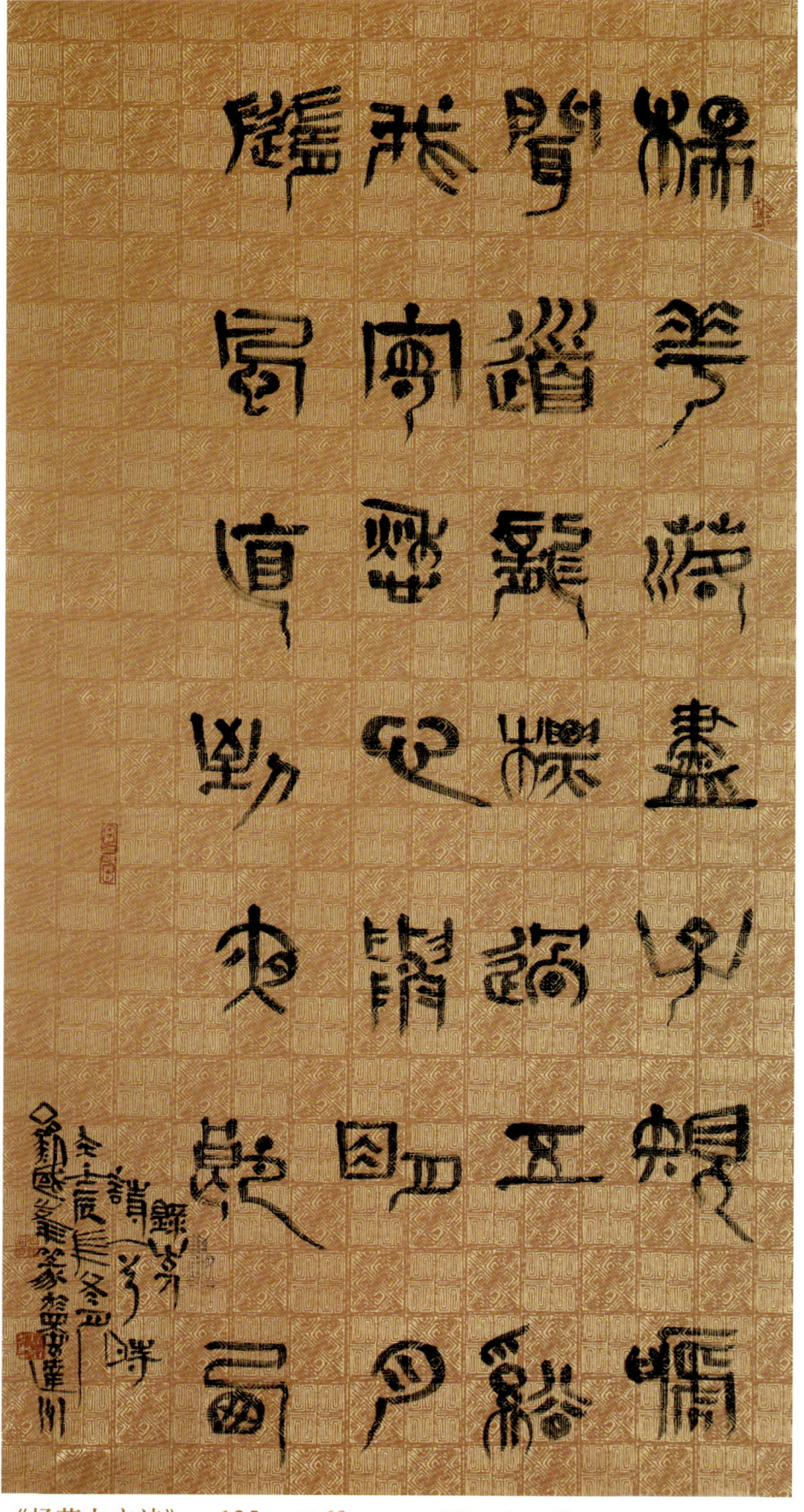

《杨花七言诗》　　135cm×69cm　　*"Yanghwa Seven-word poem"*

# 苏健  *Su Jian*

苏健，1962年生，山东单县人，现为中国文物学会会员，中国美术家协会山东分会会员，山东省单县美术家协会主席，博物馆研究员。

润笔价格：10,000元/平尺

Su Jian, born in 1962, is from Shan County, Shandong. He is member of China Heritage Society, member of Shandong branch of Chinese Artists Association, president of Dan County Artists Association in Shandong, researcher of museum.

*Reference price: 10,000 yuan / square foot*

《花鸟四条屏》　　138cm×34cm×4　　"A Set of Four Paintings of Flowers and Birds"

# 郭增善 *Guo Zengshan*

郭增善，男，1956年生，号三养斋斋主，现为中国公共关系学会艺术委员会会员，北京市朝阳区诗书画研究会会员，现供职于北京工业大学。

润笔价格：6,000元/平尺

Guo Zengshan, male, born in 1956, is also known as Moderator of Sanyang Building. He is the member of Arts Committee in China Public Relations Society, member of Poetry and Calligraphy Research Association of Chaoyang District. He is currently holding an office at Beijing University of Technology.
*Reference price: 6,000 yuan / square foot*

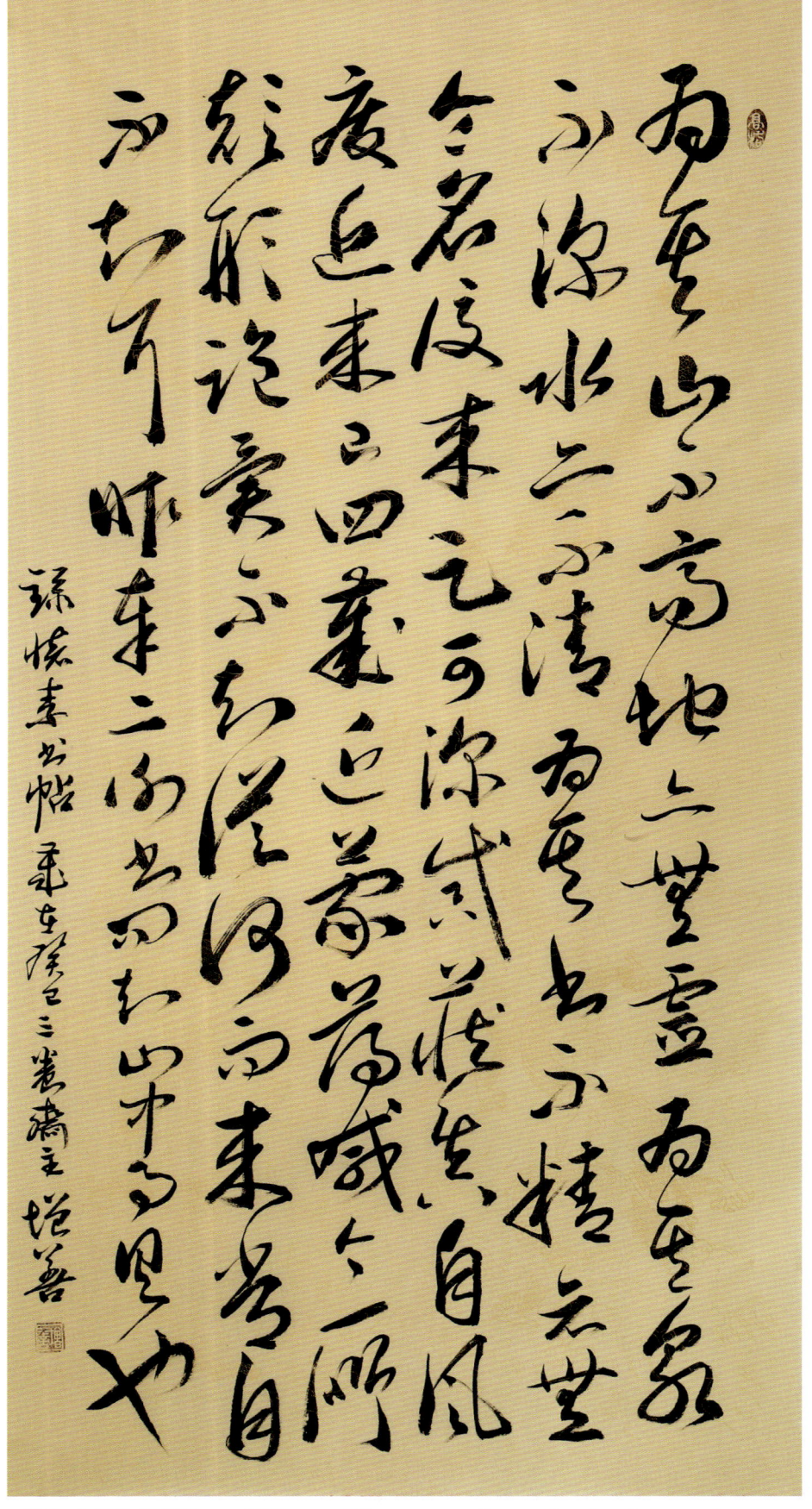

《录 怀素书帖》　　137cm×70cm　　*"Hornbook of Huasu"*

# 马忠  *Ma Zhong*

马忠，1955年生，北京人，现任中国民族书画研究院研究员，北京工笔重彩画会会员，师从国际著名花鸟画画家沈学仁博士，曾得到吴作人、白雪石等前辈大师的教诲。

润笔价格：12,000元/平尺

Ma Zhong, born in 1955, is from Beijing. He is currently the researcher of Chinese national painting academy, member of Beijing meticulous color painting society. He is the disciple of Shen Xueren, who is a internationally renowned bird painter, and taught by Wu Zuoren, Baixue and other senior masters.

*Reference price: 12,000 yuan / square foot*

《玉兰如雪》　　70cm×137cm　　"Snow-white Magnolia"

### 冯建生　*Feng Jiansheng*

冯建生，男，1953年5月24日，北京市人，汉族，中国书协会员，中国艺术家协会书画研究会理事。

润笔价格：6,000元/平尺

Feng Jiansheng, male, born on May 24, 1953, is from Beijing. He is Han nationality and member of Chinese Calligraphers Association, director of Painting Research Association in Chinese Artists Association.

*Reference price: 6,000 yuan / square foot*

海上群峯暎紫霞五雲樓觀是仙家誰吹玉笛春風起千樹碧桃都作花

明劉崧題飛霞閣詩一首癸巳春
馮建生書於獨樂齋

刘崧《题飞霞阁》　　137cm×69cm　　YF "Inscription on Feixia Pavilion"

# 牛山  *Niu Shan*

牛山，女，湖南省美协会员，湘西中国画学术研究中心理事，中原书画院院士，先后就读于怀化学院及天津美院，师从著名花鸟画家易图境、霍春阳、董振涛先生。

润笔价格：10,000元/平尺

Niu Shan, female, is member of the Hunan artists Association, director of Hunan Chinese painting academic research center, academician of Zhongyuan Academy of Painting and Calligraphy. She was graduated from Huaihua University and Tianjin Academy of Fine Arts. She is the disciple of Yi Tujing, Huo Chunyang and Dong Zhentao, who are famous painter on flowers and birds.

*Reference price: 10,000 yuan / square foot*

《山深云满屋》 70cm×139cm  *"Houseful Cloud in Remote Mountain"*

## 郭志坚　*Guo Zhijian*

郭志坚，男，字尧远，号紫塞堂主人，1960年生，天津人，中国艺术家协会书画研究会理事，天津印社社员，天津开发区、保税区、河西区书法家协会会员。

润笔价格：8,000元/平尺

Guo Zhijian, male, born in 1960, is from Tianjin. He possesses pen names as Yao Yuan and Holder of Zizhai Hall. He is the director of Painting Research Association in China Artists Association, member of Tianjin Seal club, member of Calligraphers Association in Tianjin Development Zone, bonded zone and Hexi district.

*Reference price: 8,000 yuan / square foot*

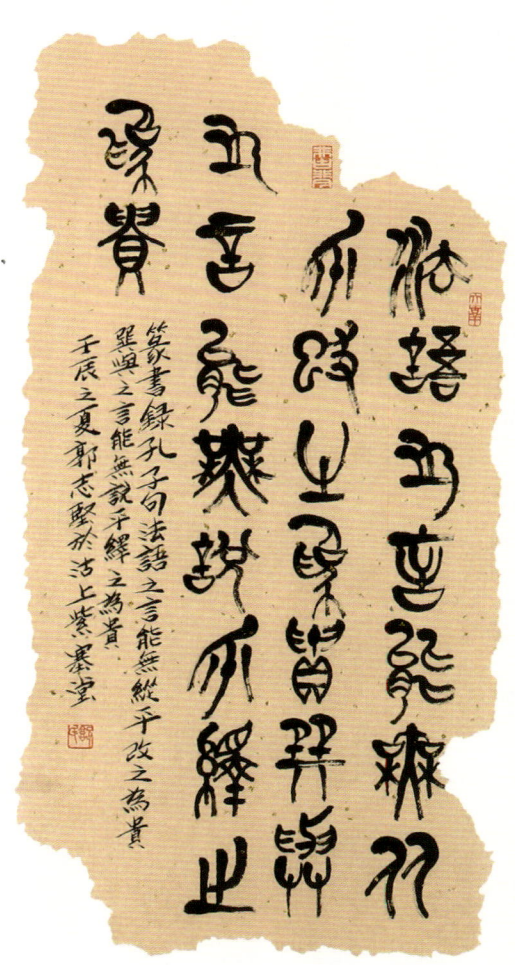

《录孔子句》　125cm×40cm　　"Sentences of Confucius"

# 牛珺辉  *Niu Junhui*

牛珺辉，男，内蒙古美术家协会会员，内蒙古书法家协会会员，包头市东河区美协秘书长。
润笔价格：14,000元/平尺

Niu Junhui, male, is member of Artists Association of Inner Mongolia, member of Inner Mongolia Calligraphers Association, Secretary General of East River District Artists Association in Baotou City.
*Reference price: 14,000 yuan / square foot*

《秋实图》　　83cm×180cm　　*"Painting of Autumn"*

# 韩奇明  *Han Qiming*

韩奇明，男，1943年，北京人，现为中国艺术家协会书画研究会会长，中国书画家联谊会会员，中华浩瀚书画院特邀院士，东城区书画研究会会员。

润笔价格：4,000元/平尺

Han Qiming, male, born 1943, is from Beijing. He is chairman of Chinese Painting Research Association Artists Association, member of Chinese Painting and Calligraphy Association, invited academician of the Chinese Haohan Painting and Calligraphy Institute, member of Dongcheng District Painting Research Association.

*Reference price: 4,000 yuan / square foot*

《诗有烟霞气》　　137cm×69cm　　"Hazy Poetry"

# 张渤涛　*Zhang Botao*

张渤涛，男，1968年生，河北雄县人，现任雄县机关事务管理局局长，河北省美术家协会会员，河北省书法家协会会员，中国画家协会理事。

润笔价格：6,000元/平尺

Zhang Botao, male, born in 1968, is from Xiong County, Hebei. He is currently the chief of Xiong County government affairs office, member of Hebei Province Artists Association, member Hebei Calligraphers Association, director of Chinese painters Association.

*Reference price: 6,000 yuan / square foot*

《锦上添花》　　138cm×68cm　　*"Icing on the Cake"*

# 王国卿 *Wang Guoqing*

王国卿，男，1947年出生，湖北省天门市人，历任行财股长，县书协主席、美协主席，创建县文联任第一任副主席，工会副主席、主席，竹林诗社副社长，市书协常务理事、顾问。

润笔价格：7,000元/平尺

Wang Guoqing, male, born in 1947, is from Tianmen, Hubei. He served as financial section chief, president of county Calligraphers Association and artists Association, the first vice-chairman of County literary Federation, vice president and president of the union, vice chairman of the bamboo poetry, executive director and consultant of City Calligraphers Association.

*Reference price: 7,000 yuan / square foot*

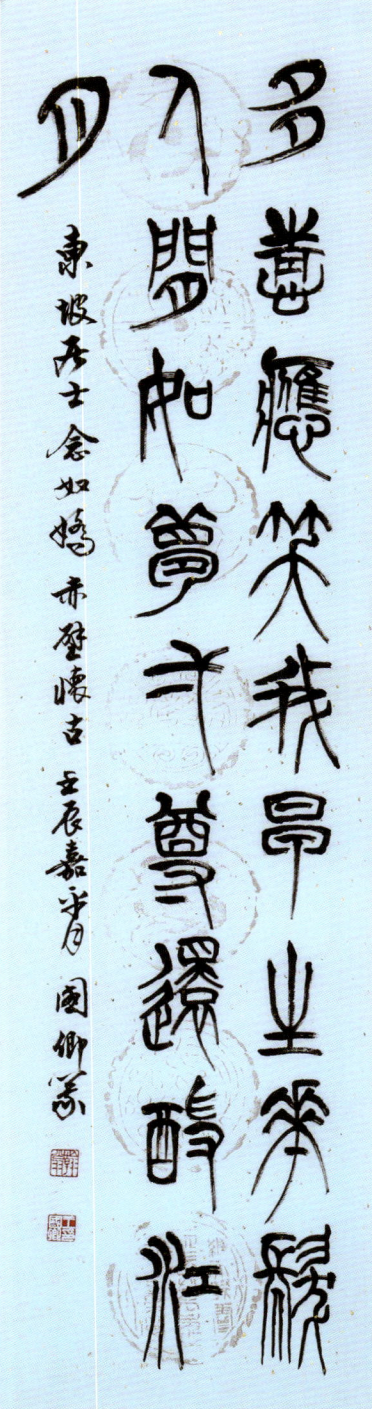

苏轼《赤壁怀古》四条屏　133cm×32cm×4　*A Set of Four Paintings of Su Shi's "Chi Bi"*

## 何学芬　*He Xuefen*

何学芬，四川眉山人，斋号怡心阁。现为美中文化教育经济基金会特聘画家，中国艺术家协会书画研究院理事。数幅作品被国务院北戴河服务局、全国人大、总参、总政、总装及众多博物馆和中华慈善总会收藏，引起了收藏家的广泛关注。

润笔价格：10,000元/平尺

He Xuefen, from Meishan, Sichuan, is also known as Yi Xinge. Now he serves as the distinguished painter of United States and Chinese Culture Education Economics Foundation, director of Chinese Academy of Painting and Calligraphy Artists Association. Several paintings are kept by the State Bureau of services in Beidaihe, the NPC, the General Staff, General Political Department, General Armament Department and the China Charity Federation, and many museums, which attracted wide attention.

*Reference price: 10,000 yuan / square foot*

《伴居青山》　68cm×138cm　*"Living next to Mountains"*

### 贺振涛　　*He Zhentao*

贺振涛，男，现为广州市萝岗区青年联合会委员，广州市萝岗区书法家协会理事。

润笔价格：8,000元/平尺

He Zhentao, Male, is now commissary of Luogang Youth Federation, director of Luogang Calligraphy Association.
*Reference price: 8,000 yuan / square foot*

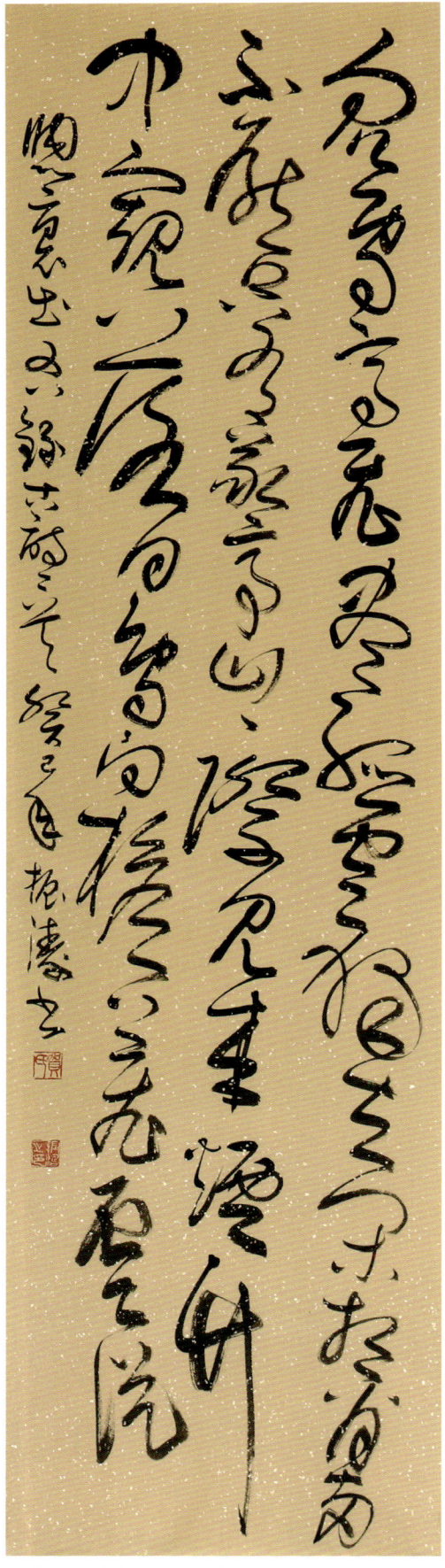

《众鸟高飞尽》　　175cm×47cm　　"The Birds Flew Away"

# 唐明芳 *Tang Mingfang*

唐明芳，号青龙居士，生于四川彭山县青龙镇山秀水灵之地，自幼习画，深受苏东坡和前来彭山久留的张大千、董寿平、徐悲鸿等大师的影响，现为中国国画家协会理事，一级画师，中国文联书画艺术交流中心创作员，中国书法美术艺术创作中心副教授，国际羲之书画院副院长。

润笔价格：10,000元/平尺

Tang Mingfang with a pan name as Lay Buddhist of QingLong, was born in Pengshan, Sichuan. He began studying painting at an early age, and was effected by Su Dongpo, Zhang Daqian, Dong Shouping and Xu Beihong, etc. he is now director of Chinese painting Association, A-level artist, painter of painting and calligraphy art exchange center in China literary Federation , Associate professor of Chinese calligraphy and Art Center, vice president of International Xizhi painting academy.
*Reference price: 10,000 yuan / square foot*

《桃献千寿》  68cm×138cm  *"Long Life Represented by Peach"*

# 吕哲　　*Lvzhe*

吕哲，男，斋号醉墨轩，现为国家一级书法家，中华全国书画家联合会常务副主席，中国书画院高级院士，文化部徐悲鸿书画院特聘书法家，中都书画院客座教授。

润笔价格：4,000元/平尺

*Lvzhe, Male, is also known as Zui Moxuan. He is now a national A-level calligrapher, vice president of China painter Federation, Senior academician of Chinese Painting and Calligraphy Institute, Distinguished calligrapher of the Xu Beihong painting academy in Ministry of Culture, visiting professor in Zhongdu painting and calligraphy academy.*

*Reference price: 4,000 yuan / square foot*

祖咏《终南望余雪》　　70cm×136cm　　*Zu Yong "View Snow in Zhongnan Mountain"*

# 何玉超　HE Yuchao

何玉超，男，1969年生于四川眉山，若水阁阁主。中国文联书画艺术交流中心创作员，中国和合画院一级创作员，中国艺术家协会会员，中国艺术家协会书画研究会理事，河北省经典书画艺术研究院理事，常州南城寺佛教文化艺术馆艺术部主任。

润笔价格：10,000元/平尺

HE Yuchao, male, born in 1969 in Meishan, Sichuan, is the holder of Ruoshui pavilion. He is the painter of art exchange center in China Federation of painting and calligraphy, A-level painter of China Hehe Painting academy, member ofChina Artists Association, director of Research Association in China Artists Association, director of Heibei art research academy of classical painting and calligraphy, head of Art Department of Changzhou Nan Temple Buddhist Culture Museum.

*Reference price: 10,000 yuan / square foot*

《紫气东来》　68cm×138cm　　"Purple Air Comes from the East"

# 张文魁  *Zhang Wenkui*

张文魁，男，山西平定人，中国美术家协会、北京美术家协会会员，中国齐白石艺术研究会副会长，中国禅佛书画院副院长，北京古岸画院院长，敬梅堂主人。

润笔价格：6,000元/平尺

Zhang Wenkui, male, is from Pingding, Shanxi. He is the member of Chinese Artists Association, member of Beijing Artists Association, vice president of China Qi Baishi Art Research Association, vice president of Chinese Zen Buddhism Paintings, president of Beijing Guan Painting Academy, holder of Jing Mei Hall.
*Reference price: 6,000 yuan / square foot*

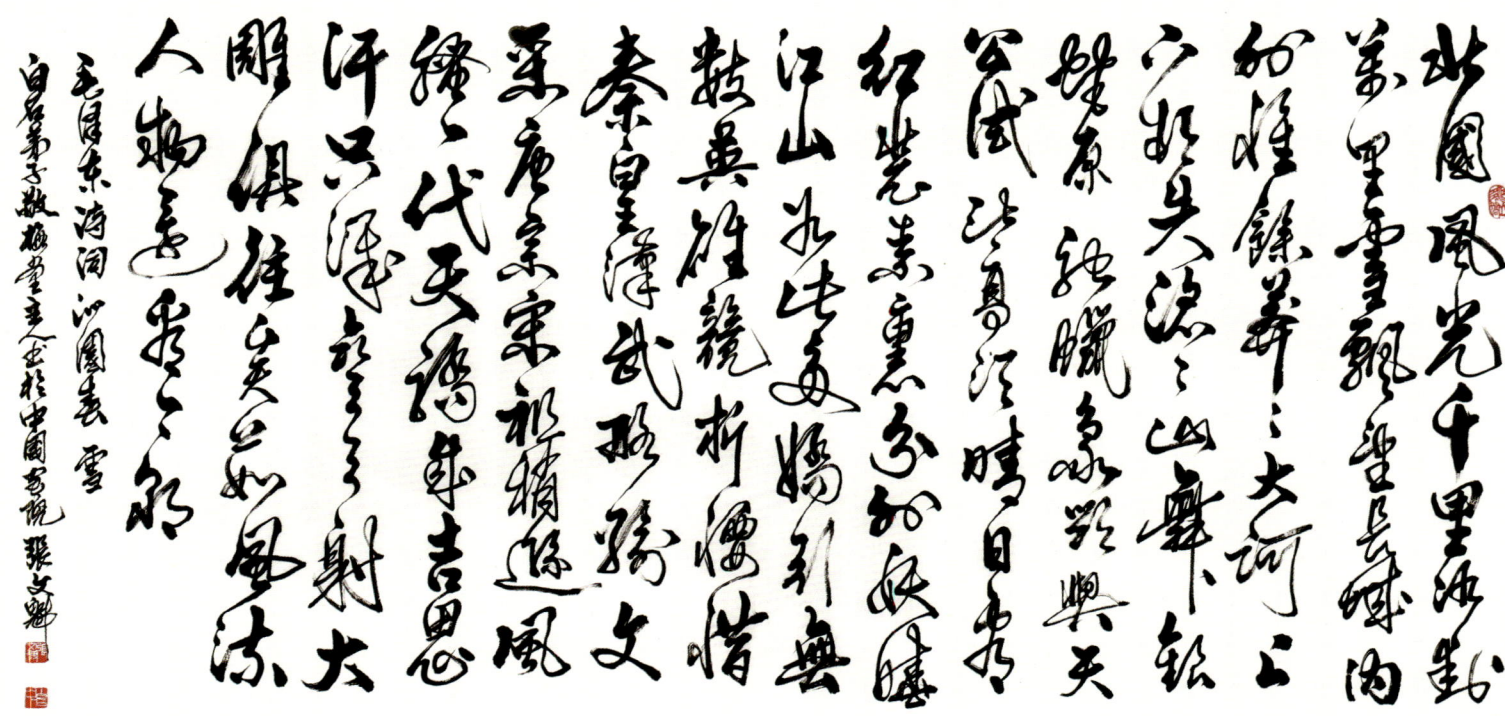

《沁园春·雪》   68cm×138cm   *"To the Tunes of Qin Yuan Chun - Snow"*

# 彭钧  *Peng Jun*

彭钧，男，50年代生于中原禹州，现为专职画家，任中国年代书画院院长、中国美协会员，石河子大学美术系客座教授，《中国美术家》编辑。

润笔价格：10,000元/平尺

Peng Jun, male, was born in 1950 in Yuzhou. He is now a full-time painter. He served as the president of China Niandai paintings academy, member of the Chinese Artists Association, visiting professor of art School of Shihezi University, editor of "Chinese Artists

*Reference price: 10,000 yuan / square foot*

《石榴》　68cm×138cm　　*"Pomegranate"*

# 邓新江　*Deng Xinjiang*

邓新江，1962年6月生，中国书法家协会会员，国家二级美术师，东莞市樟木头镇书法协会会长。

润笔价格：7,000元／平尺

Deng Xinjiang was born in June 1962. He is member of the Chinese Calligraphers Association, National B-level artists, president of Zhangmutou Calligraphy Association.

*Reference price: 7,000 yuan / square foot*

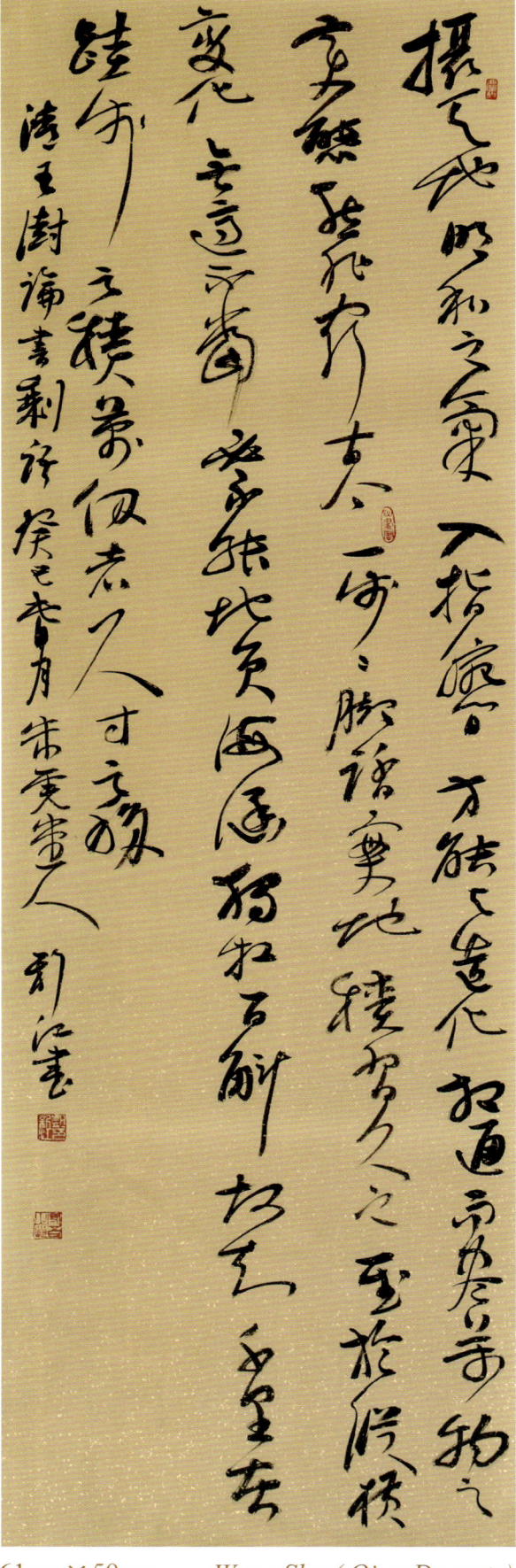

清·王树《论书剩语》　　161cm×50cm　　*Wang Shu ( Qing Dynasty) "Experience on Calligraphy"*

# 葛凤兰 *Ge Fenglan*

葛凤兰，女，汉族，1944年生于陕西定边县。陕西省美术家协会会员，西安市美术家协会会员，陕西省黄河文化艺术研究院副秘书长，西安精英女子画院副秘书长。

润笔价格：8,000元/平尺

Ge Fenglan, female, Han nationality, was born in 1944. she is the member of Shaanxi Artists Association, member of Xi'an Artists Association, deputy secretary-general of the Yellow River Culture and Arts Research Institute, deputy secretary-general of Xi'an elite women's painting academy.

*Reference price: 8,000 yuan / square foot*

《金秋硕果》　　138cm×69cm　　"Fruit in Autumn"

## 金鸣 *Jin Ming*

金鸣，男，笔名拓野，斋号佑文斋、一元斋。1976年8月出生，湖南邵阳人。曾任中国书画函授大学伊犁分校副校长、副教授，任教于北京大学。
润笔价格：5,000元/平尺

Jin Ming, male, is also known as Tuoye, Youwen Zhai and Yiyuan Zhai. He was born in August 1976 in Shaoyang, Hunan. He was Former vice president and associate professor of campus of Yili in Chinese painting and calligraphy correspondence university, and is teaching at Peking University.
*Reference price: 5,000 yuan / square foot*

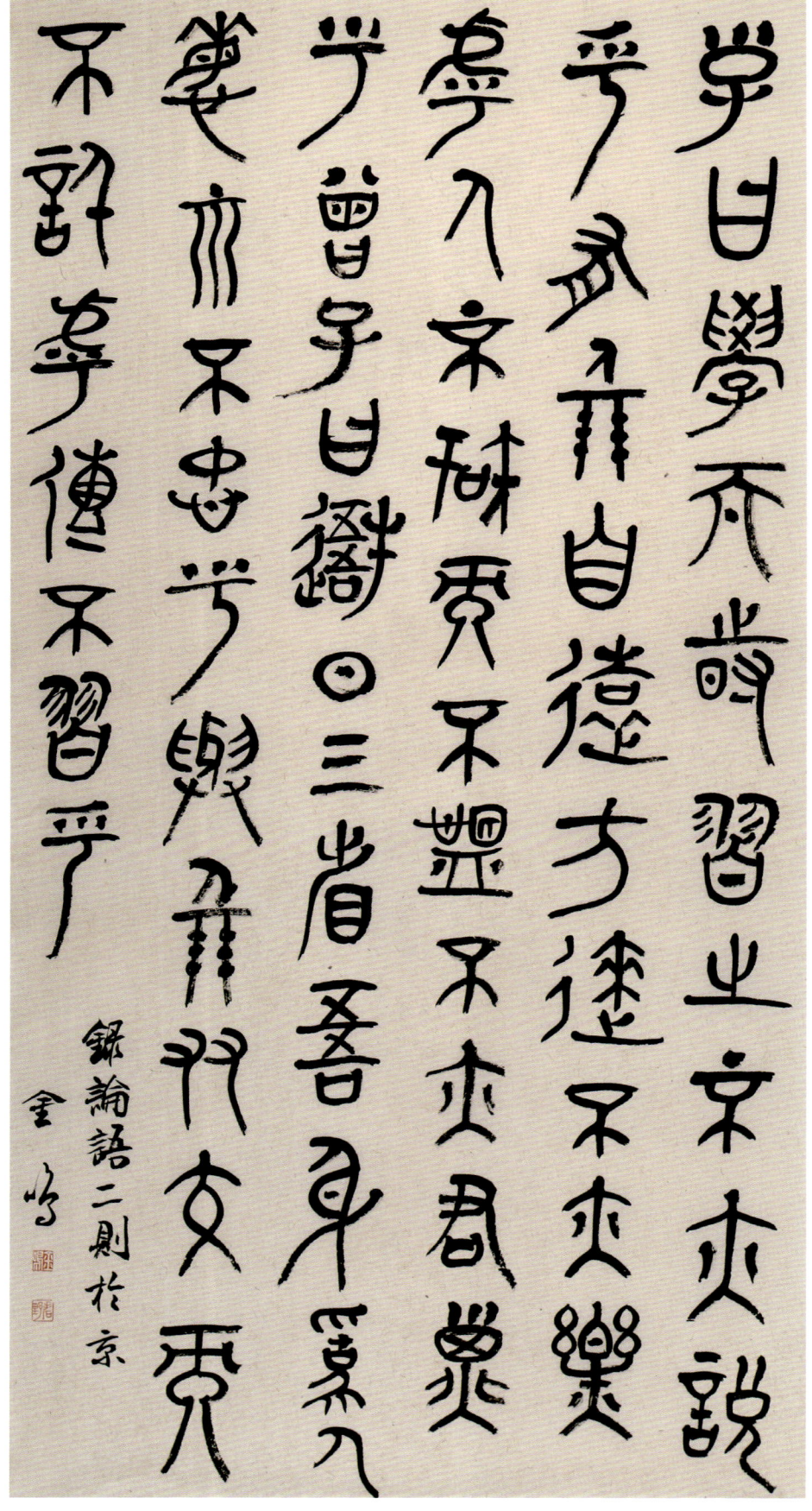

《论语两则》　137cm×70cm　"Two Paragraphs of The Analects"

# 贾宝山　*JIA Baoshan*

贾宝山，笔名沐山，1956年生于陕西西安，陕西省美术家协会会员、西安市美术家协会会员、中国民主促进会会员，主攻山水，兼工花鸟。

润笔价格：10,000元/平尺

JIA Baoshan, with pen name as Mu Shan, was born in 1956 in Xi'an. He is the member of Shaanxi Artists Association, member of Xi'an Artists Association, member of China Association for Promoting, mainly majoring in landscapes, flowers and birds.

*Reference price: 10,000 yuan / square foot*

《秦岭云烟》　138cm×69cm　　*"Cloud and Mist of Qin Ling"*

# 崔长才  *Cui Changcai*

崔长才，男，汉族，1940年3月生，内蒙古人，内蒙古书协会员，鄂尔多斯市书协顾问、鄂尔多斯市政协书画院院士，伊金霍洛旗书协主席。

润笔价格：4,000元/平尺

CUI Changcai, male, Han nationality, was born in March 1940 in Inner Mongolia. He is the member of Inner Mongolia Calligraphers Association, consultant of Ordos City Calligraphers Association, academician of fine art academy of Ordos City CPPCC, chairman of Yijinhuoluo Calligraphers Association.
*Reference price: 4,000 yuan / square foot*

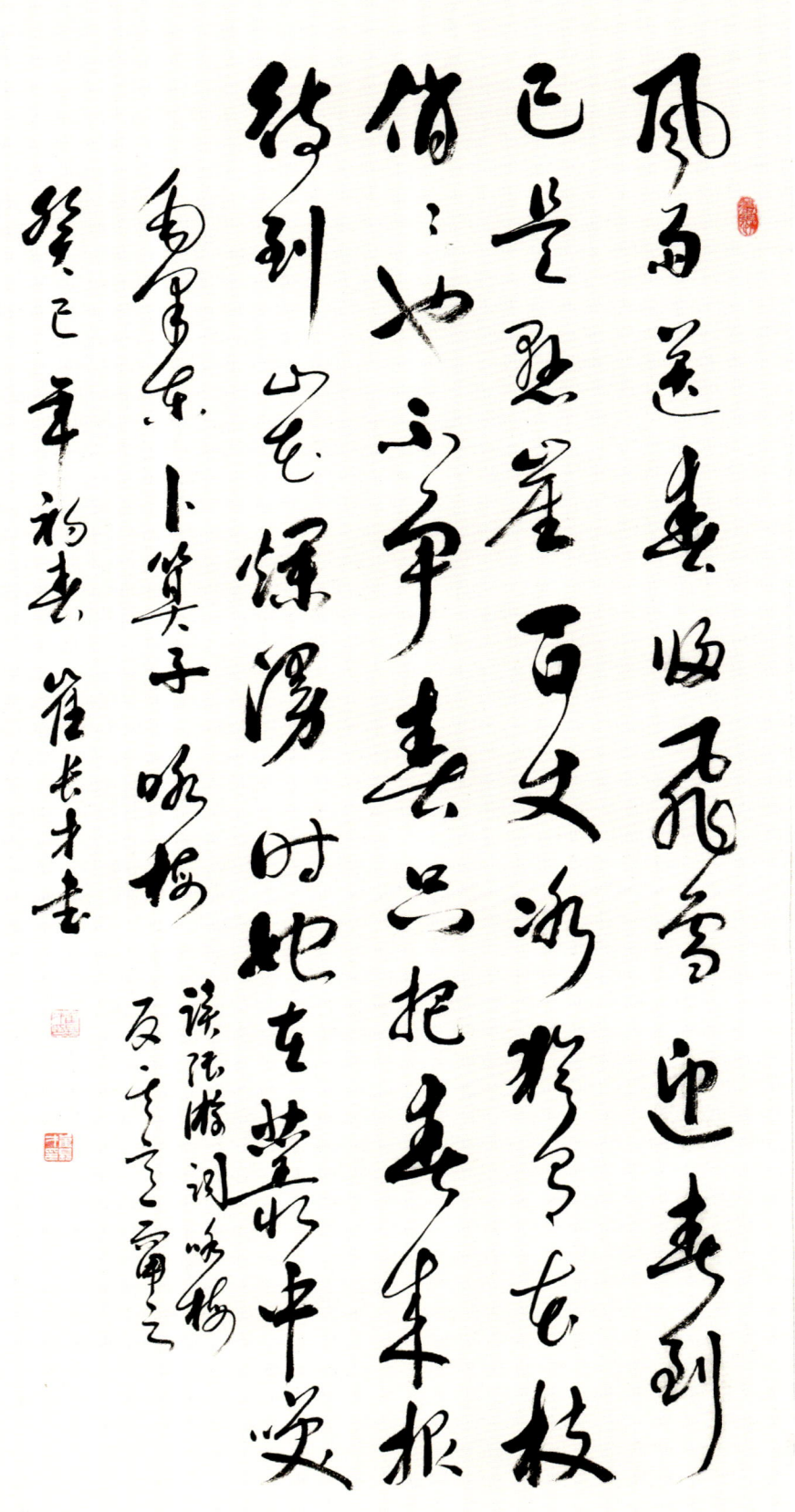

《卜算子·咏梅》　　138cm×68cm　　"To the Tunes of Pu Suan Zi - Plum"

# 李玲  *Li Ling*

李玲，女，1955年出生于西安，现为文化部侨联文华阁书画院画师，西安市美术家协会会员，陕西省书画艺术委员会副主任，西安市山水画研究会副主席，陕西省山水画研究会常务理事。

润笔价格：10,000元/平尺

Li Ling, female, born in 1955 in Xian, is now the painter of Painting and Calligraphy Institute in Ministry of Culture, member of Xi'an Artists Association, deputy director of the Shaanxi Provincial art Committee, deputy president of Xi'an Landscape Painting Research Association, and executive director of Shaanxi Landscape Painting Research Association.

*Reference price: 10,000 yuan / square foot*

《厚土情》　138cm×69cm　*"Love for Thick Soil"*

## 刘如意　*Liu Ruyi*

刘如意，男，号九痴时人，现为北京名人翰墨书画院副院长，河北省书法家协会会员，中华书画报社特聘书法家，承德市硬笔书协理事。

润笔价格：4,000元/平尺

Liu Ruyi, male, is also known as Jiuchi Shiren. He is the vice president of Beijing celebrity calligraphy painting academy, member of Hebei Calligraphers Association, Distinguished calligrapher of Chinese painting and calligraphy newspaper, director of Chengde Hard-Pen Calligraphers Association.

*Reference price: 4,000 yuan / square foot*

《佛》　138cm×68cm　　"Buddha"

# 史国霖　*Shi Guolin*

史国霖，男，1940年生于西安，自幼喜欢绘画，现任陕西西北书画研究院副院长、中国书画家研究院理事。

润笔价格：8,000元/平尺

Shi Guolin, male, was born in 1940 in Xi'an. He was fond in drawing from early age and is the vice president of Shaanxi Northwest Painting and Calligraphy Research Institute, director of Chinese Painting and Calligraphy Institute.
*Reference price: 8,000 yuan / square foot*

《骏马图》　69cm×138cm　　*"Painting of Horses"*

## 谢光辉　*Xie Guanghui*

谢光辉，男，中国书法家协会会员，桂林市书协主席团成员、副秘书长，桂林电子科技大学艺术与设计学院教授。

润笔价格：4,000元/平尺

Xie Guanghui, male, is the member of Chinese Calligraphers Association, member and deputy Secretary-General of the Bureau of Guilin Calligraphers Association, professor of Electronic Science and Technology College of Art and Design of Guilin University.

*Reference price: 4,000 yuan / square foot*

《唐人诗两首》　138cm×68cm　"Two Poems of People in Tang Dynasty"

# 王立文 Wang Liwen

王立文，1940年9月生，河南温县人，军旅画家，国际中国书画家交流促进会艺委会秘书长，曾参与组织多次全国书画大展，任画册主编、艺术顾问等职。

润笔价格：10,000元/平尺

Wang Liwen, born in September 1940, is from Wen country, Henan. He is a military painter, and is the Secretary-General of China International Exchange Association of calligrapher Arts. He has been involved in several organized national painting and calligraphy exhibition, holds the office as book editor and art consultant.

*Reference price: 10,000 yuan / square foot*

《惠风和畅》　　69cm×138cm　　*"Pretty Breeze"*

# 张邦文  *Zhang Bangwen*

张邦文，男，1945年生，陕西安康人，中国硬笔书法家协会会员，青海省硬笔书法家协会副主席，中国书法家协会会员。

润笔价格：6,000元/平尺

Zhang Bangwen, male, born in 1945, is from Ankang, Shaanxi. He is the member of Chinese Hard-Pen Calligraphers Association, vice chairman of Qinghai hard-pan Calligrapher Association, member of the Chinese Calligraphers Association.
*Reference price: 6,000 yuan / square foot*

《将进酒》四条屏    178cm×48cm×4    *A Set of Four Paintings of "Bringing the Wine"*

# 王勇智  *Wang Yongzhi*

王勇智，陕西省人大书画研究会副会长兼办公室主任、陕西省美术家协会会员、陕西省军旅美术家协会副秘书长、西安市雁塔区美术家协会副主席。

润笔价格：8,000元/平尺

Wang Yongzhi is the vice president and director of Shaanxi Painting Research Association of People's Congress, member of the Shaanxi Artists Association, deputy Secretary-General of the Shaanxi Provincial Military Artists Association, and vice Chairman of Yanta District Artists Association.

*Reference price: 8,000 yuan / square foot*

《竹子》　　138cm×69cm　　"Bamboo"

## 王文学　　*Wang Wenxue*

王文学，男，汉族，1958年生，字渊之，号芦荻斋主、三养斋主等，生于安徽宿州市，中国书法家协会会员，江苏省书法家协会会员，新燕都画院院长，中国毛体书法家协会顾问。

润笔价格：4,000元/平尺

Wang Wenxue, male, Han nationality, was born in 1958. He is also known as Hanzhi, Moderator of Ludi, and Moderator of Sanyang. He was born in Suzhou City, Anhui. He is the member of China Calligraphers Association, member of Jiangsu Provincial Calligraphers Association, president of the Xin Yandu painting academy, consultant of Chinese Mao's style Calligraphers Association.
*Reference price: 4,000 yuan / square foot*

《大风歌》　　180cm×50cm　　*"Wind Song"*

# 于福岭 *Yu Fuling*

于福岭，男，笔名金沙，现任中国书画协会理事、中国书画家协会一级美术师、中国美术研究院理事、陕西省美术家协会会员、西安市美术家协会会员。

润笔价格：8,000元/平尺

Yu Fuling, male, is also known as Jinsha, is the member of Chinese Painting and Calligraphy Association, A-level artist of Chinese Calligraphers Association, director of China Art Research Institute, member of Shaanxi Province Artists Association and Xi'an Artists Association.

*Reference price: 8,000 yuan / square foot*

《吉星高照》 138cm×69cm "Best Wishes"

## 桑吉仁谦  *Sangji Renqian*

桑吉仁谦，甘肃省作家协会会员，甘肃少数民族作协理事，当代作家协会会员，甘肃省书法家协会会员，中国国际书画艺术协会会员，中国土族研究会特邀常务理事。

润笔价格：7,000元/平尺

Sangji Renqian is the member of Gansu Writers Association, director of Gansu Minority Writers Association, member of Contemporary Writers Association, member of Gansu Provincial Calligraphers Association, member of China International Fine Arts Association, invited executive director of China Soil Family Research Institution.

*Reference price: 7,000 yuan / square foot*

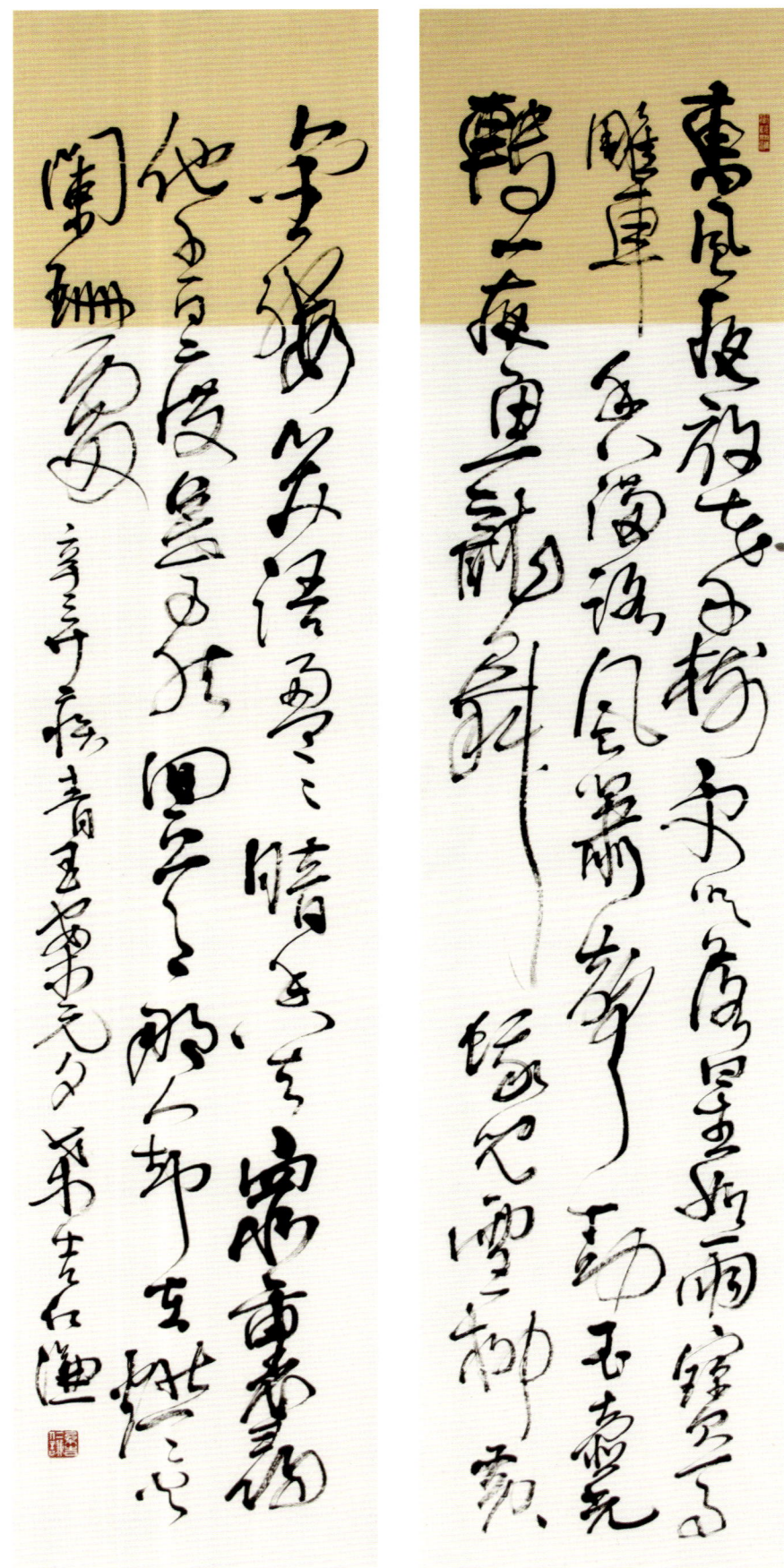

辛弃疾《青玉案·东风夜放花千树》　　165cm×34cm×2　　*Xin Qiji " Gray Jade Table"*

# 于振莲 *Yu Zhenlian*

于振莲，1950年出生于山东文登，有幸师承长安画派名家何海霞先生，现为陕西省美协会员、文化部中华艺术交流中心理事、陕西书画艺术研究院理事、西安精英女子画院副院长。

润笔价格：10,000元/平尺

Yu Zhenlian was born in 1950 in Shandong. She was taught by He Haixia, a famous painter of Changan Style. She is now the member of Shaanxi Province Artists Association, director of China Arts Exchange Center of the Ministry of Culture, director of Shaanxi Calligraphy and Painting Research Institute, vice president of Xi'an woman elite painting academy.

*Reference price: 10,000 yuan / square foot*

《青坡十里》　138cm×69cm　"Ten Mile of Green Slope"

# 周彬　　*Zhou Bin*

周彬，男，1940年9月9日生，安徽省淮北市人，安徽省书法家协会会员，淮北书协会员，淮北市书画研究会理事。

润笔价格：5,000元/平尺

Zhou Bin, male, born on September 9, 1940, is from Huaibei, Anhui. He is currently the member of Anhui Calligraphers Association, member of Huaibei Calligraphers Association, director of Huaibei City Painting Research Association.

*Reference price: 5,000 yuan / square foot*

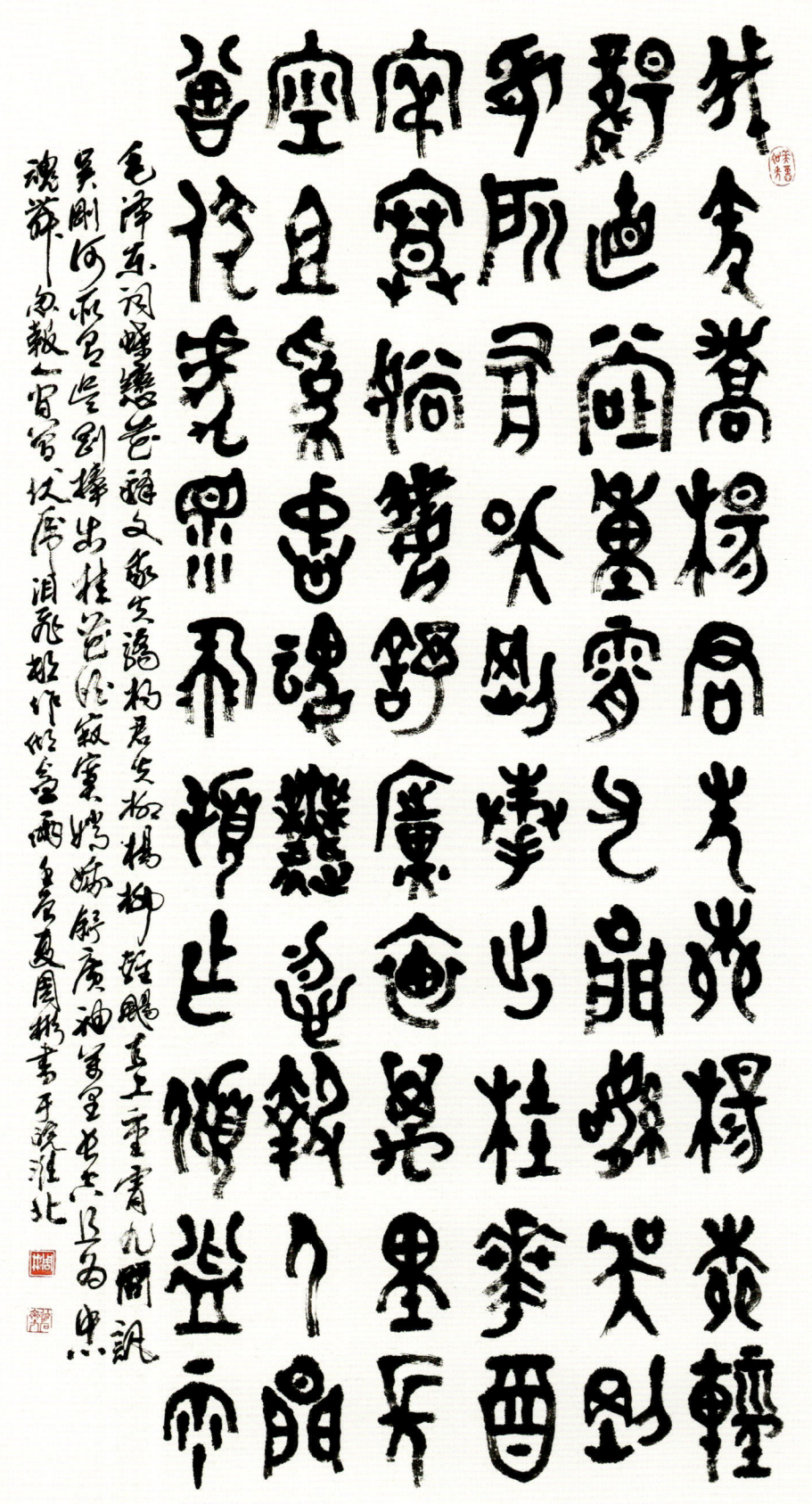

《蝶恋花·答李淑一》　　137cm×69cm　　"Butterflies Loving Flowers – Reply to Li Shuyi"

# 张晓民　*Zhang Xiaomin*

张晓民，男，1954年12月生于陕西西安。陕西省美术家协会会员，西安市美术家协会会员，陕西省山水画研究会理事，西安汉唐书画学会常务副会长，陕西政法系统书画协会艺术顾问。

润笔价格：10,000元/平尺

Zhang Xiaomin, male, was born in December 1954 in Xi'an. He is the member of Artists Association of Shaanxi Province, member of Xi'an Artists Association, director of Shaanxi Province Landscape Research Association, executive vice president of Hantang Painting Association, art consultant of political and legal system in Shaanxi Calligraphy Association,.

*Reference price: 10,000 yuan / square foot*

《铁骨神韵》　　138cm×69cm　　"Strong Mind"

## 涂正康  *Tu Zhengkang*

涂正康，男，1936年6月生，江苏泗阳人，中国书法家协会会员，一级书法师，洛阳市颜真卿研究会名誉会长。

润笔价格：5,000元/平尺

Tu Zhengkang, male, born in June 1936, is from Jiangsu Siyang. He is the member of Chinese Calligraphers Association, an A-level calligrapher, honorary president of Luoyang Yen Zhenqing Research Institution,.

*Reference price: 5,000 yuan / square foot*

《念奴娇·赤壁怀古》　　69cm×137cm　　"To the Tunes of Nian Nujiao - Chibi"

## 甄德贤  *Zhen Dexian*

甄德贤，1950年9月生，祖籍河北邢台。1969年参军到中央警卫团，历任战士至正师职副团长，大校军衔。2000年3月转业到人民大会堂管理局任正局级副局长、纪委书记、党委副书记。现为中央国家机关书法家协会常务理事，北京市摄影家协会会员。

润笔价格：10,000元/平尺

Zhen DeXian, born in September 1950, is a native of Xingtai, Hebei. He joined the army to the central Guards Regiment in 1969, served as warrior and positive division level to deputy head of the rank, and now has the level of colonel. He transferred to be the deputy director of board-level, Secretary of the Discipline Inspection Commission, and deputy Secretary of the Party committee in March 2000. he is Currently the executive director of the Calligraphers Association in central state organs, member of Beijing Photographers Association.

*Reference price: 10,000 yuan / square foot*

《多寿》　　138cm×69cm　　"Longevity"

## 艾创奇  *Ai Chuangqi*

艾创奇，男，汉族，1956年9月生，湖南省江平县牛寨人，现为中国书画家协会理事，北京东方名家书画院永久性高级专业书画家。

润笔价格：4,000元/平尺

Ai Chuangqi, male, Han nationality, was born in September 1956. He is the director of Chinese Calligraphers Association, permanently senior professional calligrapher of Beijing Oriental Painting and Calligraphy Institute.
*Reference price: 4,000 yuan / square foot*

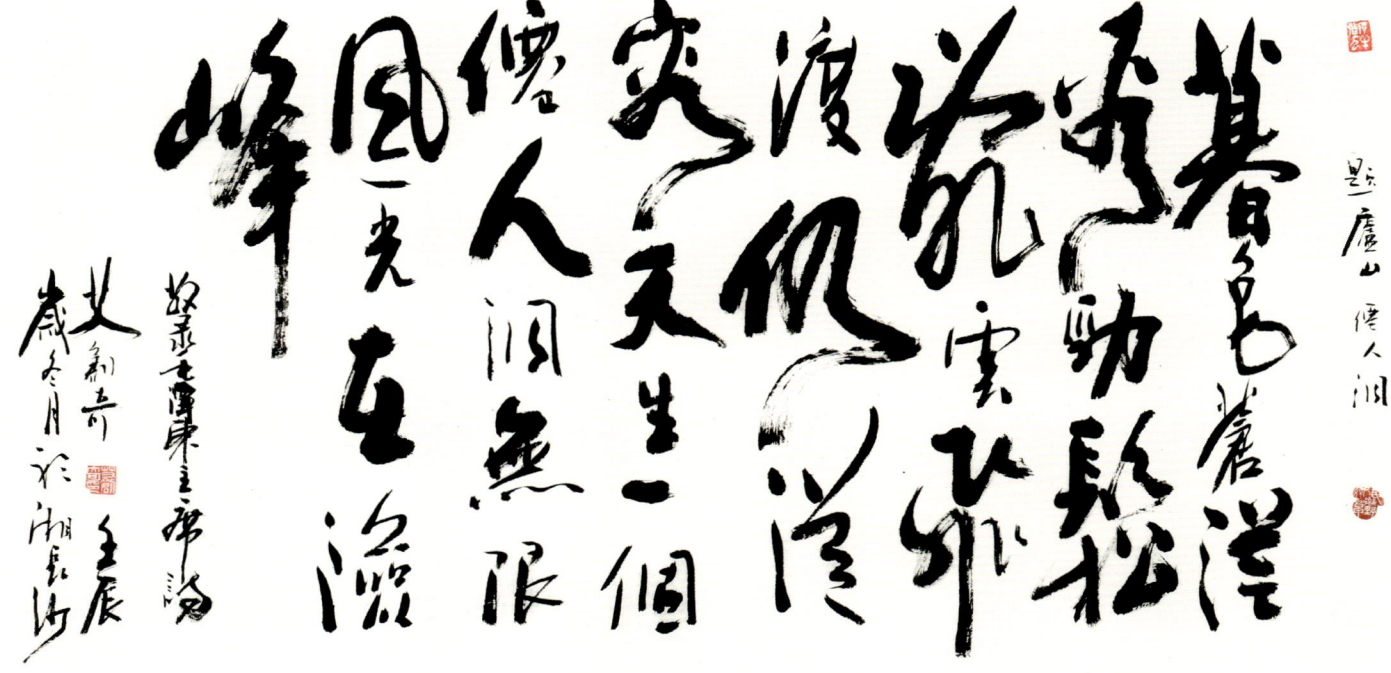

《题庐山仙人洞》　　68cm×136cm　　*"Inscription on the Fairy Cave of Lushan"*

# 贾建国  *Jia Jianguo*

贾建国，字鉴闻，号见山堂主人，工艺美术师，北京市美术家协会会员，中国文化艺术发展促进会艺术会员，北京装帧艺术研究会理事，现为中国图书文化展览馆馆长。

润笔价格：14,000元/平尺

Jia Jianguo, also known as the Holder of Jianshan Hall and Jianwen, is a craft artist, and the member of Beijing Artists Association, member of Chinese Culture and Arts Development Association, director of Beijing Binding Art Research Association. Now he holds the office as the curator of the Chinese book culture exhibition.
*Reference price: 14,000 yuan / square foot*

《西山春晓》　　138cm×69cm　　" Spring of Western Hills "

# 冯尚信　*Feng Shangxin*

冯尚信，男，1940年生，河北省高邑县人，中国书画家协会理事、高邑县老干部书协副主席。
润笔价格：5,000元/平尺

Feng Shangxin, male, was born in 1940 in Gao Yi County, Hebei. He is the director of China Calligraphers Association, vice chairman of Gao Yi county veteran Calligraphers Association.
*Reference price: 5,000 yuan / square foot*

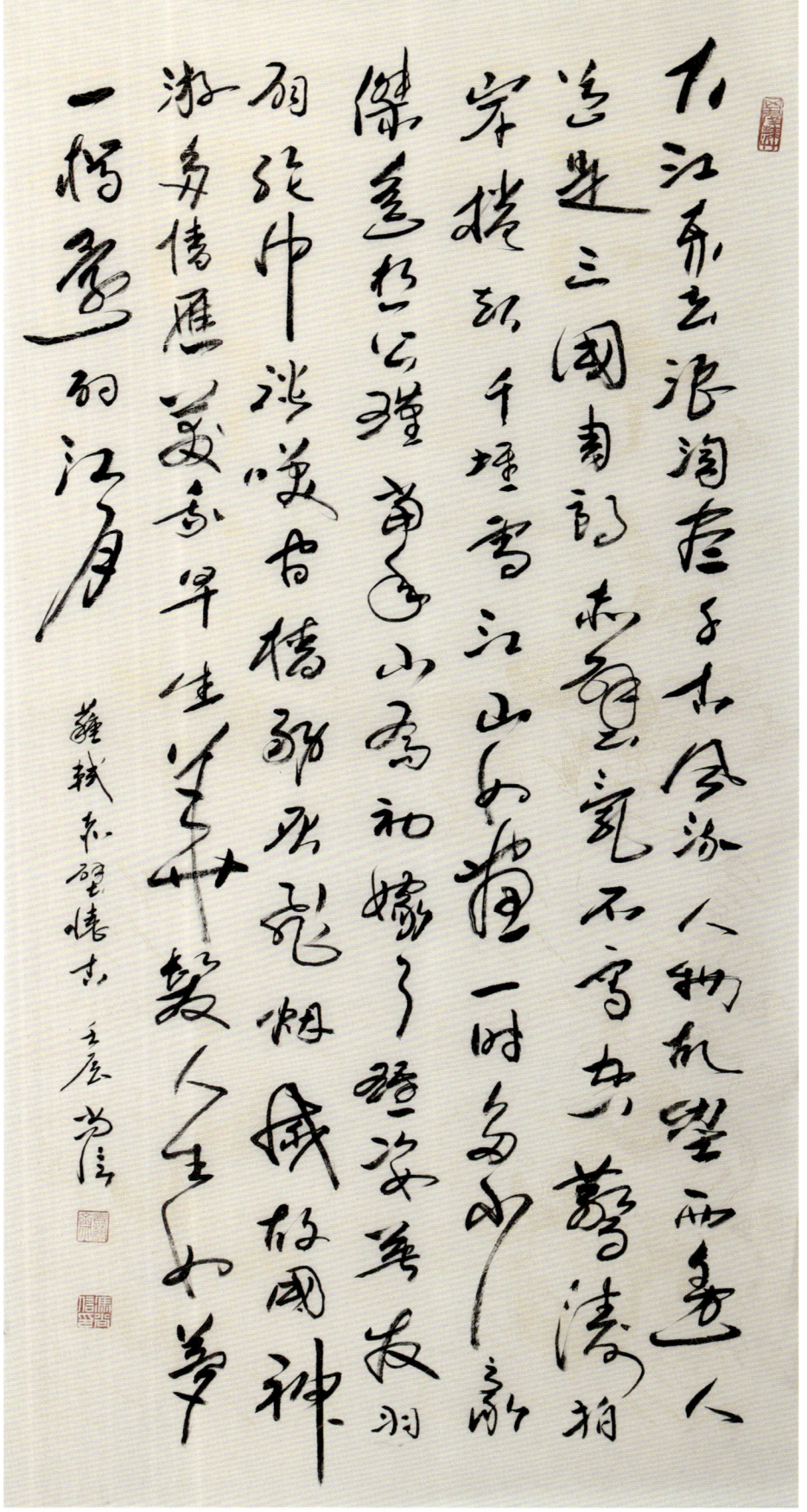

《念奴娇·赤壁怀古》　　136cm×68cm　　"To the Tunes of Nian Nujiao - Chibi"

## 紫荷   *Zihe*

紫荷，原名李怡静，现任翰林书画院院长，北科院教授，中国书画界联合会会员，中国国际书画院理事，中国绿化基金会艺术委员会委员，中国徐悲鸿画院画师，华夏东方杰书画院名誉副院长。

润笔价格：12,000元/平尺

Zihe, formerly known as Li Yijing, is now the president of the Imperial Painting and Calligraphy Institute, professor of the North EPRI, member of Federation of Chinese calligraphy and painting, director of Chinese International Association of Painting and Calligraphy, commissary Art Committee of China Green Foundation, painter of Chinese Xu Beihong Painting academy, Honorary vice president of China Oriental Jie Painting and Calligraphy Institute.

*Reference price: 12,000 yuan / square foot*

《境由心生》   102cm×66cm   "Environment from the Heart"

### 张源太 *Zhang Yuantai*

张源太，男，1928年生，山东德州人，现为书法艺术家中外书法鉴赏家，淮海书法艺术学校导师，楚天书画艺术研究院院士。

润笔价格：4,000元/平尺

Zhang Yuantai, male, born in 1928, is from Dezhou, Shandong. He is currently an artist and the connoisseurs of Chinese and foreign calligraphy, instructors of Huaihai calligraphy art school, academician of Chutian Painting Art Research Academy.

*Reference price: 4,000 yuan / square foot*

《书以载道》　　132cm×34cm　　"The Book as a Vehicle"

# 陈锡安　*Chen Xi'an*

陈锡安，字山翁，留云堂主，1952年生于北京，毕业于教育学院美术系，现任京海书画艺术研究院副院长，中国禅学艺术研究院研究员，作品被企业家、个人收藏。

润笔价格：16,000元/平尺

Chen Xi'an, also known as Shanweng and Holder of Liuyun Hall, was born in in 1952 in Beijng. He was graduated from the Fine Arts Department of Education College, and is now the vice president of Jinghai Calligraphy Art Research Institute, researcher of Chinese Zen arts research Institution. His works are collected by the entrepreneurs and individuals.
*Reference price: 16,000 yuan / square foot*

《山居图》　　138cm×69cm　　*"Mountains"*

# 李安儒  *Li Anru*

李安儒，男，1932年3月，陕西省商州人，现为中国老年书画研究会北京市分会和北京市老年书画联谊会会员，任长沙羲之国际艺术中心顾问。

润笔价格：5,000元/平尺

Li Anru, male, born in March 1932, is from Shangzhou, Shaanxi. He is the member of elderly Painting Research Association (Beijing Branch) and Beijing elder painter fraternity, consultant of Changsha Xizhi international art center.

*Reference price: 5,000 yuan / square foot*

四条屏《满江红》　　136cm×17cm×4　　A Set of Four Paintings of "The River All Red"

# 朱淑玉  *Zhu Shuyu*

朱淑玉，女，四川眉山市人，职业画家。现为中国文联书画艺术交流中心创作员，四川省美术家协会会员，四川省工笔画学会会员。

润笔价格：8,000元/平尺

Zhu Shuyu, female, from Meishan City, Sichuan, is a professional painter. She is currently a creative personnel of the China Federation of calligraphy art exchange center, member of Sichuan Artists Association, member of Sichuan claborate-style painting Society.

*Reference price: 8,000 yuan / square foot*

《樱花颂》　　69cm×69cm　　*"Sakura Song"*

# 江太生  *Jiang Taisheng*

江太生，男，1958年5月生，安徽太湖人，现为中国收藏家协会会员、中国书画家协会理事、中国硬笔书法协会会员、中国金融书法家协会会员、安徽书法家协会会员。

润笔价格：5,000元/平尺

Jiangtai Sheng, male, born in May 1958, is from Taihu, Anhui. He is member of China Collectors Association, director of the Chinese Calligraphers Association, member of Chinese Hard-Pen Calligraphy Association, member of Chinese financial Calligraphers Association, member of Anhui Calligraphers Association.
*Reference price: 5,000 yuan / square foot*

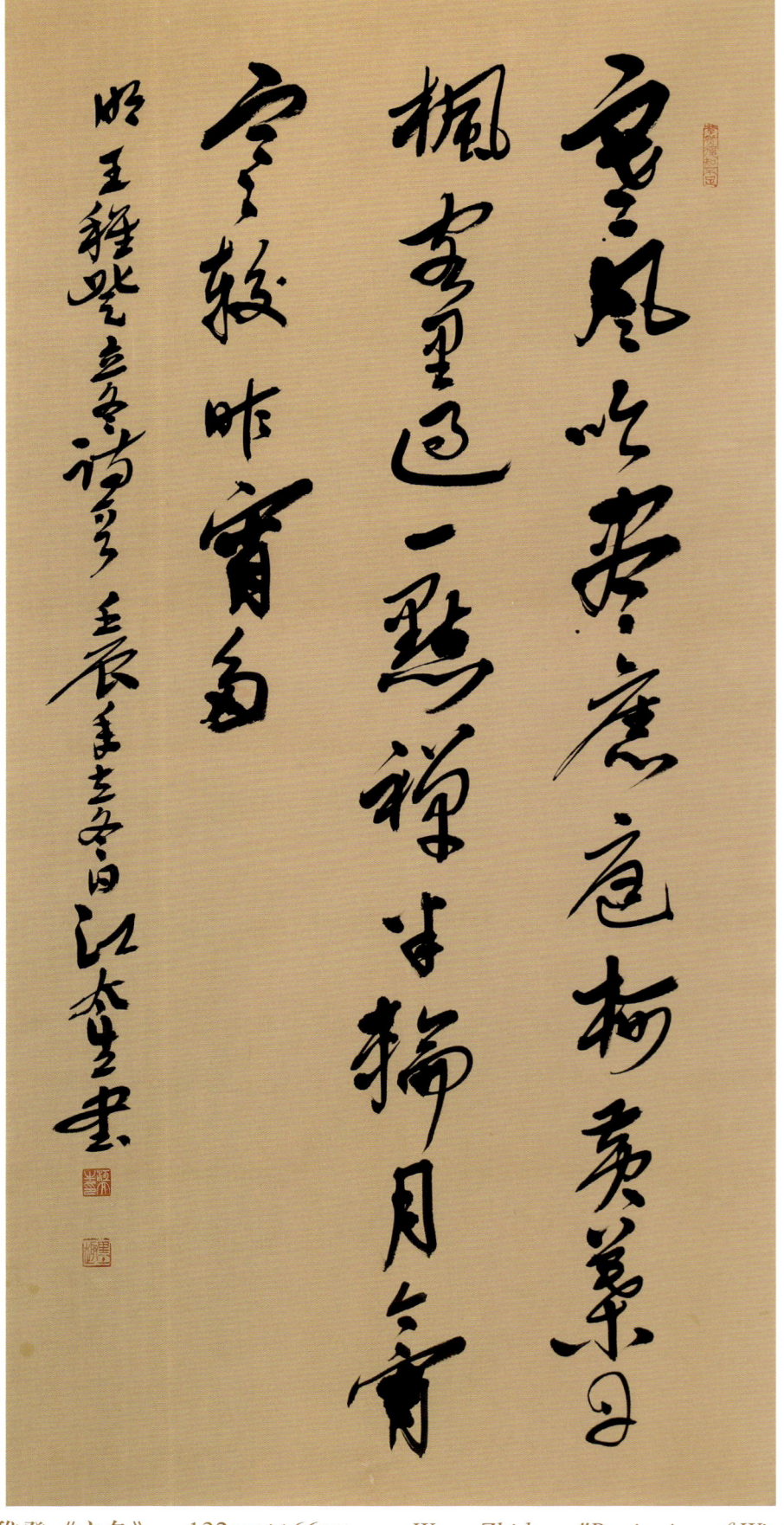

王稚登《立冬》　　132cm×66cm　　*Wang Zhideng "Beginning of Winter"*

# 李修举  *Li Xiuju*

李修举，男，1941年生，山东青岛人，现为山东潍坊教育学院教授、中国美协会员、山东省美协会员、青岛市书画联谊会会长、青州市美协副主席、金陵书画院名誉院长。

润笔价格：8,000元/平尺

Li Xiuju, male, born in 1941, is from Qingdao, Shandong. He is the professor of Weifang education Institution, member of Chinese Artists Association, member of Shandong Province Artists Association, president of Qingdao painting Friendship Association, vice president of Qingzhou City Artists Association, honorary president of Jinling Painting and Calligraphy Institution.

*Reference price: 8,000 yuan / square foot*

《三思图》　　137cm×69cm　　*"Painting of Thinking Twice"*

# 张本堂　*Zhang Bentang*

张本堂，男，山东人，山东省书法家协会会员。

润笔价格：4,000元/平尺

Zhang Bentang, male, is from Shandong Province. He is the member of Shandong Calligraphers Association.
*Reference price: 4,000 yuan / square foot*

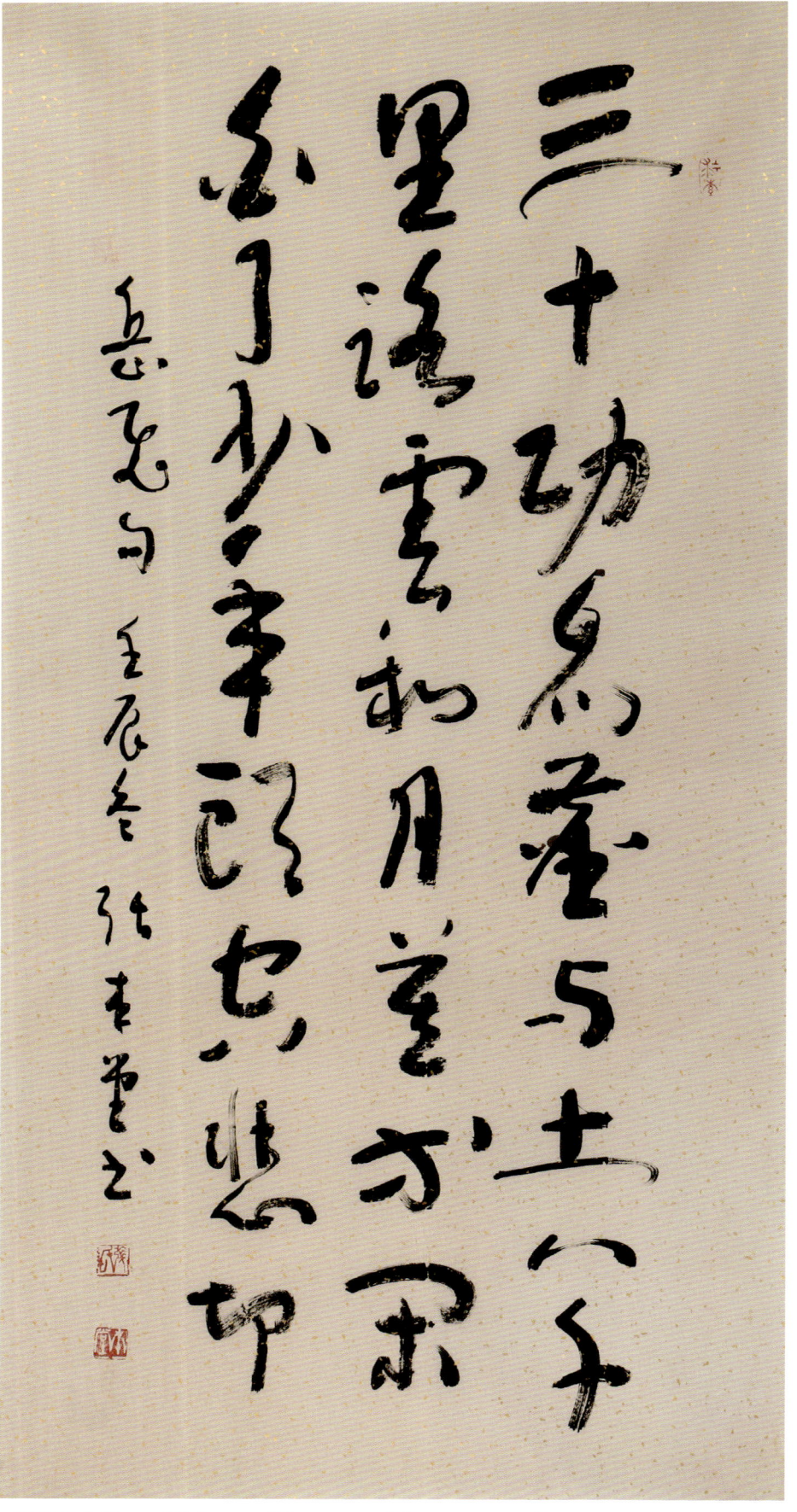

《岳飞句》　　134cm×67cm　　*"Sentences of Yue Fei"*

# 余斯清  *Yu Siqing*

余斯清，男，1932年出生，福州市人，微书"滕王阁序"被第三届"世界华人艺术大会"评为特别奖，国画作品"小品扇面四扇屏"被中国书画研究院评为"传世金奖"。

润笔价格：14,000元/平尺

Yu Siqing, male, born in 1932, is from Fuzhou. His micro Calligraphy work "Preface to Tengwang Pavilion" was commented as special award by the third "World Chinese art conference", and his painting work "a set of four paintings of fans" is commented as " Gold award to be handed down. " by Chinese Painting and Calligraphy Institute.

*Reference price: 14,000 yuan / square foot*

《小品扇面四扇屏》　　24cm×28cm×4　　*" A Set of Four Paintings of Fans "*

# 卢振先 *Lu Zhenxian*

卢振先，1949年生，广西兴业县人，广西硬笔书法协会理事，广西对外友好交流书法家协会理事，广西玉林市文联书法家协会理事，中国书画院特聘名誉院长，国家书画院委任书画院副院长。

润笔价格：4,000元/平尺

Lu Zhenxian, born in 1949, is from Xingye, Guangxi. He is the director of Guangxi Hard-Pen Calligraphy Association, director of Guangxi Calligraphy Association for Friendship with Foreign Exchange, director of Guangxi Yulin Literature and Arts Calligraphy Association, honorary president of Chinese Painting and Calligraphy Institute Chair, vice president of National Painting and Calligraphy Institute.

*Reference price: 4,000 yuan / square foot*

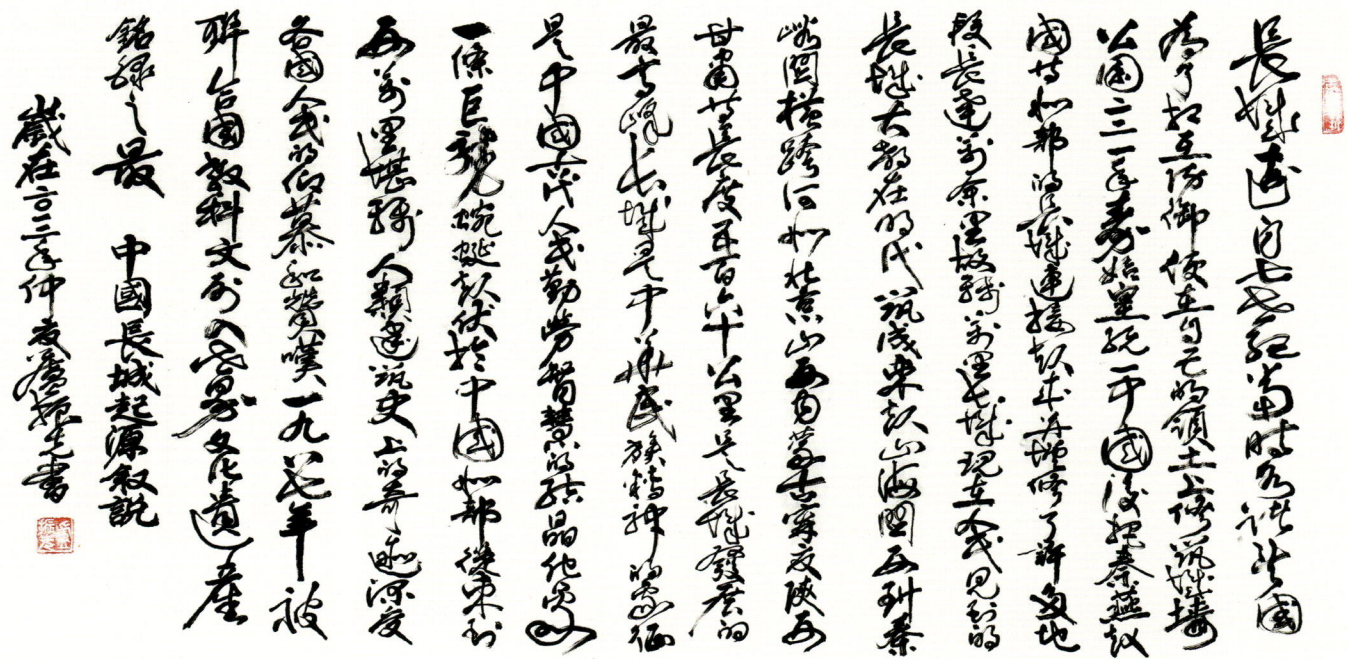

《中国长城起源叙说》　　178cm×96cm　　*" Origin of the Great Wall"*

# 佘汉武　She Hanwu

佘汉武，男，湖南人，中华诗词学会会员，中国楹联协会会员，中华书画家协会副主席，湖南靖港古镇画院院长。

润笔价格：8,000元/平尺

She Hanwu, male, is from Hunan. He is the She Hanwu China Poetry Society, member of Chinese couplets Association, vice Chairman of Chinese Calligraphers Association, president of Hunan jinggang town Painting Academy.

*Reference price: 8,000 yuan / square foot*

《马到成功》　　53cm×230cm　　"Instant Success"

## 袁康年　*Yuan Kangnian*

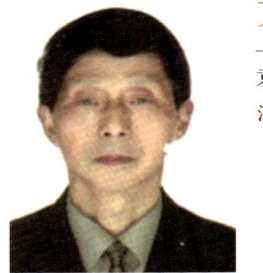

袁康年，男，1959年，作品先后多次被港澳台、新加坡、澳大利亚领导人、华人等收藏。
润笔价格：4,000元/平尺

Yuan Kangnian, male, was born in 1959. His works have repeatedly been collected by leaders of Hong Kong, Macao, Taiwan, Singapore and Australia, as well as by other Chinese.
*Reference price: 4,000 yuan / square foot*

王昌龄《黄沙百战穿金甲》　　136cm×69cm　　*Wang Changling "Force Armed with Golden Armor"*

# 史文青 *Shi Wenqing*

史文青，男，1947年5月4日生，河北省大名县人，辽宁美术家协会会员，中国书画研究院院士，一级美术师，南京颜真卿文化研究会名誉主席。

润笔价格：6,000元/平尺

Shi Wenqing, male, born on May 4, 1947, is from Daming Country, Hebei. He is the member of Liaoning Artists Association, academician of Chinese Academy of Painting and Calligraphy Institution, A-level artist, and honorary chairman of Nanjing YanZhenQing Culture Research Association.
*Reference price: 6,000 yuan / square foot*

《富贵雍容》　　70cm×137cm　　*"Rich and Grace"*

## 吴继海  *Wu Jihai*

吴继海,男,1940年,河南省范县人,现为中国五体书法研究会副会长兼行书专业委员会常务委员会委员,中国书法家协会和中国书画家协会会员、国家一级书法师。

润笔价格:5,000元/平尺

Wu Jihai, Male, born in 1940, is from Fan country, Henan. He is now vice president of China five bodies' calligraphy Research Committee and commissary of running cursive Committee, member of China Calligraphers Association and the Chinese paintings and Calligraphers Association, national A-level calligrapher.

*Reference price: 5,000 yuan / square foot*

《笔情墨趣》　　138cm×68cm　　*"Taste of Ink Pen"*

# 何悦丰  *He Yuefeng*

何悦丰，男，1976年11月11日，广东省揭阳市人，上海民族画院院士，内蒙古青年书画院院士。
润笔价格：6,000元/平尺

He Yuefeng, male, born on November 11, 1976, is from Jieyang City. He is the academician of Shanghai National Painting Academy of Sciences, academician of Inner Mongolia Academy of youth painting.
*Reference price: 6,000 yuan / square foot*

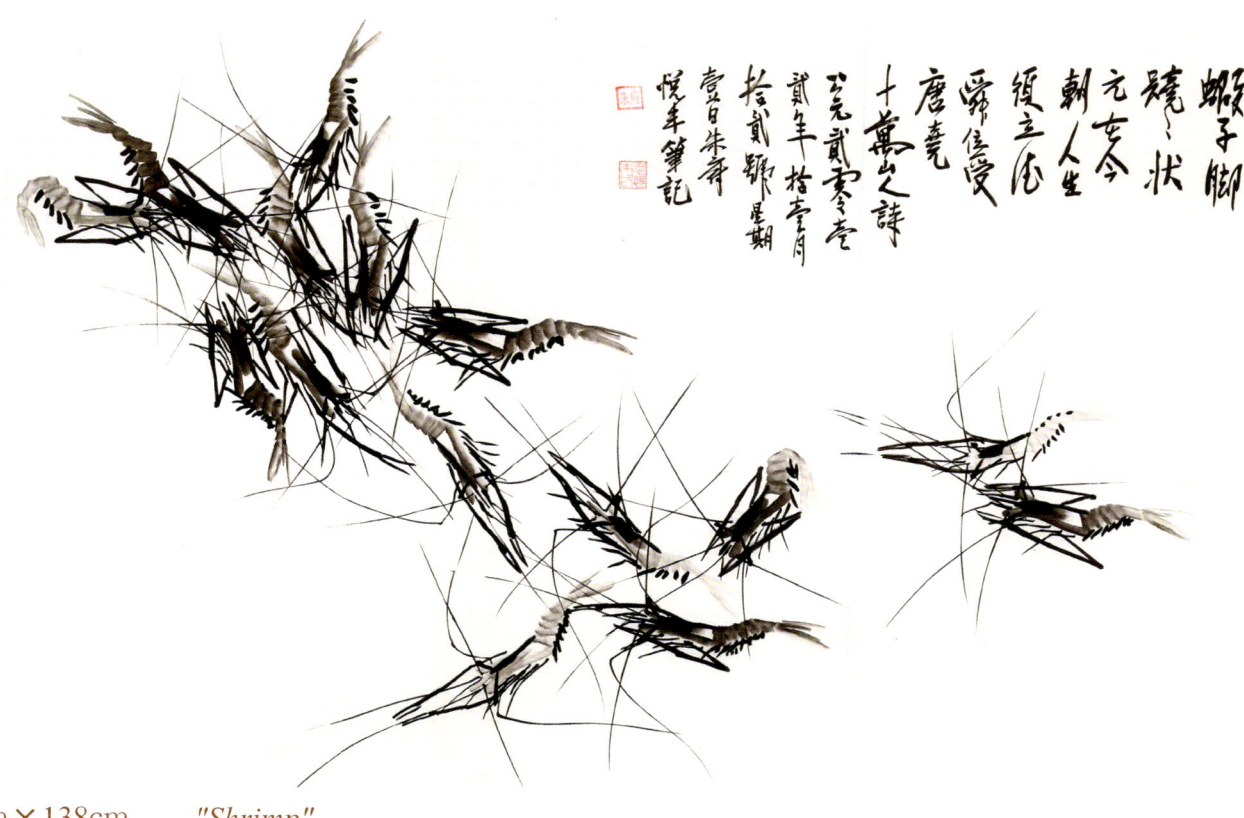

《虾》　67cm×138cm　　"Shrimp"

## 陈品睿　*Chen Pinrui*

陈品睿，男，1951年生，湖南人，中国艺术创作院理事，中国书法家艺术家协会理事，湖南省书法家协会会员。

润笔价格：4,000元/平尺

Chen Pinrui, male, born in 1951, is from Hunan, he is the director of China artistic Academy, director of Chinese calligrapher Art Association, member of Hunan Calligraphers Association.
*Reference price: 4,000 yuan / square foot*

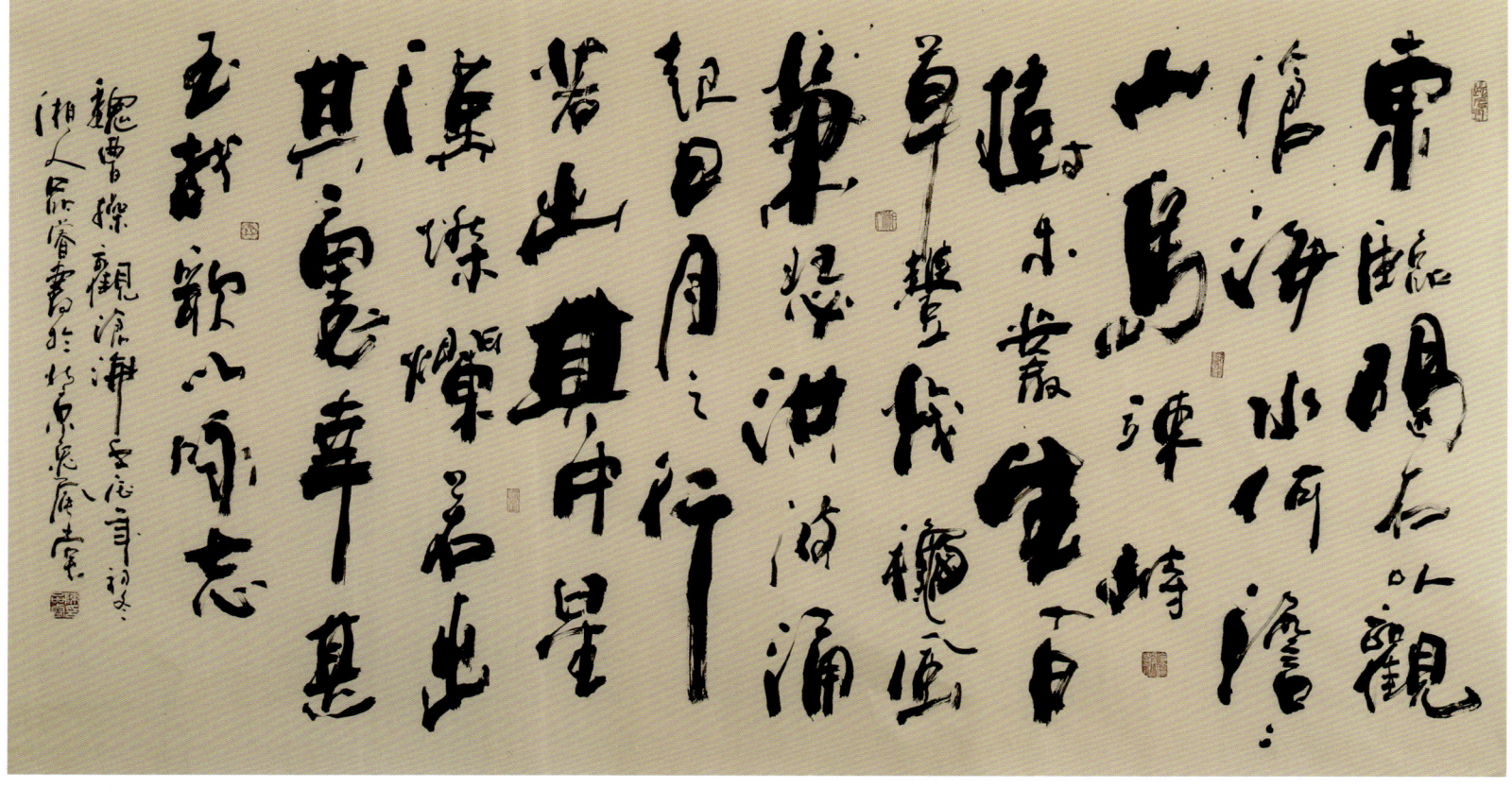

《观沧海》　96cm×178cm　" View of Sea "

# 李爱民　*Li Aimin*

李爱民，男，1954年，重庆云阳人，笔名村人，现任专职书画师，高级书画师，峡江画院副院长。

润笔价格：10,000元/平尺

Li Aimin, Male, 1954, also known as Cunren, is from Yunyang, Chongqing. He is a full-time painter, senior artist, painting, vice president of the Xiajiang painting academy.

*Reference price: 10,000 yuan / square foot*

《别有天地》　134cm×67cm　　"Another World"

# 张春生  *Zhang Chunsheng*

张春生，男，1957年，福建人，现为中国书法家协会会员。

润笔价格：7,000元/平尺

Zhang Chunsheng, Male, 1957, Fujian province, is a member of Chinese Calligraphers Association.
*Reference price: 7,000 yuan / square foot*

宋·史铸《咏翻集句》　　134cm×65cm　　*Shizhu of Song Dynasty "Sentences of Yongfan"*

# 郝书文  *Hao Shuwen*

郝书文，男，笔名艺文，1958年生于辽宁大连，现为中国书画研究会会员、辽宁省美术家协会会员、大连市美术家协会会员、瓦房店市美术家协会副主席。

润笔价格：12,000元/平尺

Hao Shuwen, male, also known as YIwen, was born in 1958 in Dalian, Liaoning. He is now a member of Chinese calligraphy and painting research Institution, member of Liaoning Province Artists Association, member of Dalian City Artists Association, vice chairman of Wafangdian City Artists Association.
*Reference price: 12,000 yuan / square foot*

《居高图》　　137cm×68cm　　"The High Figure"

# 陈飞云　*Chen Feiyun*

陈飞云，男，字起后，湖南人1927年生，中国书画家协会理事。

润笔价格：4,000元/平尺

Chen Feiyun, male, with a pen name of Qihou, was born in Hunan Province in 1927. he is now the director of Chinese Calligraphers Association.
*Reference price: 4,000 yuan / square foot*

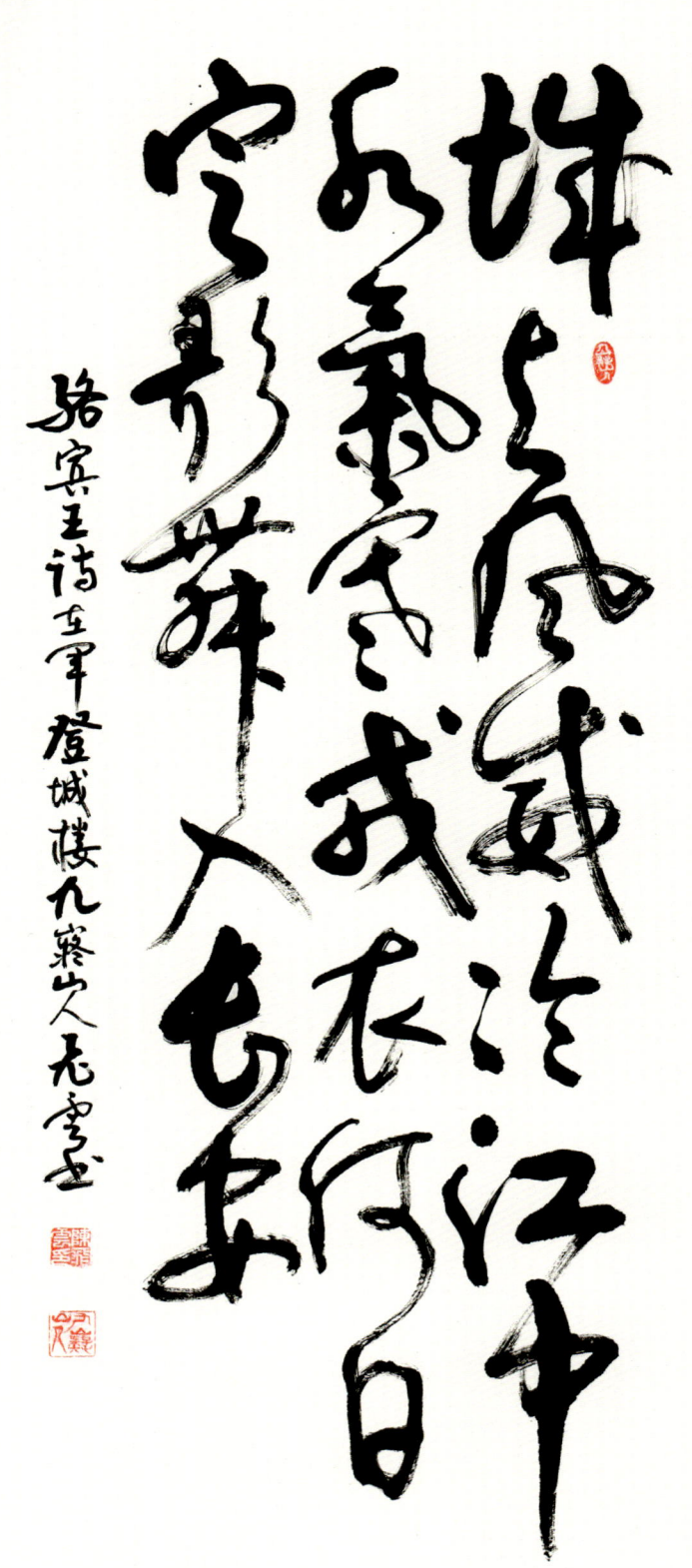

骆宾王《在军登城楼》　　136cm×69cm　　*Luobin Wang "At the Jundeng tower"*

# 李玉清 *Li Yuqing*

李玉清，男，生于1938年，河北人，现为中国书画家协会名誉会长、中国艺术名家交流协会常务副会长、中国艺术名家研究院常务理事、中国国学学会副会长、高级美术师。

润笔价格：12,000元/平尺

Li Yuqing, male, born in 1938, is from Hebei Province. He is now the honorary president of China Calligraphers Association, vice president of Chinese virtuoso Association, executive director of China Academy of Art Masters, vice president of Chinese Sinology Institute, senior artist.

*Reference price: 12,000 yuan / square foot*

《山峦春色》　　137cm×69cm　　"Mountain Spring"

# 萧辉　　*Xiao Hui*

萧辉，男，1957年9月3日生，山西芮城县永乐镇历山人。现任中国书法研究院会员、中国书画艺术家协会理事、中国国学研究会名誉会长等职务。

润笔价格：4,000元/平尺

Xiao Hui, male, born on September 3, 1957 born, is from Lishan, Yongle Town, Ruicheng Country, Shanxi. He is currently the member of Chinese Calligraphy Institute, director of Chinese Painting and Calligraphy Artists Association, honorary president of Chinese Sinology research Institution.

*Reference price: 4,000 yuan / square foot*

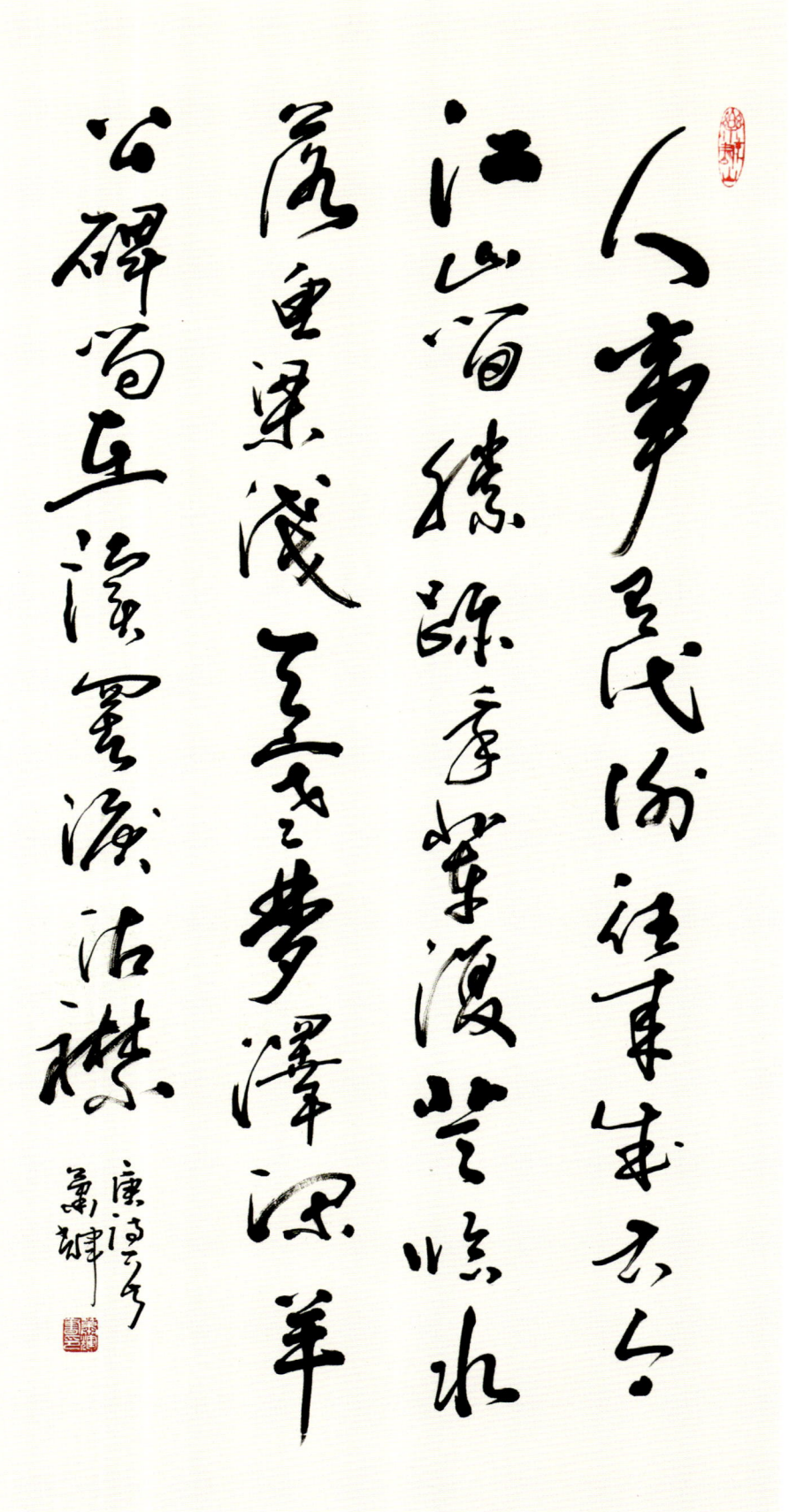

**孟浩然《与诸子登岘山》**　　136cm×68cm　　*Meng Haoran "Climbing Xianshan with Certain People"*

# 洪国林　*Hong Guolin*

洪国林，男，字清远，1960年生于杭州西子湖畔。现为浙江省美协会员、杭州市美协会员、中国国际书画研究院研究员、浙江省逸仙书画院专职画家、浙江四味斋特聘画家。

润笔价格：8,000元/平尺

Hong Guolin, male, also known as Qingyuan, was born in 1960 beside the West Lake in Hangzhou. He is now the member of Zhejiang Fine Arts Association, member of Hangzhou Fine Arts Association, researcher at the International Institute of Painting and Calligraphy, full-time painter of Zhejiang Province Yixian Calligraphy and painting academy, distinguished painter of Siwei Pavilion.
*Reference price: 8,000 yuan / square foot*

《竹雀图》　　70cm×137cm　　*"Bamboo Bird"*

## 邱天章  *Qiu Tianzhang*

邱天章，号静怡轩主人，男，1942年2月生，福建省泉州人，国家一级书法师，中国书法家协会会员，中国书画家协会理事，国家人事部人才所中国书画人才研修中心特邀中级研究员，中国艺术研究院文化艺术中心创作委员。

润笔价格：5,000元/平尺

Qiu Tianzhang, also known as Holder of Jingyi Xuan, male, born in February 1942, is from Quanzhou, Fujian. He is national A-level callgraphier, member of Chinese Calligraphers Association, director of Chinese Calligraphers Association, invited Intermediate researchers of the talent training center of the Chinese Ministry of Personnel, creative commissary of Art Centre of China Academy of Art Culture.

*Reference price: 5,000 yuan / square foot*

《莫道夕阳暂》　134cm×65cm　*"Permenant Sunset"*

# 张汉　　*Zhang Han*

张汉，男，字清桂，道明崇君，道号玄丹、古梅道人，齐名"汉风堂"。1936年生于墨子的故里山东滕州。现为中国美术学会常务副主席、中国文化艺术家协会名誉会长、中国文学艺术工作者联合会副主席。

润笔价格：10,000元/平尺

Zhang Han, male, possesses pen names as Qing Gui, Dominic Chongjun, Xuan Dan, Gumei Daoren and Hanfeng Tang. He was born in 1936 in Shandong Tengzhou which is the home town of Mozi. He is currently the executive vice chairman of the Chinese Artists Association, honorary president of Chinese Culture Artists Association, vice president of China Federation of Literary and Artist.
*Reference price: 10,000 yuan / square foot*

《墨梅》　　137cm×68cm　　"Plum"

## 陈肇新　*Chen Zhaoxin*

陈肇新，字步栋，温州市人，1937年生，国家一级书法师、中国紫禁城书画院副院长、北京人民画院院士、中国艺术学会常委、中国民族文艺家协会常务副会长。

润笔价格：4,000元/平尺

Chen Zhaoxin, also known as Budong, is from Wenzhou City, born in 1937. he is a national A-level callgraphier, vice president of Chinese Forbidden City painting and calligraphy Institution, academician of Beijing People's Art Academy, member of standing committee of Chinese Society of Arts Committee, executive vice president of China national artists Association.

*Reference price: 4,000 yuan / square foot*

对联《高风亮节　浩然正气》　135cm×35cm×2　　*Couplet "Ethical Uprightness"*

# 贺伟国　*He Weiguo*

贺伟国，男，字逊之，号繁荫，当代著名山水画家，1943年生于北京书画世家。现为北京专业画家、一级美术师、北京美术家协会会员、北京燕京书画院副院长。

润笔价格：12,000元/平尺

He Weiguo, Male, also known as Xunzhi and Fanyi, is a famous contemporary landscape painter. He was born in Beijing in 1943 in a painting family. He is currently a professional painter in Beijing, an A-level artist, member of Beijing Artists Association, vice president of Beijing Yanjing painting Institution.

*Reference price: 12,000 yuan / square foot*

《屋前绿树吟风雨》　　137cm×69cm　　"Trees in Front of the House Reflecting Wind and Rain"

## 赵元华  Zhao Yuanhua

赵元华，男，北京军区离休干部，1942年加入中国共产党并参加八路军，曾任编辑、记者、新闻处长、师政委，现任国礼艺术家。

润笔价格：4,000元/平尺

Zhao Yuanhua, male, is a retired cadres of Beijing Military Region. He joined the Chinese Communist Party and participated in the Eighth Route Army in 1942, served as editor, reporter, news director, division political commissary. He currently is an artist of Guoli.
*Reference price: 4,000 yuan / square foot*

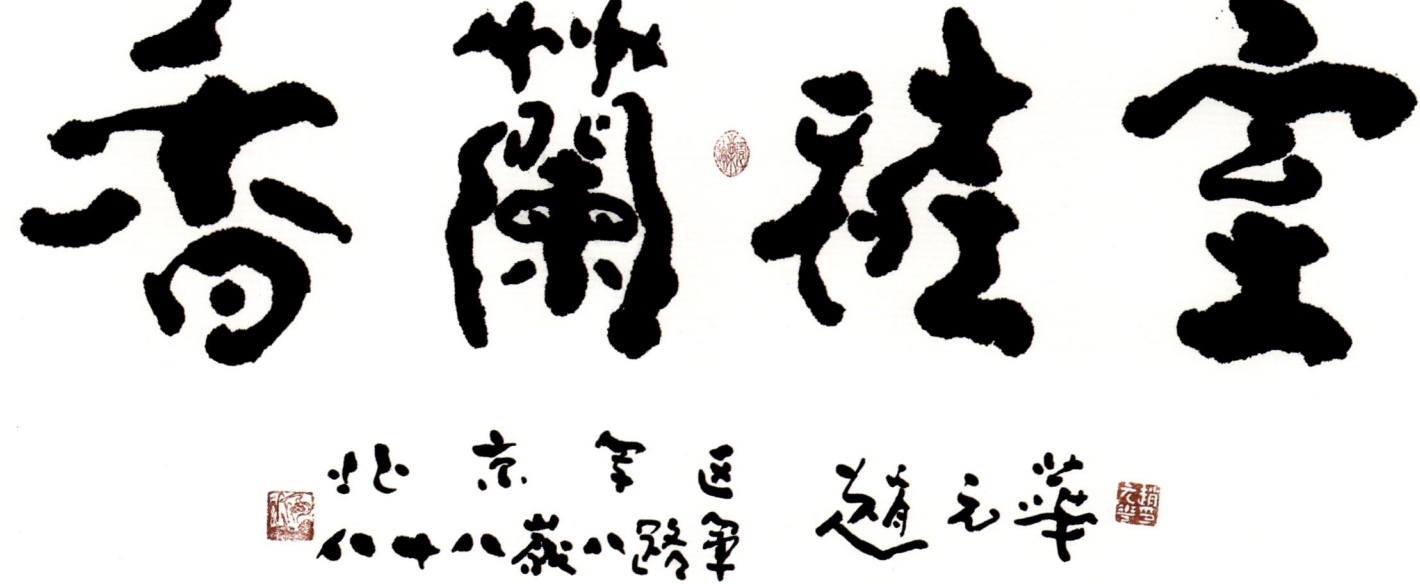

《室雅阑香》　　69cm×136cm　　"Fragrant Room"

# 许振华　*XU Zhen-hua*

许振华，男，字雍君，号悟一斋斋主，五行居士，法号如华，现为山东省美术家协会会员、泰山中国画研究院研究员、中国佛教协会会员。

润笔价格：6,000元／平尺

XU Zhen-hua, male, with pan names of Yongjun, Monerator of YiZhai, Lay Buddhist of Wuxing and Ruhua, is the member of Shandong Province Artists Association, researcher of Taishan Chinese painting research Institution, member of the Chinese Buddhist Association.

*Reference price: 6,000 yuan / square foot*

《平安富贵图》　　131cm×66cm　　"Peace and Wealth"

# 辛德翔  Xin Dexiang

辛德翔，又谓辛亚翔，笔名羊羽、微尘，福建霞浦人，现为福建省宁德市文联、霞浦县政协委员、宁德市霞浦空海研究会常务理事，系福建省书法家协会、中国硬笔书法家协会会员。

润笔价格：4,000元/平尺

Xin Dexiang, also known as Xin Yaxiang, Yangyu, Weichen, is from Xiapu, Fujian. He is currently the commissary of Ningde Literary Federation, Xiapu County CPPCC, executive director of Ningde Xiapu Konghai Research Association, member of the Department of Fujian Provincial Calligraphers Association and China Hard-Pen Calligrapher Association.

*Reference price: 4,000 yuan / square foot*

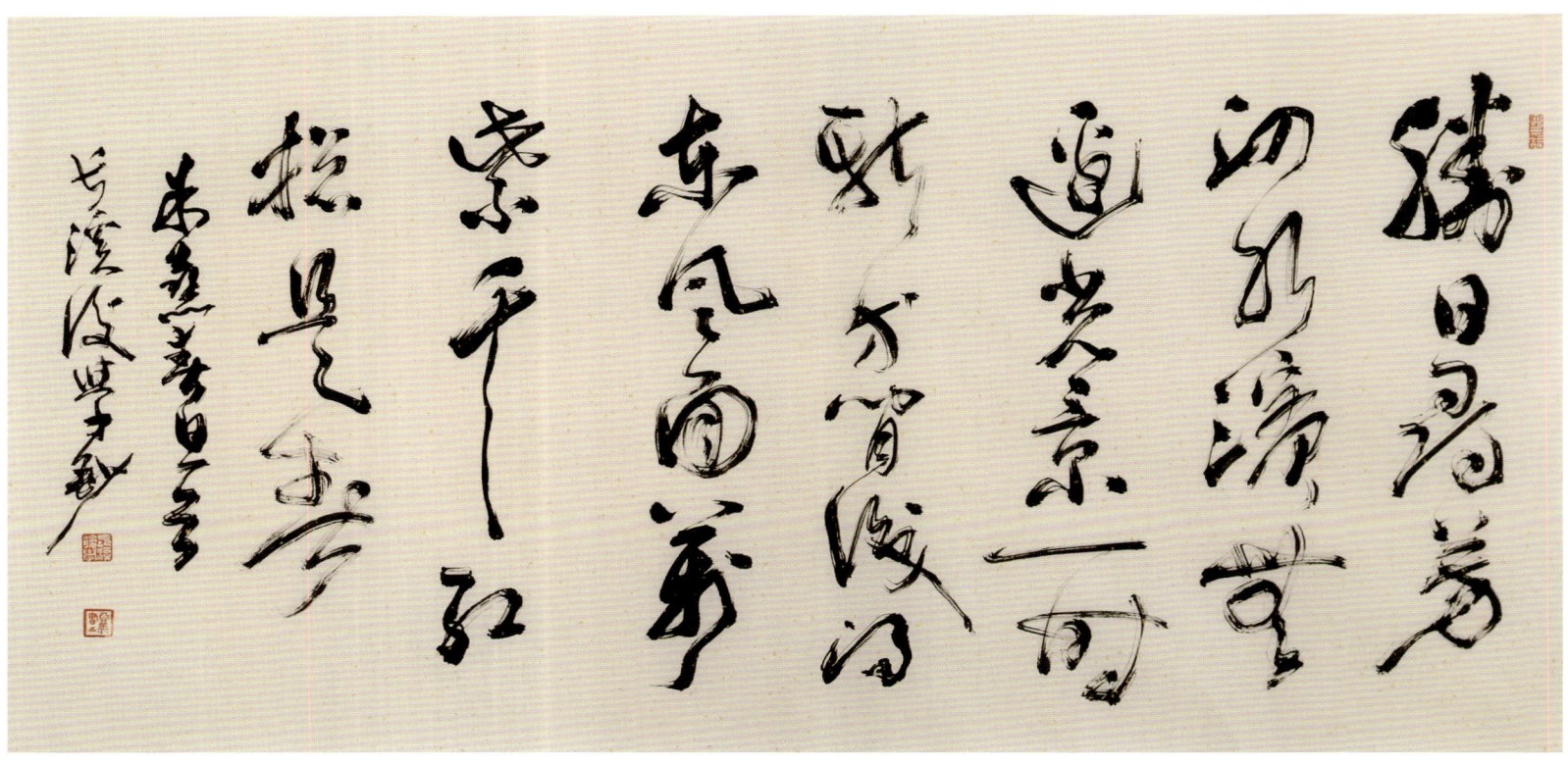

朱熹《春日》　66cm×133cm　　*Zhu Xi "Spring"*

# 张建中 *Zhang Jianzhong*

张建中，男，1964年生于甘肃静宁，西北师范大学美术系毕业，学士学位。现为甘肃画院创作研究部副主任、国家一级美术师、中国国画家协会常务理事、甘肃当代书画院副院长。

润笔价格：14,000元/平尺

Zhang Jianzhong, male, born in 1964 in Jingning, Gansu, was graduated from Department of Fine Arts of Northwest Normal University and possesses the bachelor's degree. He is now the deputy director of Gansu Painting Creation Research, national A-level artist, executive director of China National Artists Association, vice president of Gansu contemporary painting Institution.

*Reference price: 14,000 yuan / square foot*

《观梅图》　70cm×136cm　　*"Viewing Plum"*

## 刘永志  *Liu Yongzhi*

刘永志，男，汉族，1938年生于江苏淮安，2007年加入淮安市楚州区书法协会和江苏老年书画研究会。2008年起，参加全国书画大赛，多次获得金奖和银奖。

润笔价格：5,000元/平尺

Liu Yongzhi, male, Han nationality, was born in 1938 in Huaian, Jiangsu. He joined Huaian Chuzhou District Calligraphy Association and Jiangsu elderly Painting Research Association in 2007. He has participated in national Fine Arts Competitions sice 2008 and won several gold and silver medals.

*Reference price: 5,000 yuan / square foot*

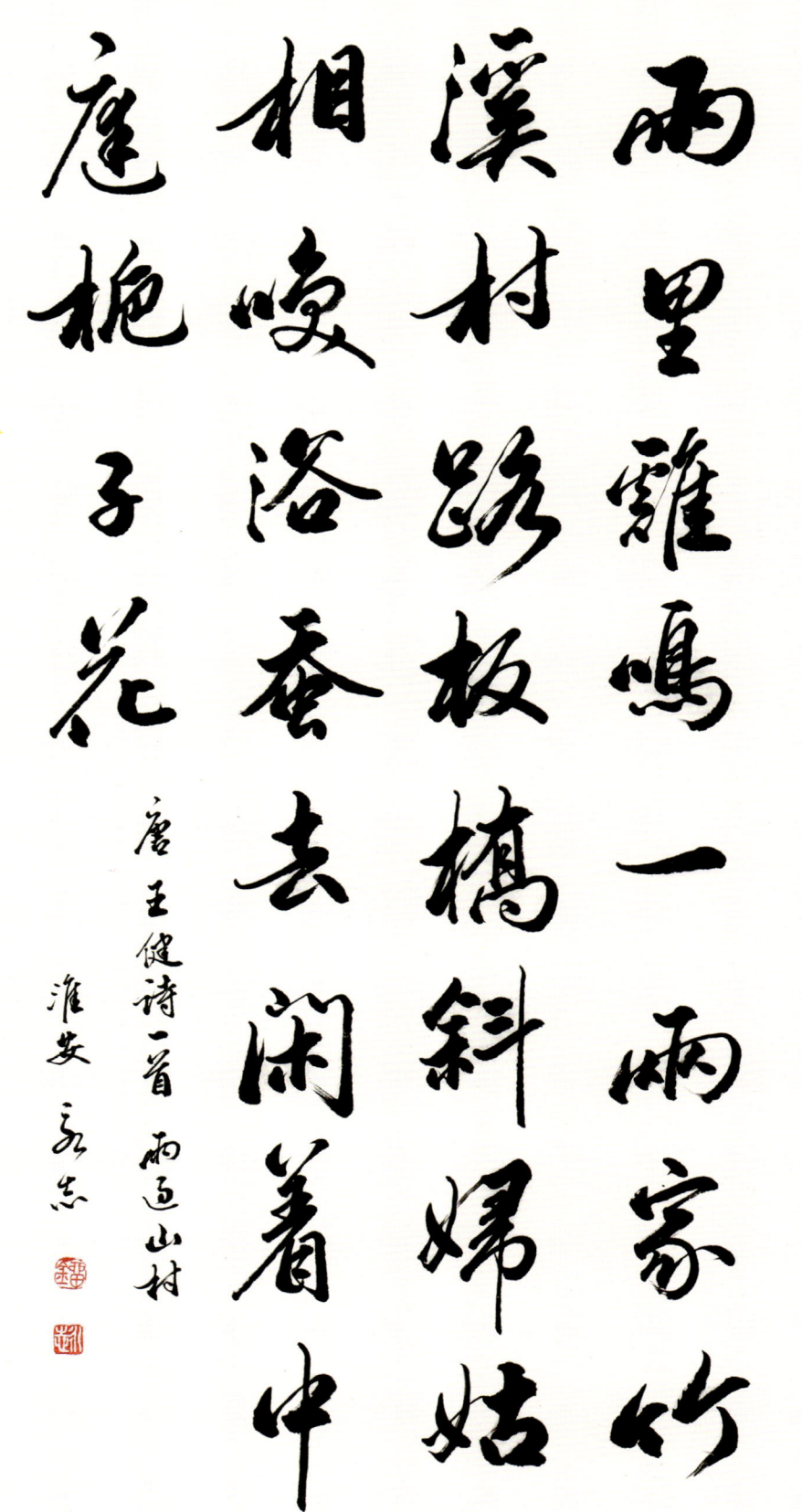

王健《雨过山村》　　137cm×69cm　　Wang Jian "Raining Village"

# 王根顺 *Wang Genshun*

王根顺，男，笔名王大宇，河南开封人，中国书画艺术交流协会常务理事，中原书画院客座教授，河南省美术家协会会员。

润笔价格：12,000元/平尺

Wang Genshun, male, with pen name as Wang Dayu, is from Henan Kaifeng. He is the executive director of China Painting and Calligraphy Association, visiting professor at the Central Plain Calligraphy Institute, member of Henan Artists Association.

*Reference price: 12,000 yuan / square foot*

《细雨濛濛过海来》　140cm×70cm　　"Rain across the Sea"

### 刘希舜  *Liu Xishun*

刘希舜，男，1930年11月，山东人，现为北大荒老年书画研究会会员、老年书画协会副会长，被授予中国红色书画名家、中华民族接触艺术家等荣誉称号。

润笔价格：5,000元/平尺

Liu Xishun, male, born in November 1930, is from Shandong Province. He is currently a member of the Study Institution on the painting and calligraphy for old people, vice president of Study on the painting and calligraphy in old people, was commented as the master of Chinese red painting and calligraphy, Chinese contacter with artists and other honorary titles.

*Reference price: 5,000 yuan / square foot*

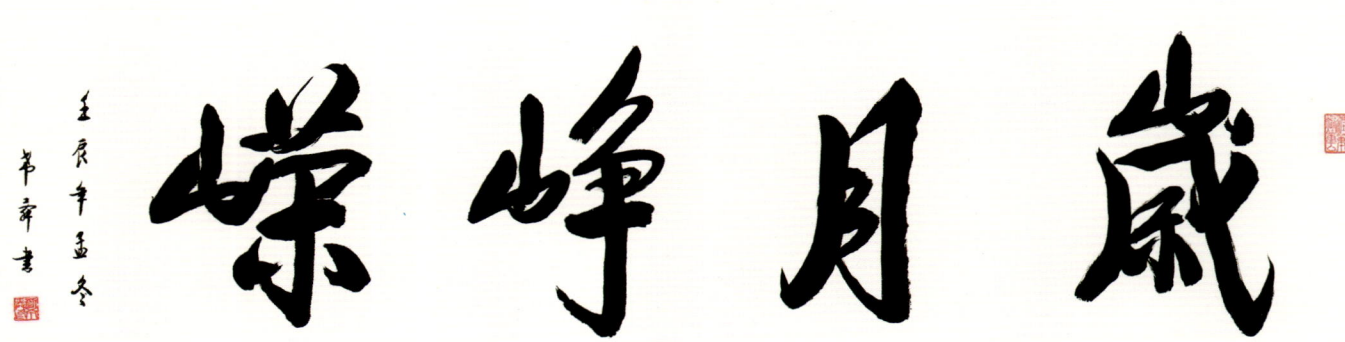

《岁月峥嵘》　　69cm×178cm　　*"Outstanding Years"*

# 陈鸿娟　*Chen Hongjuan*

陈鸿娟，女，艺名寒梅，江苏宝应人，现为东方名家书画院高级专业书画家。

润笔价格：6,000元/平尺

Chen Hongjuan, female, known as Hanmei, is from Jiangsu Baoying. She is the senior professional calligrapher of Oriental famous painters Institute.

*Reference price: 6,000 yuan / square foot*

《连年有余》　137cm×69cm　　*"Surplus Year after Year"*

# 翟鸿藻　*Zhai Hongzao*

翟鸿藻，男，汉族，1936年4月生于山东，现为书刻艺术家协会会员、烟台市书法家协会会员，被聘为河南王铎书画院院长。

润笔价格：4,000元/平尺

Zhai Hongzao, male, Han nationality, was born in April 1936 in Shandong. He is a member of calligraphy and seal Artists Association, Yantai City Calligraphers Association, and was hired to be the president of Henan Wang Duo painting academy.
*Reference price: 4,000 yuan / square foot*

《三国演义开篇词》　　137cm×69cm　　"Opening Passage of Three Kingdoms "

# 王天成 *Wang Tiancheng*

王天成，男，笔名左乐，1940年生，河南人，现为中国老年书画艺术委员会会员、中国人才研究会艺术家学部委员。

润笔价格：8,000元/平尺

Wang Tiancheng, male, known as Zuole, born in 1940, is from Henan Province. He is the member of the painting and calligraphy art committee for old people and commissary of artist department of China Talent Research Institution.

*Reference price: 8,000 yuan / square foot*

《迎春》　69cm×137cm　　"Welcoming Spring"

## 刘世铮　*Liu Shizheng*

刘世铮，男，字玄之，1939年生于天津市，现为中国书画院副院长、中国黄河书画研究院顾问、中国海峡两岸书画家协会副主席、中国榜书研究会研究员、人民艺术家协会常务理事。

润笔价格：4,000元/平尺

Liu Shizheng, male, known as Xuanzhi, was Born in 1939 in Tianjin. He is now vice president of Chinese Painting and Calligraphy, advisor of Chinese Yellow River Painting and Calligraphy Institute, vice president of Chinese Cross – strait Calligraphers Association, Researcher of Chinese callgraph research Institution, executive director of People's Artist Association.

*Reference price: 4,000 yuan / square foot*

《见贤思齐》　67cm×137cm　　*" Emulate Those Better than Oneself "*

# 潘振德  *Panzhen De*

潘振德，男，字述仁，河北省深州市人，1945年9月生，中国书画家协会会员，中国书画收藏研究院高级院士。

润笔价格：8,000元/平尺

Panzhen De, male, known as Shuren, from Shenzhou, Hebei, was born in September 1945. He is the member of Chinese Calligraphy Association, Senior academician of Chinese Painting and Calligraphy Institute.
*Reference price: 8,000 yuan / square foot*

《太行佳景》　　137cm×69cm　　*"Taihang Scene"*

# 吴庆瑞 *Wu Qingrui*

吴庆瑞，男，1963年生于扬州，现为中国标准草书学社社员，现为扬州大明寺佛学院书法教师，大明寺鉴真书画院住会常务理事。

润笔价格：6,000元/平尺

Wu Qingrui, male, born in 1963 in Yangzhou, is the member of Chinae standard cursive Society, calligraphy teacher of Yangzhou Daming Temple Buddhist Institute, executive director of Daming Jianzhen painting academy.
*Reference price: 6,000 yuan / square foot*

汉·蔡邕《论书》　　138cm×70cm　　*Cai Yong "Book"*

# 王敬  *Wang Jing*

王敬，男，1964年生，广西桂林人，一级美术师，中国书画家协会理事，中华当代书画研究会名誉会长，中国书画艺术研究会常务理事。

润笔价格：6,000元/平尺

Wang Jing, male, born in 1964, is from Guangxi Guilin, an A-level artist. He is the director of Chinese Calligraphers Association, honorary president of China Contemporary Painting Research Association, executive director of Chinese Painting and Calligraphy Art Research Association.

*Reference price: 6,000 yuan / square foot*

《铁骨生春》　　69cm×137cm　　*"Spring on Steel"*

# 何海生  He Haisheng

何海生，男，广东佛山人，现系佛山市书法家协会会员，佛山市禅城区书法家协会会员，石湾书画协会常务理事，禅城平远文化艺术协会会长等。

润笔价格：6,000元/平尺

He Haisheng, male, from Foshan, Guangdong province, is now the member of Calligraphers Association of Foshan City, member of Foshan Calligraphers Association, executive director of Shiwan Calligraphy Association, president of Chancheng Ping Yuan Culture and Arts Association.

*Reference price: 6,000 yuan / square foot*

《般若波罗密经》  68cm×137cm  "The Heart of Perfect Wisdom"

# 杨启运  *Yang Qiyun*

杨启运，男，陕西黄陵人，1948年生，现为陕西省老年书画学会会员，轩辕黄帝文化研究会会员。

润笔价格：10,000元/平尺

Young Qiyun, male, from Huangling, was born in 1948. He is a member of Shanxi Study on the painting and calligraphy in old people, member of Huangdi Culture Research Association.

*Reference price: 10,000 yuan / square foot*

《乔山古柏》　　137cm×68cm　　*" Cooper on Qiao Mountain"*

# 张耀宗　Zhang Yaozong

张耀宗，男，现任中国书画家协会理事、华夏夕阳红书画艺术院名誉院长。
润笔价格：7,000元/平尺

Zhang Yaozong, male, is currently the director of Chinese Calligraphers Association, honorary president of China sunset red calligraphy art research Institution.
*Reference price: 7,000 yuan / square foot*

《明月几时有》　130cm×67cm　　"How Long will the Full Moon Appear"

# 谢石山　*Xie Shishan*

谢石山，男，1953年生，湖南祁阳人，中国文人美术家协会理事，中国书画家联谊会会员，江苏省唐伯虎书画研究院副院长。

润笔价格：6,000元/平尺

Xie Shishan, male, born in 1953 in Hunan Qiyang, is the director of Chinese Artists Association, member of Chinese Painting and Calligraphy Association, vice president of Jiangsu Tang Bohu Painting Research Institute.
*Reference price: 6,000 yuan / square foot*

《圳上林花昨日开》　137cm×68cm　　"Flowers Bloomed Yesterday"

## 赵明奇　*Zhao Mingqi*

赵明奇，男，1949年出生，天津华侨书画院理事，北京东方名家书画院高级书画家，书法作品在全国书画展中获奖。

润笔价格：6,000元/平尺

Zhao Mingqi, male, was born in 1949. He is the director of Tianjin Chinese Painting and Calligraphy Institute, senior painter of Beijing Oriental famous painters Institute. His calligraphy paintings have won award in national calligraphy exhibitions.
*Reference price: 6,000 yuan / square foot*

李白《清平乐》　　136cm×70cm　　*Li Bai, "To the Tunes of Qingping"*

# 张明宇　Zhang Mingyu

张明宇，1962年出生，浙江台州人，斋号"问耕室"，现为国家一级美术师，甘肃省中国画研究院画家，中国国画艺术研究院画家。
润笔价格：6,000元/平尺

Zhang Mingyu, born in 1962, is from Taizhou, Zhejiang. He is also known as "Wen Geng Shi" and is an A-level national artist, painter of Gansu Chinese Painting Research Institute, painter of China Academy of Art painting.
*Reference price: 6,000 yuan / square foot*

《晴山疏雨后》　47cm×98cm　　*"Mountains after Rain"*

# 王义 *Wang Yi*

王义，男，山西省人，现任中国书画艺术促进会常务理事，被授予"海峡两岸艺术交流大使"荣誉称号。

润笔价格：5,000元/平尺

Wang Yi, male, from Shanxi, is currently the executive director of Chinese Painting and Calligraphy Association, and was awarded the "Cross-Strait art exchange ambassadors" honorary title.

*Reference price: 5,000 yuan / square foot*

《回文旋图诗》　　137cm×66cm　　*"Poem of Huiwen Xuantu"*

# 王烨 *Wang Ye*

王烨，生于河南内黄，号黑白斋主，中国美术家协会河南分会会员，河南省书画院特聘画家，安阳师范学院兼职教授，中国东方书画院副院长。

润笔价格：8,000元/平尺

Wang Ye, born in Henan Province, known as Holder of Black and White, is member of Chinese Artists Association, Henan branch, distinguished Artist of Painting and Calligraphy Institute of Henan Province, professor of Anyang Teachers College, vice president of China Eastern painting Institute.
*Reference price: 8,000 yuan / square foot*

《众山可览》　69cm×137cm　　*"Views on Hills"*

# 欧作兴　*Ou Uoxing*

欧作兴，男，广东广宁人，工艺美术师，现为中国轻工业美术家协会理事，中国工艺美术家协会会员，广东省书法家协会会员，肇庆市美协、书协常务理事。

润笔价格：6,000元/平尺

Ou Uoxing, male, Guangdong, is from Quang Nin. He is a craft artist, member of China Light Industry Artists Association, member of China Arts and Crafts Association, member of the Guangdong Provincial Calligraphers Association, executive director of Zhaoqing City Artists Association and Calligraphers Association.
*Reference price: 6,000 yuan / square foot*

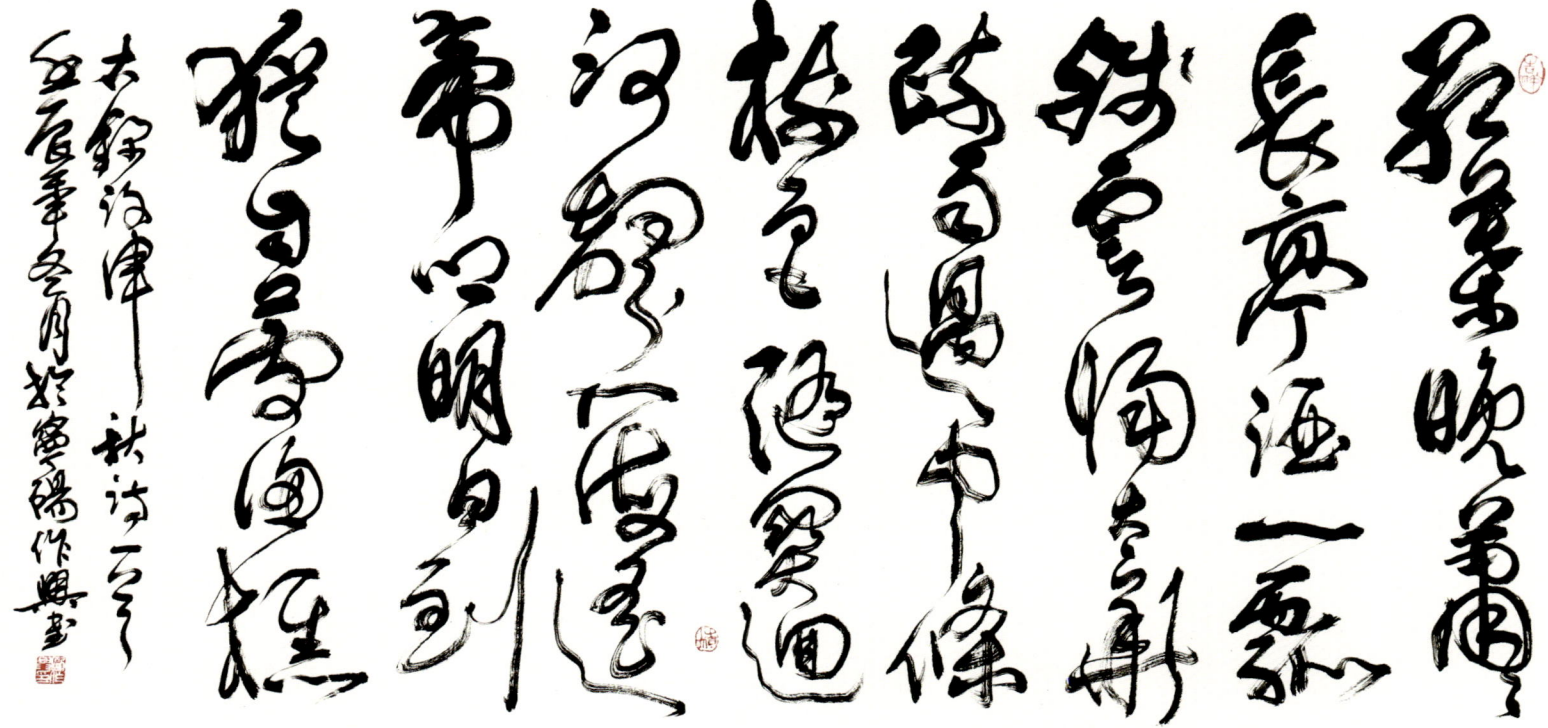

许浑《秋诗》　　136cm×69cm　　*Xu Hun "Peom on Autumn"*

# 韩伟  *Han Wei*

韩伟，号书剑斋主人，生于1969年，山东济宁人，现为中国书画家协会理事，中国青年美术家协会会员，中国国画院院士，荷辕书画研究院副院长。

润笔价格：10,000元/平尺

Han Wei, known as Holder of Jian Building, born in 1969, is from Jining, Shandong. He is now director of China Calligraphers Association, member of the China Youth Artists Association, academician of Chinese calligrapghy Institute, vice president of Heyuan Painting Research Institute.

*Reference price: 10,000 yuan / square foot*

《秋风有余香》　　137cm×69cm　　"Autumn is Fragrance"

# 何松枝　*He Songzhi*

何松枝，字弘文，男，1950年11月生，获各种荣誉称号，受聘多家书画院。

润笔价格：6,000元/平尺

He Songzhi, known as Hongwen, male, was born in November 1950. he has many honorary titles, and was employed by many painting and calligraphy acadamies..
Reference price: 6,000 yuan / square foot

《大唐道因法师碑》　　34cm×230cm　　"Stone Tabel of Master Daoyin "

《大唐道因法师碑》　　局部　　"Stone Tabel of Master Daoyin " Partly

## 魏军民 *Wei Junmin*

魏军民，男，字山泉，河南人，现居山东，任中国画家协会理事，中国国画家协会会员，泰安岱宗书画院副院长。

润笔价格：10,000元/平尺

Wei Junmin, male, known as Shanquan, is from Henan and now living in Shandong. He serves as director of paintings Association, member of China Association of Chinese painter, vice president of Taian Dai Zong Calligraphy Institute.

*Reference price: 10,000 yuan / square foot*

《泰山桃花峪》　137cm×70cm　　*"Peach Bloosm in Taishan Mountain"*

## 刘尧彬　*Liu Yaobin*

刘尧彬，男，满族，1942年9月生，陕西长安人，中国美术家协会北京分会会员，中国文化艺术发展促进会会员，中国北京文化艺术交流中心书画家，高级书法、美术教师。

润笔价格：4,000元/平尺

Liu Yaobin, male, Man nationality, born in September 1942, is from Shaanxi Chang'an. He is the member of the Chinese Artists Association, member of Chinese Culture and Arts Development Association (Beijing branch), painter of China Beijing Culture and Arts Exchange Centre, senior calligraphier and art teachers.

*Reference price: 4,000 yuan / square foot*

《爱国创新　包容厚德》　　136cm×70cm　　"Patriotism, Innovation, Inclusion, Social Morals"

# 段庆昌  *Duan Qingchang*

段庆昌，男，1965年生，号惺月墨人，现为中国书画家学会副主席，中国书法美术协会理事，中国画家协会理事，中国文艺家协会理事，中国书法家协会会员。

润笔价格：12,000元/平尺

Duan Qingchang, male, born in 1965, known as Xingyue Moren, is now vice chairman of the Society of Chinese painting, director of Chinese calligraphy art Association, director of Association of Chinese painting, member of Chinese Literary Association, Chinese Calligraphers Association.

*Reference price: 12,000 yuan / square foot*

《旷达怀远对弈图》　68cm×68cm　"Kuangda and Huaiyuan Playing Chess"

## 孟凡荣　Meng Fanrong

孟凡荣，男，笔名小青，1946年11月生，河北省书法家协会会员。

润笔价格：4,000元/平尺

Meng Fanrong, male, known as Xiaoqing, was born in November 1946. He is member of Hebei Calligraphers Association.
*Reference price: 4,000 yuan / square foot*

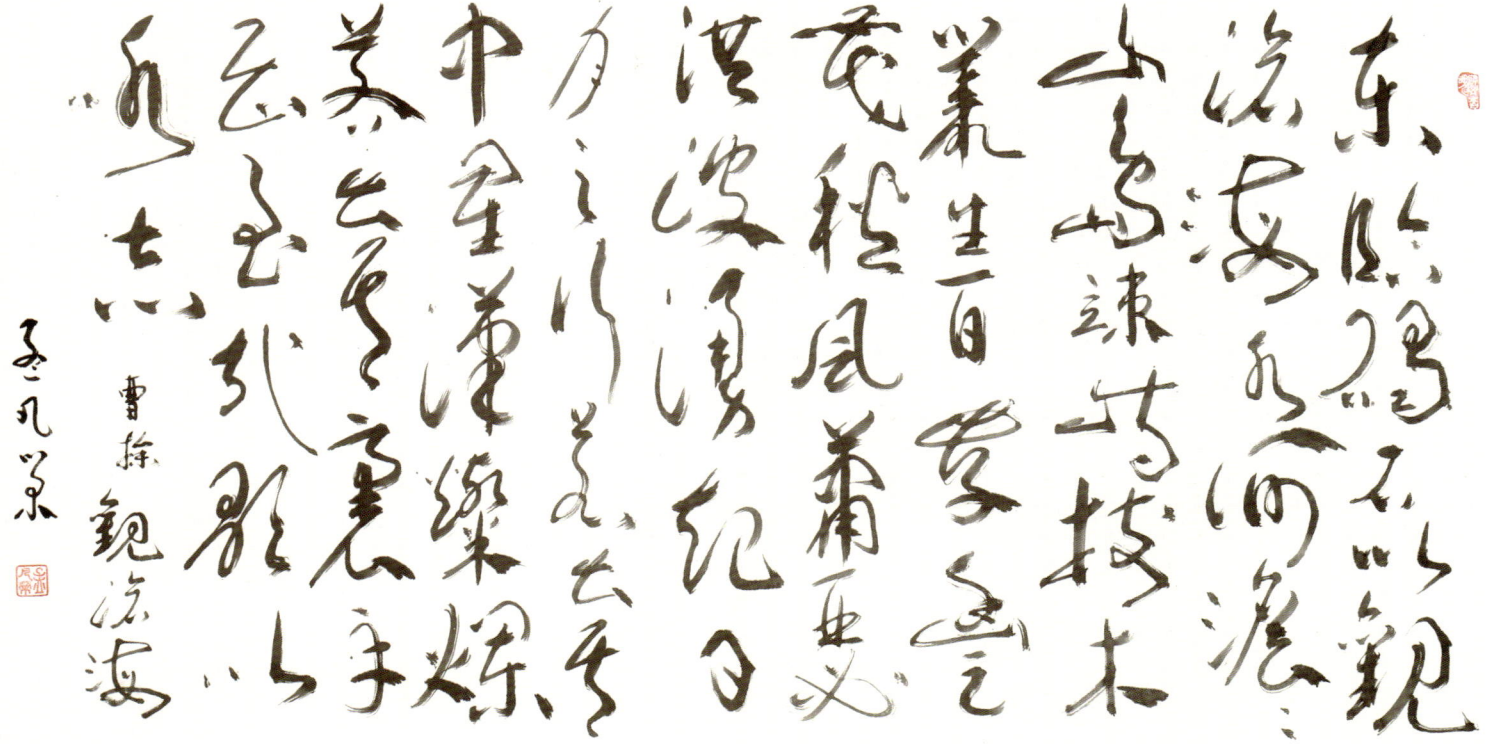

曹操《观沧海》　　96cm×178cm　　Cao "View of the Sea"

# 刘天鹏 Liu Tianpeng

刘天鹏，男，别名拙甫，聚艺斋主，黄河乌金峡人，国家一级美术师，中华书画研究院名誉院长。
润笔价格：6,000元/平尺

Liu Tianpeng, male, known as Zhufu and Wujinxia of the Yellow River, is an A-level national artist, honorary president of Chinese Painting and Calligraphy Institute.
*Reference price: 6,000 yuan / square foot*

《双鸡图》　69cm×136cm　　*"Double Chickens"*

# 张明康  *Zhang Mingkang*

张明康，男，笔名张更，汉族，1935年9月生，北京延庆人，中国艺术名家协会理事，中国书画家协会会员，内蒙古书画研究院院士，王铎故里书画院名誉院长。

润笔价格：6,000元/平尺

Zhang Mingkang, male, Han nationality, with a pen name as Zhanggeng, was born in September 1935 in Yanqing, Beijing. He is the director of China Art Name Association, member of Chinese Calligraphy Association, academician of Inner Mongolia Academy of Painting and Calligraphy Institute, honorary president of Wang Duo hometown painting and calligraphy Institute.

*Reference price: 6,000 yuan / square foot*

《道德经句》　136cm×69cm　　"Moral Sentences"

# 杨柏林 *Yang Bailin*

杨柏林，男，土家族，1946年4月生，湖南省凤凰县人，现为中国汉唐画院画师，中国国画院客座教授，北京京华兰亭书画院名誉院长。

润笔价格：8,000元/平尺

Yang Bailin, male, Tujia ethnic minority, was born in April 1946. He is from Fenghuang County, Hunan and is an art artist in Han and Tang Dynasties of China Painting Institution, visiting professor of Chinese Painting Institution, honorary president of Beijing Jing Hua Lanting Calligraphy academy.

*Reference price: 8,000 yuan / square foot*

《乾坤清气》　97cm×178cm　　*"Universe Clear Air"*

## 张学范　*Zhang Xuefan*

张学范，男，1965年生，甘肃天水人，笔名墨泉，现为中国书画函授大学优秀学员，中国书画家协会会员，北京宝延轩书画院院士，天水书协理事。

润笔价格：7,000元/平尺

Zhang Xuefan, male, born in 1965, is from Gansu Tianshui. With a pen name of Moquan, he is an outstanding student of Chinese painting and calligraphy correspondence university, member of Chinese Calligraphers, academician of Beijing Yan Bao Xuan fine art academy, director of Tianshui Calligraphers Association.
*Reference price: 7,000 yuan / square foot*

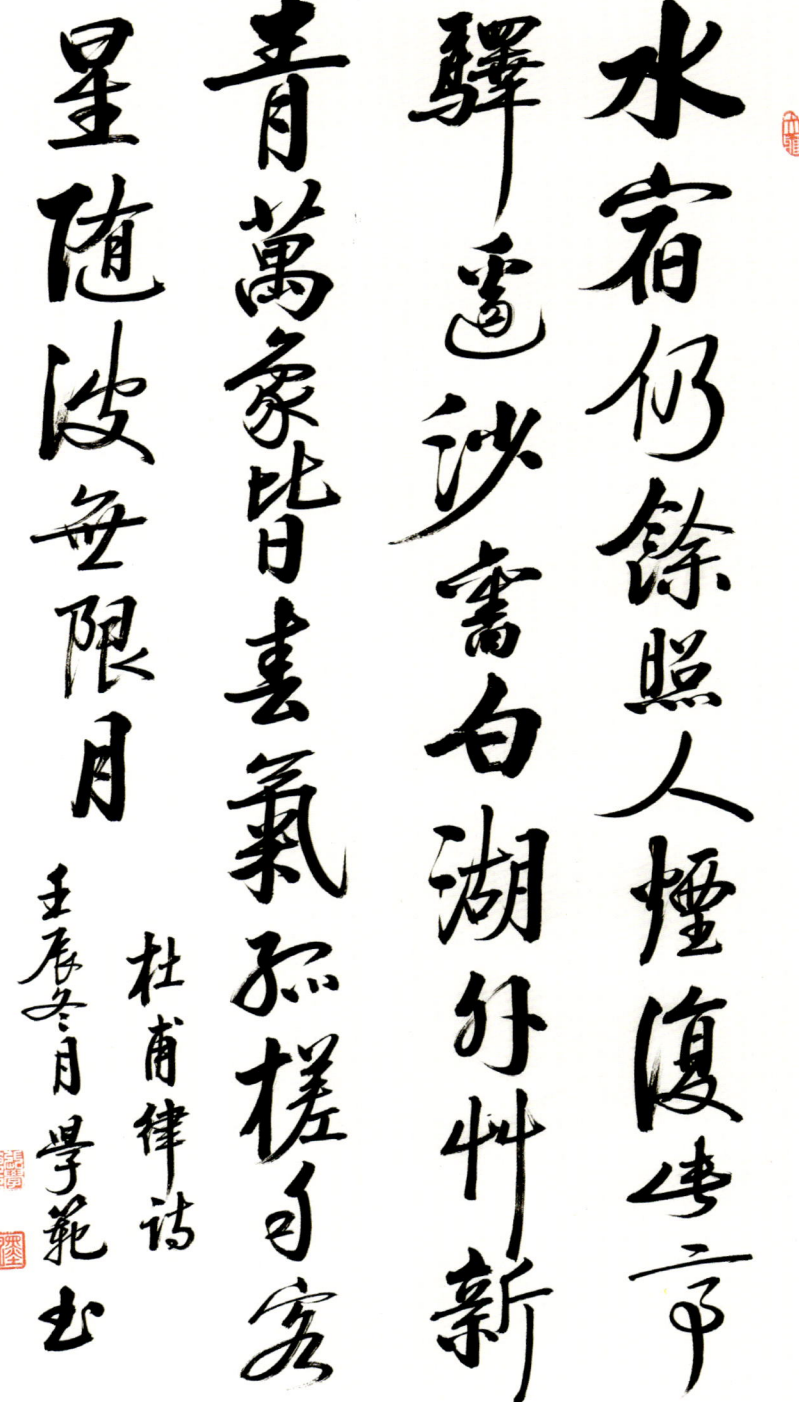

《杜甫律诗》　136cm×67cm　*"Du Fu's Poems"*

# 胡甫英  *Hu Fuying*

胡甫英，男，1951年生，山东曹县人，现为山东省书法家协会会员，山东美术家协会会员，中国书画研究院院士，山东省新泰市美术馆副馆长。

润笔价格：6,000元/平尺

Hu Fuying, male, born in 1951, is from Cao country, Shandong. He is now the member of Shandon Calligraphers Association, member of Shandong Artists Association, academician of Chinese Academy of Painting and Calligraphy Institute, deputy president of Xintai art museum.
*Reference price: 6,000 yuan / square foot*

《一代枭雄》　136cm×70cm　　"Hero"

### 邢顺华　*Xingshun Hua*

邢顺华，男，汉族，1935年生，保定人，现为中国书画家协会会员、中国书画艺术研究会理事、南京市长江书画家协会名誉主席。
润笔价格：5,000元/平尺

Xingshun Hua, male, Han nationality, was born in 1935 in Baoding. He is now member of China Calligraphy Association, member of Chinese Painting and Calligraphy Art Research Association, honorary chairman the Nanjing Yangtze River Calligraphers Association.
*Reference price: 5,000 yuan / square foot*

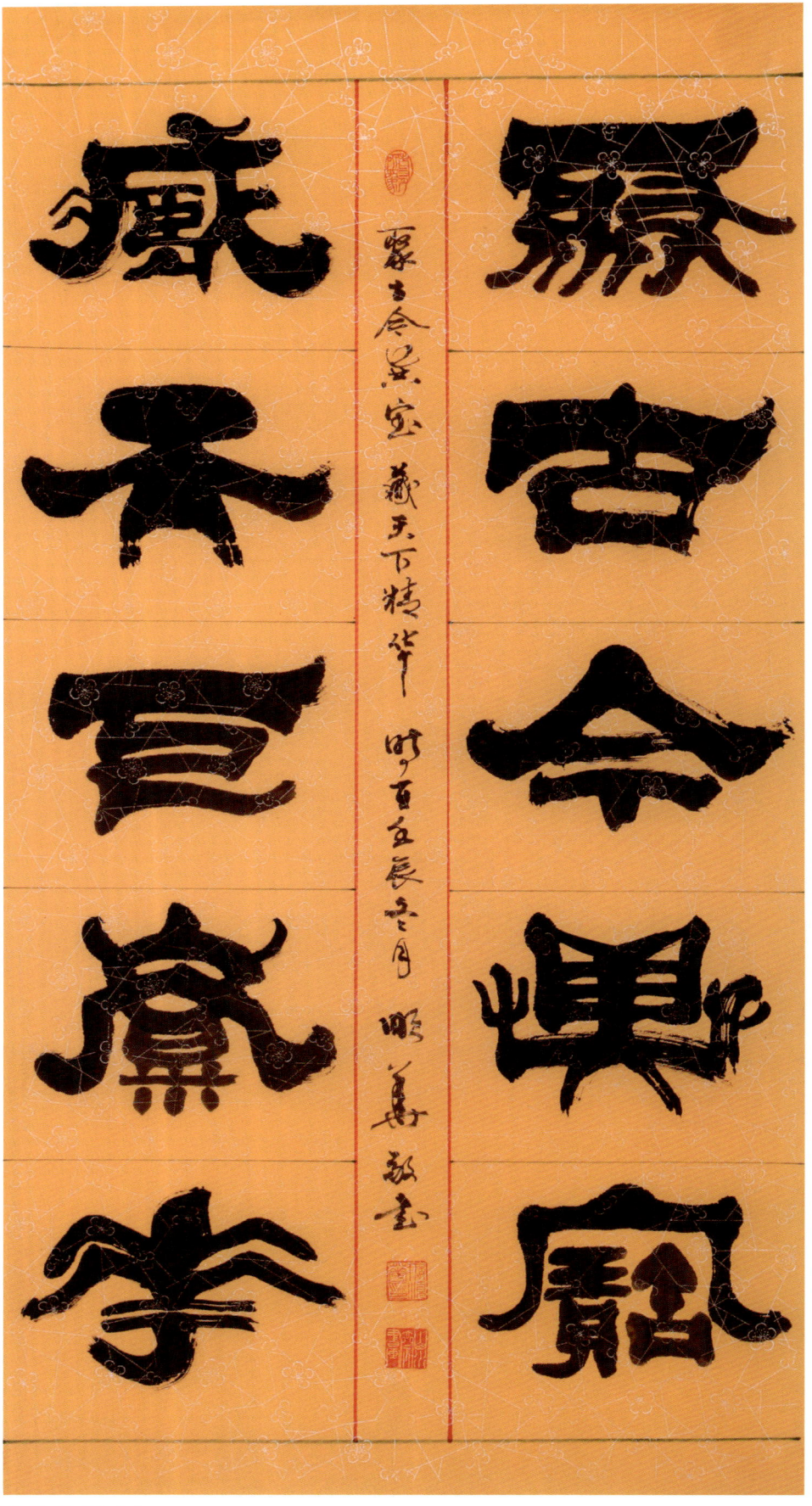

《聚古今异宝》　137cm×68cm　"Treasure through Ancient and Modern"

# 蔡云飞  *Cai Yunfei*

蔡云飞，男，浙江绍兴市人，1946年2月生，号墨井散人，一级美术师，中国国画院副院长、绍兴分院院长，绍兴市宝云轩书画院院长，中国国画家协会理事，中国书法美术家协会理事，中国收藏家协会会员，中国兰亭书画院名誉院长。

润笔价格：8,000元/平尺

Cai Yunfei, male, from Zhejiang Shaoxing City, was born in February 1946. He is known as Mojin Sanren and he is an A-level artist, vice president of Chinese painting Institute, president of Shaoxing branch, president of Shaoxing Bao Yun Xuan painting academy, director of China country artist Association, director of Chinese Calligraphy Artists Association, member of China Collectors Association, honorary president of Chinese Lanting Painting and Calligraphy Institute.

*Reference price: 8,000 yuan / square foot*

《湖山翠峦》　70cm×137cm　"Lakes and Mountains"

# 郑吕荣  *Zheng Lvrong*

郑吕荣，男，汉族，1933年生，浙江临海市人，现为中国画家协会理事，浙江省书法家协会会员，中国画虎艺术研究院名誉院长，江南书画家联谊会副会长。

润笔价格：4,000元/平尺

Zheng Lvrong, male, Han nationality, born in 1933, is from Linhai City. He is currently a director of Chinese Painting Association, member of Zhejiang Calligraphers Association, honorary president of China tiger Art Research Institute, vice president of the Association of South painter.

*Reference price: 4,000 yuan / square foot*

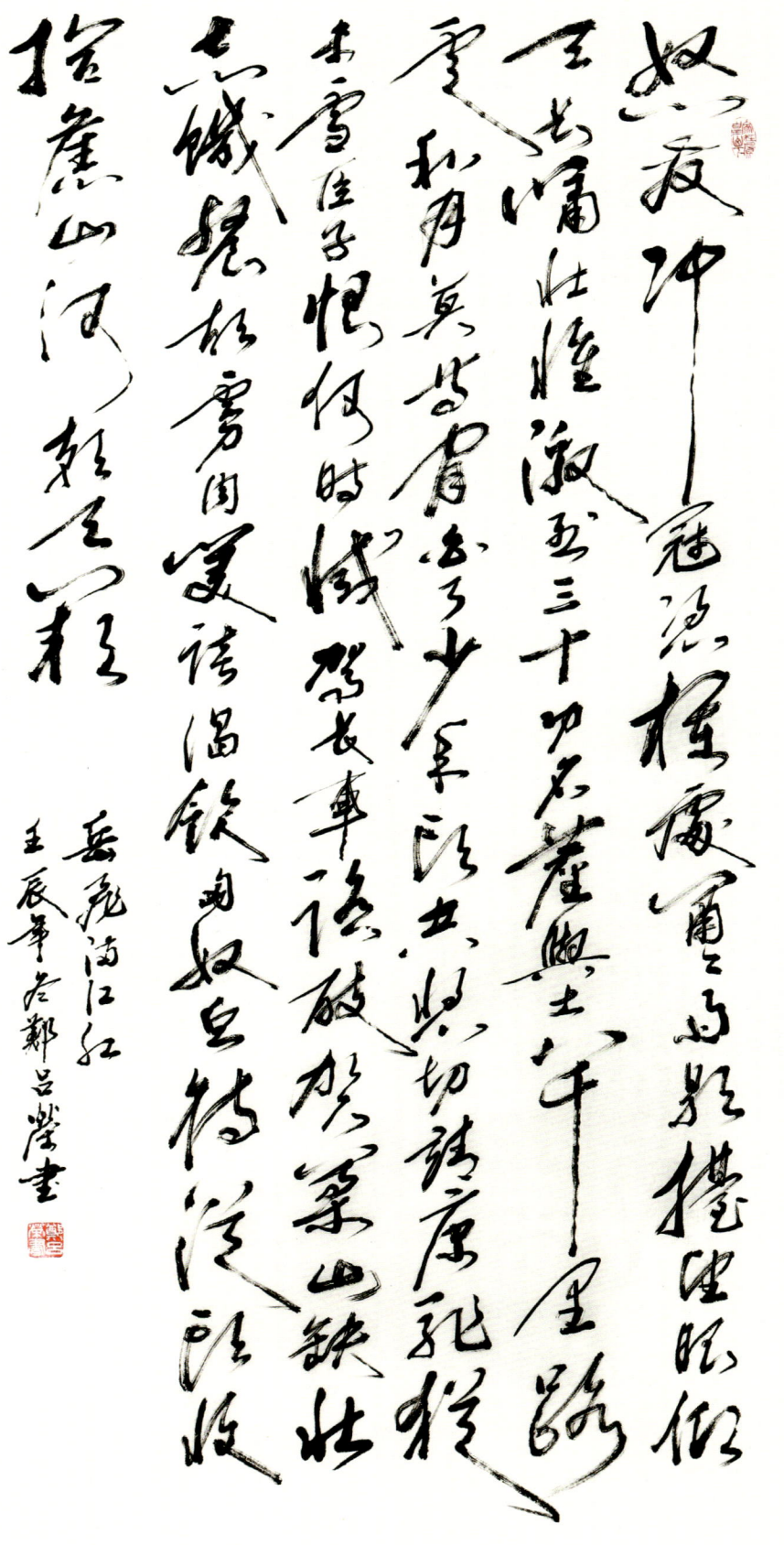

岳飞《满江红》　　138cm×70cm　　"To The Tunes of Manjianghong"

# 龚云江  *Gong Yunjiang*

龚云江，又名龚云、江浩、字墨缘，墨香阁主人，河北石家庄市人，现任中国艺术委员会委员、中国国际书画艺术家协会副会长、中国国际书画研究院副院长、河北省现代美术研究会会长。

润笔价格：6,000元/平尺

Gong Yunjiang, also known as Gong Yun, Jiang Hao, Moyuan and Holder of Moxiang Hall, is from Shijiazhuang City. He is currently the commissary of China Art Committee, vice president of China International Painting and Calligraphy Artists Association, vice president of China International Painting and Calligraphy Research Institute, president of Hebei Modern Art Research Association.

*Reference price: 6,000 yuan / square foot*

《雄风卫国》　178cm×96cm　　*"Patriotism"*

## 江海滨　Jiang Haibin

江海滨，男，汉族，1974年12月，安徽省人，祖籍黄山，艺名辛墨，斋名天哺居辛堂，系安徽省书协会员，中国楹联学会书法艺术委员会委员。

润笔价格：5,000元/平尺

Jiang Haibin, male, Han nationality, was born in December 1974. He is from Anhui Province, the ancestral home is Huangshan, with pen names asXinmo and Tianbuju Xintang. He is the member of Anhui Calligraphers society, commissary of Chinese calligraphy couplets Committee.
*Reference price: 5,000 yuan / square foot*

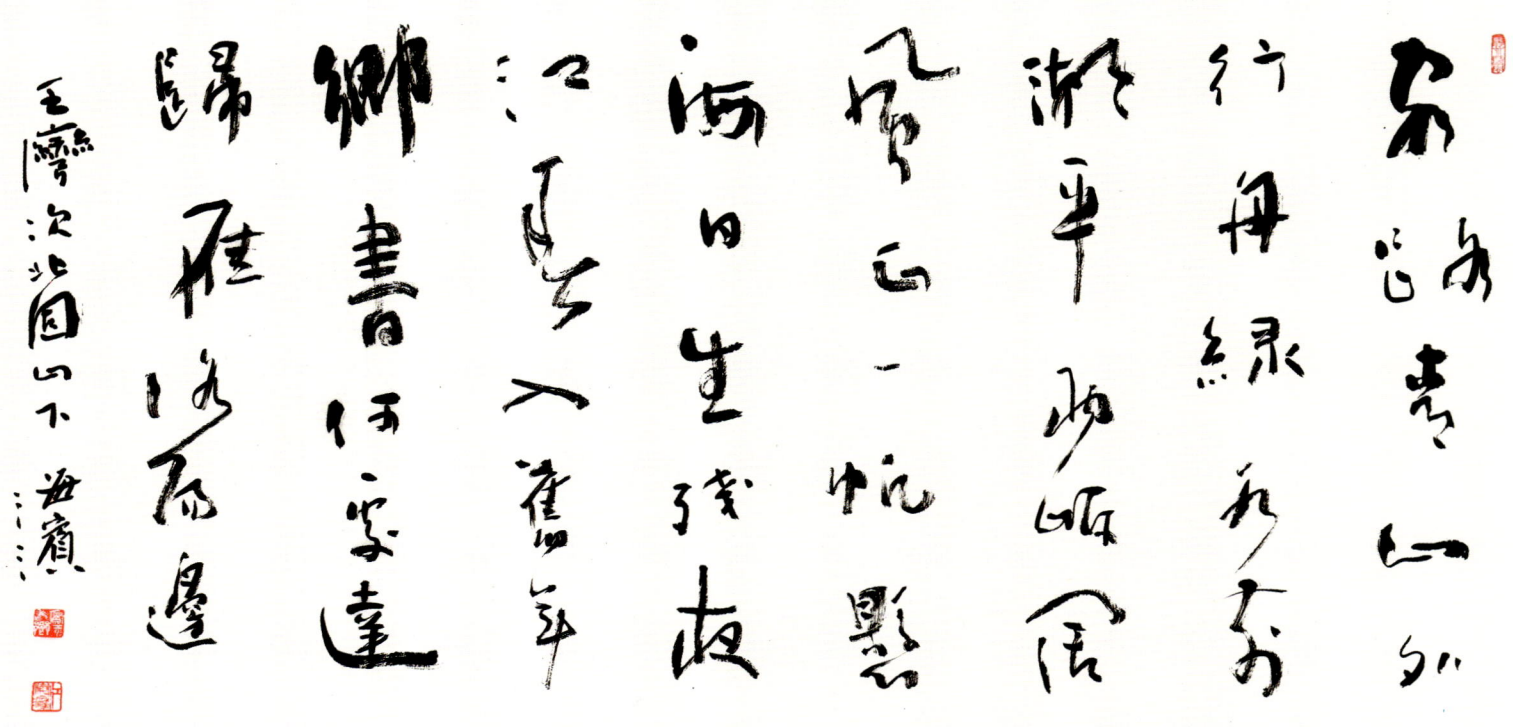

王维《次北固山下》　　138cm×67cm　　Wang Wei "Beigu Mountain"

# 张昆　　*Zhang Kun*

张昆，女，1979年生，辽宁锦州人，号水墨宫主，白石门下齐派自由画家，会意水墨画创始人著名画家王广然弟子。

润笔价格：6,000元/平尺

Zhang Kun, female, born in 1979, is from Liaoning Jinzhou. Known as Holder of Shuimo Palace, she is a free painter as Qi Baishi's disciple. She is also a disciple of Wangguagnran, who is the fonder of knowing style of calligraphy painting.

*Reference price: 6,000 yuan / square foot*

《群龙入海》　　70cm×137cm　　*"Dragons into the Sea"*

## 李永高　*Li Yonggao*

李永高，男，汉族，江苏省滨海县人，1929年8月生，现为中国人民解放军总后勤部离休干部，中国书法家协会会员，中华诗词学会会员，文化部侨联文华阁书画院院长，中华民族文化研究会诗书画艺委会名誉主席。

润笔价格：6,000元/平尺

Li Yongga, male, Han nationality, from Binhai County, Jiangsu Province, was born in August 1929. He is a retired cadres of PLA General Logistics Department, member of Chinese Calligraphers Association, member of Chinese Poetry Society, president of the painting academy of federation Mandarin Court in Ministry of Culture, honorary chairman of poetry Painting Committee of Chinese Culture Research Association.

*Reference price: 6,000 yuan / square foot*

《沁园春·雪》　96cm×178cm　　*"To the Tunes of Qin Yuan Chun- snow"*

# 潘文　　Pan Wen

潘文，男，1969年生，安徽利辛人，洛阳市美术家协会会员，洛阳书画艺术院画师。

润笔价格：8,000元/平尺

Pan Wen, male, born in 1969, is from Anhui Lixin. He is the member of Luoyang City Artists Association, artist of Art Academy of Luoyang painting Academy.

*Reference price: 8,000 yuan / square foot*

《一潭清影》　　138cm×69cm　　"Shadow in Pond"

# 李同军　*Li Tong-jun*

李同军，男，字宗轩，1946年生于河北晋县，多次在国家大型书法展上获金奖，作品被多国友人收藏。现任中艺名（北京）书法院副院长，中国国际书画研究院院士，清新书画院理事等职。

润笔价格：4,000元/平尺

LI Tong Jun, male, known as Zongxuan, was 1946 Born in Hebei Jinzhou County. He has wined gold medals several times in the national large-scale exhibition of calligraphy and his works are collected by people from different coutries. He is the vice president of Zhong YImign (Beijing) Calligraphy Academy, academician of International Painting and Calligraphy Institute, director of Qinxin Calligraphy Institute.

*Reference price: 4,000 yuan / square foot*

《剑趣》　　138cm×68cm　　"Sword Fun"

# 叶泽洲  *Ye Zezhou*

叶泽洲，男，1943年生，安徽人，现为一级美术师，中国文化艺术发展促进会艺术会员，中国美协旅游联谊中心会员，中国国画家协会理事。

润笔价格：6,000元/平尺

Ye Zezhou, male, born in 1943, is from Anhui. He is now an A-level artist, member of Chinese Culture and Arts Development Association, member of the Chinese Artists Association Travel Fellowship Center, director of Chinese Painting Association.
*Reference price: 6,000 yuan / square foot*

《和谐幽居自然美》　　70cm×137cm　　"Harmony Natural Beauty"

# 吴隆湜　*Wu Longshi*

吴隆湜，笔名陇石，生于1948年，中国文人书协会员，甘肃诗书画联谊会会员，黄石林书画院美术师，中国现代文艺出版社艺术委员会委员。

润笔价格：5,000元/平尺

WU Longshi, with a pen name as Longshi, was born in 1948. He is the member of the Chinese literati Calligraphers, member of Gansu Poetry and Calligraphy Club, artist Huang Shilin painting and calligraphy Institute, commissary of Art Committee in Chinese Modern Literature Publishing House.
*Reference price: 5,000 yuan / square foot*

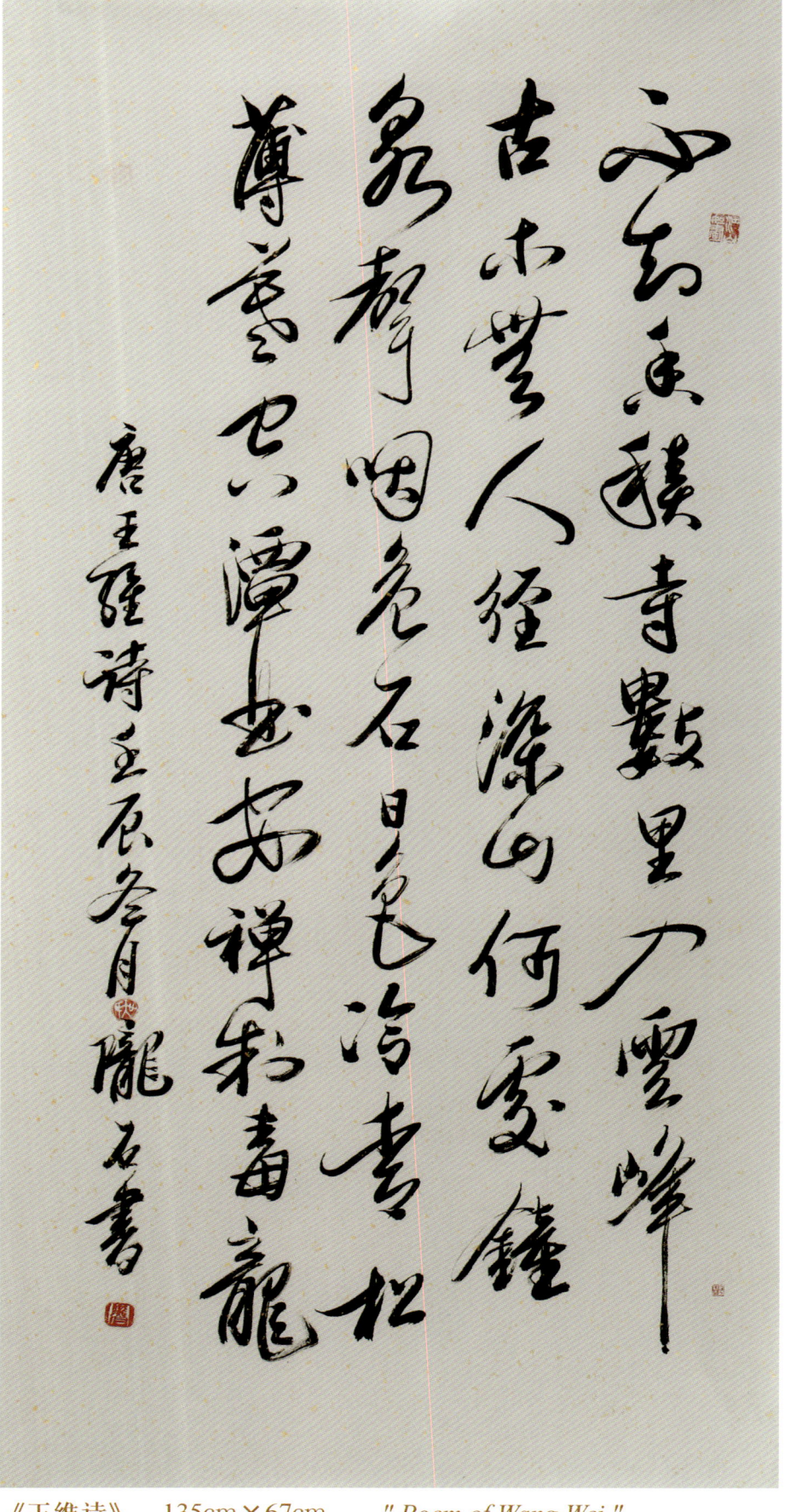

《王维诗》　　135cm×67cm　　"Poem of Wang Wei"

# 李凤楼 *Lifeng Lou*

李凤楼，男，号云台，1948年9月出生，任专业美术书法教师，一级书画师，中国书画协会会员，中华文化研究院副院长。

润笔价格：6,000元/平尺

Lifeng Lou, male, known as Yuntai, was born in September 1948. He serves as professional art and calligraphy teacher, an A-level painter, member of Chinese Painting and Calligraphy Association, president of Chinese Culture Research Institute.

*Reference price: 6,000 yuan / square foot*

《青山不老　碧水长流》　　70cm×136cm　　"Permanent Mountain and Rivers"

# 袁世煜 *Yuan Shiyu*

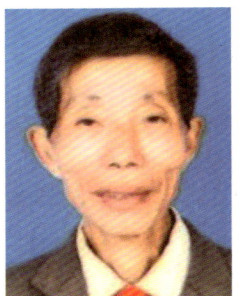

袁世煜，男，1940年3月生，江西省人，现为中国文化艺术发展促进会会员，中国书法研究院艺术委员，九州枫林国际书画院院士，北京尔康书画院院士。

润笔价格：4,000元/平尺

Yuan Shiyu, male, born in March 1940, is from Jiangxi Province. He is currently a member of Chinese Culture and Arts Development Association, commissary of Arts Committee in Chinese Calligraphy Institute, academician of Jiuzhou Fenglin International Painting and Calligraphy Academy, academician of Beijing Kang fine art academy.

*Reference price: 4,000 yuan / square foot*

苏轼《水调歌头》　　137cm×68cm　　*Su Shi's "Prelude to Water Melody"*

# 韩纪友  *Han Jiyou*

韩纪友，男，字文信，1946年生，山东日照人，现为中原书画研究院高级画师，中国书画艺术家协会会员，一级美术师。

润笔价格：8,000元/平尺

Han Jiyou, male, with a pen name as Wenxin, was born in 1946 in Rizhao. He now a senior painter of Central Institute of Fine Art, member of Chinese Painting and Calligraphy Artists Association, an A-level artist.
*Reference price: 8,000 yuan / square foot*

《梅花》　70cm×135cm　　*"Plum"*

# 王仲彦　*Wang Zhongyan*

王仲彦，男，汉族，笔名润石，斋号自在轩，1963年5月生，以行书、隶书见长，曾获《书法》风云榜提名。

润笔价格：5,000元／平尺

Wang Zhongyan, male, Han nationality, known as Runshi, Zizaixuan, was born in May 1963, good at cursive handwriting and Li calligraphy, won the "calligraphy" billboard nominations.
*Reference price: 5,000 yuan / square foot*

刘禹锡《陋室铭》　　137cm×67cm　　*Liu Yuxi "Passage for Lou Shi"*

# 张玉明 *Zhang Yuming*

张玉明，男，1960年，北京人，字汉臣，号日月斋主、梅壑道人，中国名家书画院院士，北京东城美术家协会理事，中央美术学院中国画研修班。

润笔价格：6,000元/平尺

Zhang Yuming, male, born in 1960 in Beijing, is also known as Han Chen, Moderator of Riyue, Meihe Daoren. He is the academician of Chinese Painting and Calligraphy Academy, director of Beijing Dongcheng Artists Association, working at China Central Academy of Fine Arts Painting Seminar.

*Reference price: 6,000 yuan / square foot*

《红梅一枝舞东风》　138cm×68cm　"Dancing Plum"

# 杨恒春　Yang Hengchun

杨恒春，男，1946年3月生，山东莱芜人，现为中国书法家协会会员，中国书画家协会会员，中国书画摄影家协会理事，中国当代艺术家协会会员，中国书画研究院院士。

润笔价格：8,000元/平尺

Yang Hengchun, male, born in March 1946, is from Shandong Laiwu. He is the member of Chinese Calligraphers Association, member of Chinese Calligraphy Association, director of Chinese Painting and Calligraphy Photography Association, member of Chinese Contemporary Artists Association, academician of Chinese Painting and Calligraphy Institute.
*Reference price: 8,000 yuan / square foot*

《沁园春·雪》　69cm×38cm　"To the Tunes of Qin Yuan Chun-snow"

# 赖建成　*Lai Jiancheng*

赖建成，男，字久翁，号南山居士，现为中国国家画院龙瑞工作室画家、中国山水画创作院副院长、中联书画艺术研究院常务副院长、福建省美术家协会会员。

润笔价格：16,000元/平尺

Lai Jiancheng, male, possesses pen name as Jiuweng and Lay Buddhist of Nanshan. He is the painter of the National Art Long Rui studio, vice president of Chinese landscape painting Institute, executive vice president of Federation of Calligraphy and Painting Institute, member of Fujian Province Artists Association.

*Reference price: 16,000 yuan / square foot*

《南山福地》　137cm×68cm　　*"Blessed Nanshan"*

## 张合文　*Zhang Hewen*

张合文，男，1954年生，河南郑州人，现被北京世界百家文化发展中心聘为特约编辑，中国诗词名家研究会理事，当代中国美术家书画院会员，中国书画家俱乐部副秘书长。

润笔价格：4,000元/平尺

Zhang Hewen, male, born in 1954, is from Zhengzhou. He is the distinguished editor of Beijing World Cultural Development Center, director of Chinese poetry masters Research Association, member of contemporary Chinese art academy, deputy secretary-General of Chinese painting and calligraphy clubs.
*Reference price: 4,000 yuan / square foot*

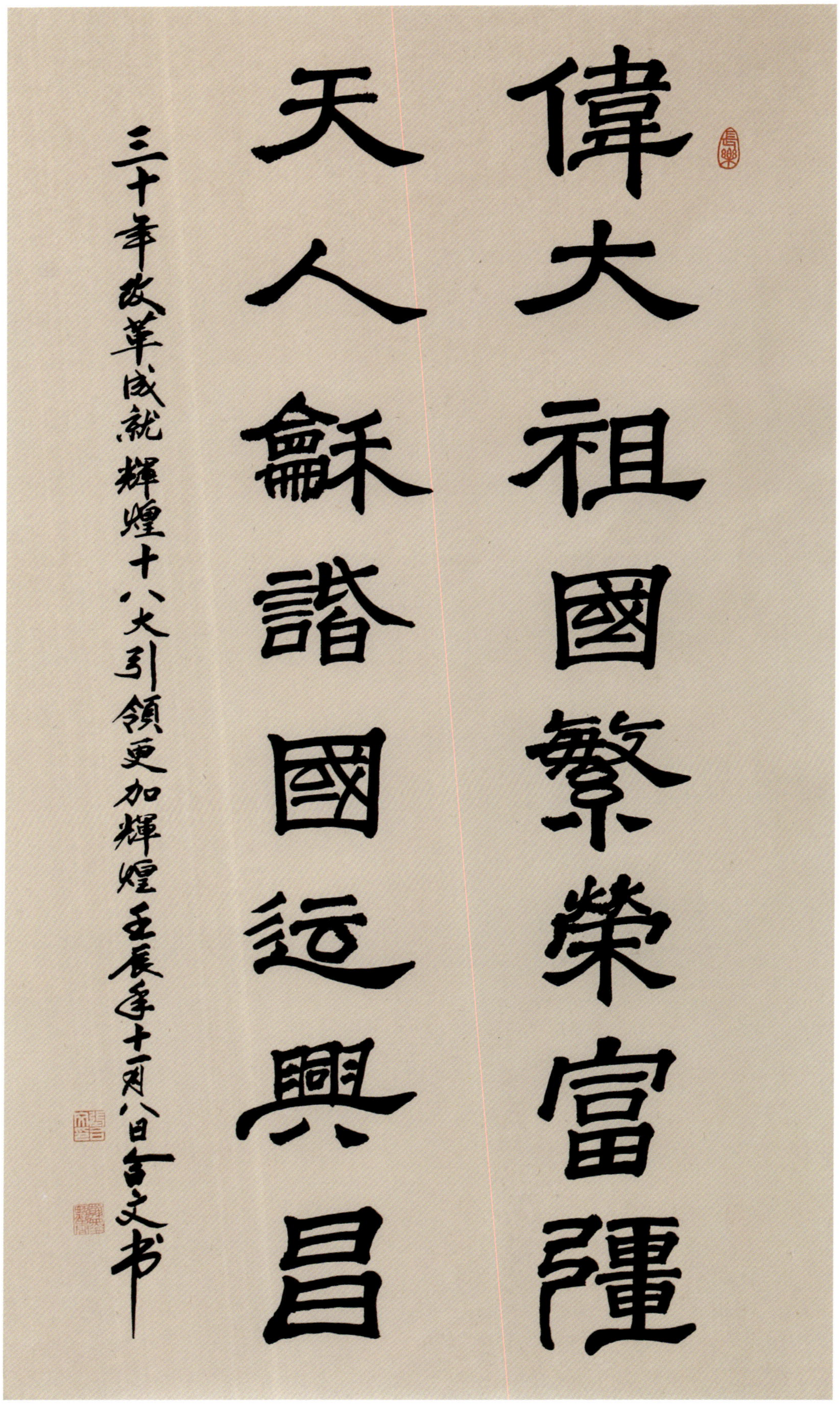

《伟大祖国》　　114cm×65cm　　"Great Motherland"

# 王乃献　*Wang Naixian*

王乃献，男，1942年生，河南人，号梅花堂主，草根画家。
润笔价格：10,000元/平尺

*Wang Naixian, male, born in 1942, from Henan Province, with a pen name of Holder of Plum Hall, he is a grassroots painter.*
*Reference price: 10,000 yuan / square foot*

《风雪高清》　　137cm×70cm　　*"Snow and Wind"*

# 徐惠中　*Xu Huizhong*

徐惠中，男，1956年3月生，江苏盐城人，现为中国书画家协会会员，上海书画院实力派书画家。
润笔价格：4,000元/平尺

Xu, male, born in March 1956, from Yancheng, is the member of China Calligraphers Association members, painter of Shanghai Painting and Calligraphy Institute.
*Reference price: 4,000 yuan / square foot*

杜牧《山行》　137cm×70cm　　*Du Mu "Trip in Mountain "*

# 麻小五　*Ma Xiaowu*

麻小五，男，现为中国国画家协会会员，中国书画研究院院士，中国画画虎艺术研究院常务理事。

润笔价格：6,000元/平尺

Ma Xiaowu, male, is the member of China National Artists Association, academician of Chinese Academy of Painting and Calligraphy Institute, executive director of China Academy of tiger Art painting.
*Reference price: 6,000 yuan / square foot*

《展雄风》　68cm×135cm　　*"Treasures Exhibition"*

# 张伯周　*Zhang Bozhou*

张伯周，男，湖南桑植县人，斋名：戏墨斋。作品在中国中老年书画名家庆澳门回归十周年书画交流展中荣获"金奖"，现为中国书画名家研究会副会长。

润笔价格：5,000元/平尺

Zhang Bozhou, male, from Hunan Sangzhi County, is also known as Ximozhai. His Works of painting and calligraphy won the "Gold Award" in the elderly Calligraphy Exhibition celebrating the tenth anniversary of Macao's return to China. He is the vice president of Chinese painting and calligraphy research Institute.

*Reference price: 5,000 yuan / square foot*

唐·韩愈《早春呈水部张十八员外》　　69cm×138cm　　*Han Yu of Tang Dynasty "Presented to Zhang in Spring"*

# 赵亦兵 *Zhao Yibing*

赵亦兵,男,1955年生,青岛人,现为中国画家协会理事、青岛市书法家协会会员、青岛美术家协会会员。

润笔价格:14,000元/平尺

Zhao Yibing, male, born in 1955, is from Qingdao. He is the director of China paintings Association, member of Qingdao City Calligraphers Association, member of Qingdao Artists Association.
*Reference price: 14,000 yuan / square foot*

《天秋百泉声》　　138cm×68cm　　" Sound of Spring Waters in Autumn "

## 蒋光前  *Jiang Guangqian*

蒋光前，男，1941年生，陕西西安人，汉族，陕西省书协会员，中国书画艺术研究会研究员，东坡书画艺术研究院顾问，长城魂当代书画家协会名誉主席，北京墨都书画院常务高级理事。

润笔价格：6,000元/平尺

Jiang Guangqian, Han nationality, male, born in 1941, is from Xi'an. He is the member of Shaanxi Provincial Calligraphers Association, researcher of Chinese Painting and Calligraphy Art Research Institute, consultant of Dongpo Calligraphy and Painting Institute, honorary chairman of the Great Wall Soul Contemporary Calligraphers, senior executive director of Beijing ink painting Institute.

*Reference price: 6,000 yuan / square foot*

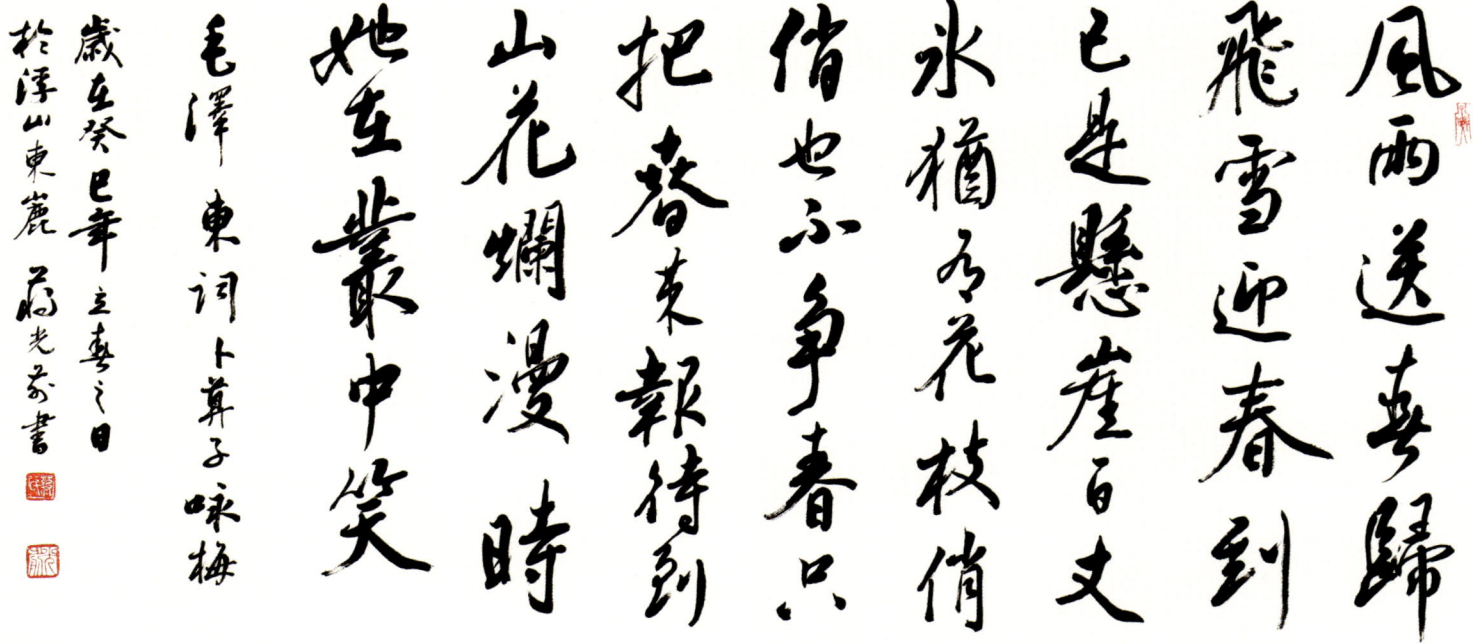

毛泽东《卜算子·咏梅》　　68cm×135cm　　*Mao Zedong "To the Tunes of Pu Suan Zi- plum"*

## 刘永林  *Liu Yonglin*

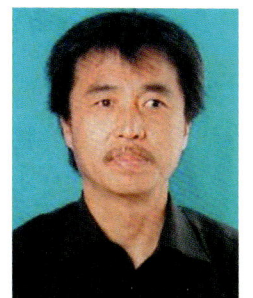

刘永林，男，汉族，1954年生，黑龙江省哈尔滨市人，贵州省美术家协会会员，贵州中山书画社副秘书长。

润笔价格：8,000元/平尺

Liu Yonglin, male, Han nationality, born in 1954, is from Heilongjiang Province, Harbin City. He is the member of Guizhou Artists Association, deputy Secretary-general of Guizhou Zhongshan painting clubs.
*Reference price: 8,000 yuan / square foot*

《草枯鹰眼疾》　　98cm×180cm　　*" Sharp Eyes of Hawk "*

## 吕渊明  *Lv Yuanming*

吕渊明，男，1956年生，上海人，先后成为潘君诺、曹简楼的弟子，绘画作品《春晓》入选庆祝建党90周年第六界上海美术大展。

润笔价格：5,000元/平尺

Lv Yuanming, male, born in 1956, is from Shanghai. He is the disciple of Pan Junnuo and Cao Jianlou. His painting "Early Spring" was selected into the sixth sector Shanghai Art Exhibition to celebrate the 90th anniversary of the Party.
*Reference price: 5,000 yuan / square foot*

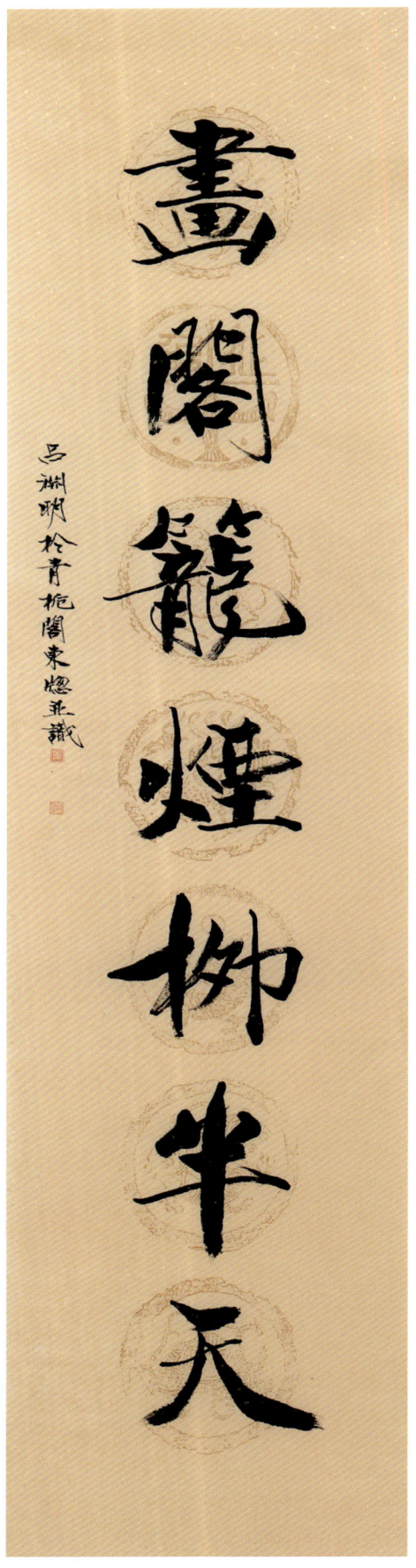

《青云拟黛山千叠，画阁笼烟柳半天》　139cm×34cm×2　"Painting of Cloud and Mist"

## 贺也频  *He Yepin*

贺也频，男，1971年生，甘肃人，国家二级美术师，中国美术家协会会员，中国油画学会会员，庆阳市美术家协会副主席，现就职于庆阳市画院。
润笔价格：10,000元/平尺

He Yepin, male, born in 1971, is from Gansu. He is the member of Chinese Artists Association, member of China Oil Painting Society, vice chairman of Qingyang City Artists Association. He is now working in Qingyang City Art Gallery, and is the National B-level artists.
*Reference price: 10,000 yuan / square foot*

《大雪》　142cm×73cm　　*"Heavy Snow"*

## 张义俊  *Zhang Yijun*

张义俊，字一丑，号慧丁，1970生，青岛人，现为中国楹联学会会员，中华全国书画联合会会员，中国硬笔书法协会会员，系历史上著名书法家张旭的后裔。

润笔价格：7,000元/平尺

Zhang Yijun, with pen names of Yichou and Huiding, was born in 1970, from Qingdao. He is member of the couplets Society, member of China National Painting and Calligraphy Association member of Chinese Pen Calligraphy Association. He is the descendant of famous calligrapher Zhang Xu.

*Reference price: 7,000 yuan / square foot*

《楷书对联》　137cm×34cm×2　　"Couplets"

# 李会妨  *Li Huifang*

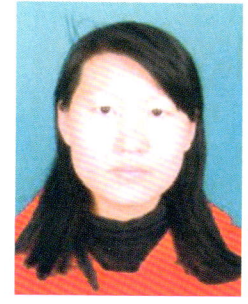

李会妨，女，1983年8月6日生，河北雄县人，河北省保定市美术家协会会员，燕南书画联谊会会员，伯平书画研究院会员。

润笔价格：12,000元/平尺

Li Huifang, female, born on 6 August 1983, is from Xiong County, Hebei. He is the member of Baoding, Hebei Province Artists Association, member of Yannan Calligraphy Association member, member of Bo-Ping Painting and Calligraphy research Institute.
*Reference price: 12,000 yuan / square foot*

《幽居山泉》　　63cm×137cm　　*"Spring in Mountains"*

# 乔士华 *Qiao Shihua*

乔士华，男，1930年12月生，河南人，现为中国艺术鉴定委员会艺术家学部委员会理事，中国国学研究会名誉会长，中国书画学会副主席，中国书画院院士。

润笔价格：6,000元/平尺

Qiao Shihua, male, born in December 1930, is from Henan Province. He is the director of the Faculty of Arts Artists Committee of the governing appraisal committee, honorary president of Chinese Sinology Research Association, vice president of Chinese Painting and Calligraphy Institute, academician of Chinese Academy of Painting and Calligraphy.

*Reference price: 6,000 yuan / square foot*

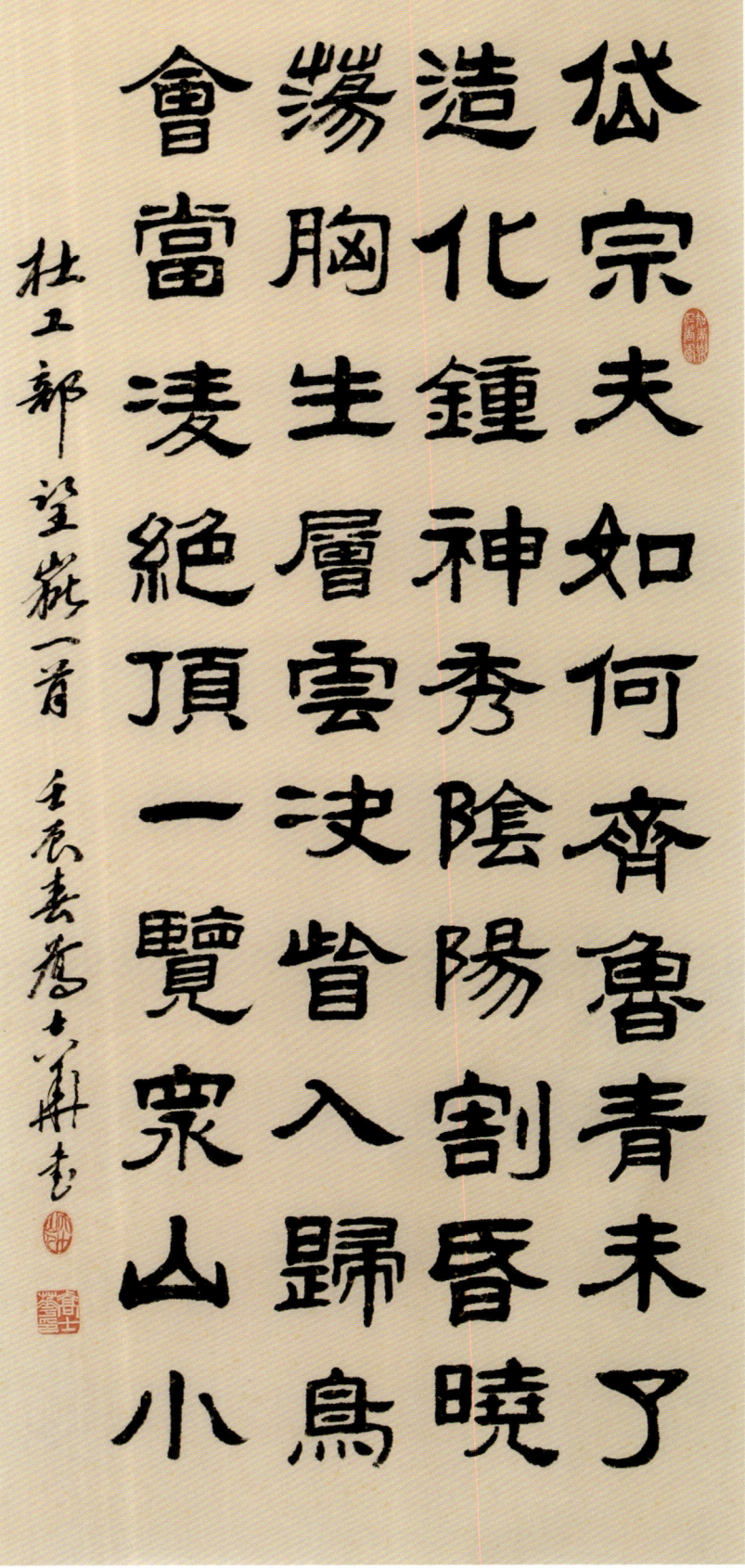

杜甫《望岳》　　115cm×53cm　　*Qiao Shihua*

# 刘建新　*Liu Jianxin*

刘建新，男，笔名阿欣，1953年生，河北人，《中国劳动保障报》河北记者站站长，现为中国画家协会会员，中国美术家协会河北分会会员，中国国际美术研究院副院长。

润笔价格：6,000元/平尺

Liu Jianxin, male, born in 1953, with a pen name as Xin, is from Hebei Province. He is the head of "China Labor and Social Security News" Hebei station, member of the Chinese Painters Association, member of Chinese Artists Association (Hebei branch), vice president of China International Art Research Institute.

*Reference price: 6,000 yuan / square foot*

《清池皓月解禅心》　　137cm×70cm　　"Water and Moon of Buddhist Mind"

# 罗少模  *Luo Shaomo*

罗少模，男，号山外人，1946年生，四川省兴文县人，现任兴文县书法家协会主席。
润笔价格：5,000元/平尺

Luo Shaomo, Male, known as Shanwairen, born in 1946, is from Sichuan Xingwen County. He is now the president of Xing Wen County Calligraphers Association.
*Reference price: 5,000 yuan / square foot*

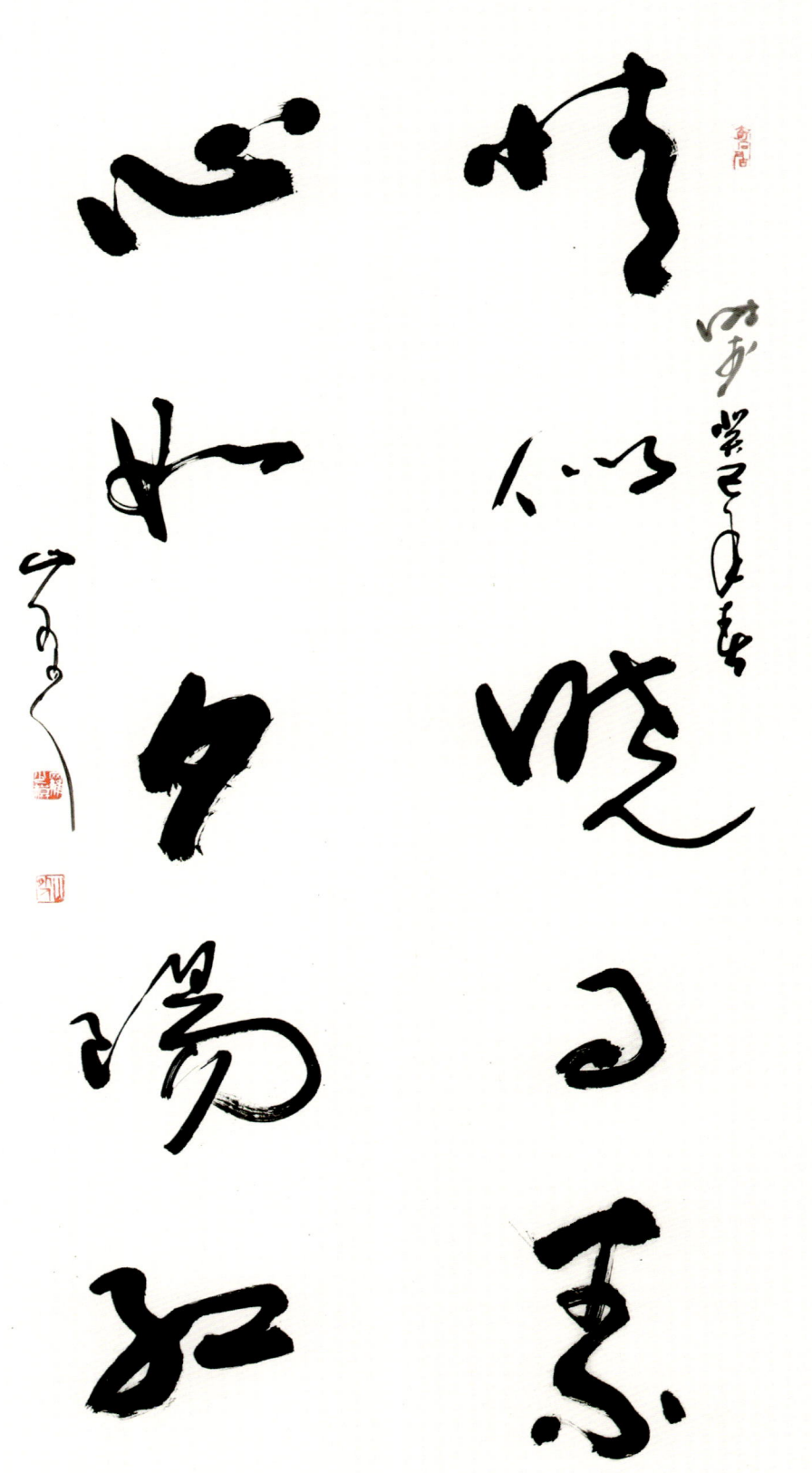

《情似小月素　心如夕阳红》　　136cm×70cm　　"Light Love and Red Heart"

# 刘茂发  *Liu Maofa*

刘茂发，男，字大有，号云峰，汉族，山东蓬莱人，现为中国书画研究会会员，终身理事，中国书画家协会理事，一级美术师，颜真卿书画院名誉院长，汕头市美协会员。

润笔价格：8,000元/平尺

Liu Maofa, male, Han nationality, with pen names as Dayou and Yunfeng, is from Shandong Penglai. He is now a member and life-long director of Chinese calligraphy and painting, director of Chinese Calligraphers Association, an A-level artist, honorary president of Yan Zhenqing painting academy, Shantou City, member of Shantou Artist Association.
*Reference price: 8,000 yuan / square foot*

《花开富贵万年春》　　134cm×67cm　　*"Blossoming"*

# 李焕然  *Li Huanran*

李焕然，男，广西桂林人，桂林市美术家协会会员，桂林市书法家协会会员。
润笔价格：4,000元/平尺

Li Huanran, male, from Guangxi Guilin, is the member of Guilin Artists Association, member of Guilin Calligraphers Association.
*Reference price: 4,000 yuan / square foot*

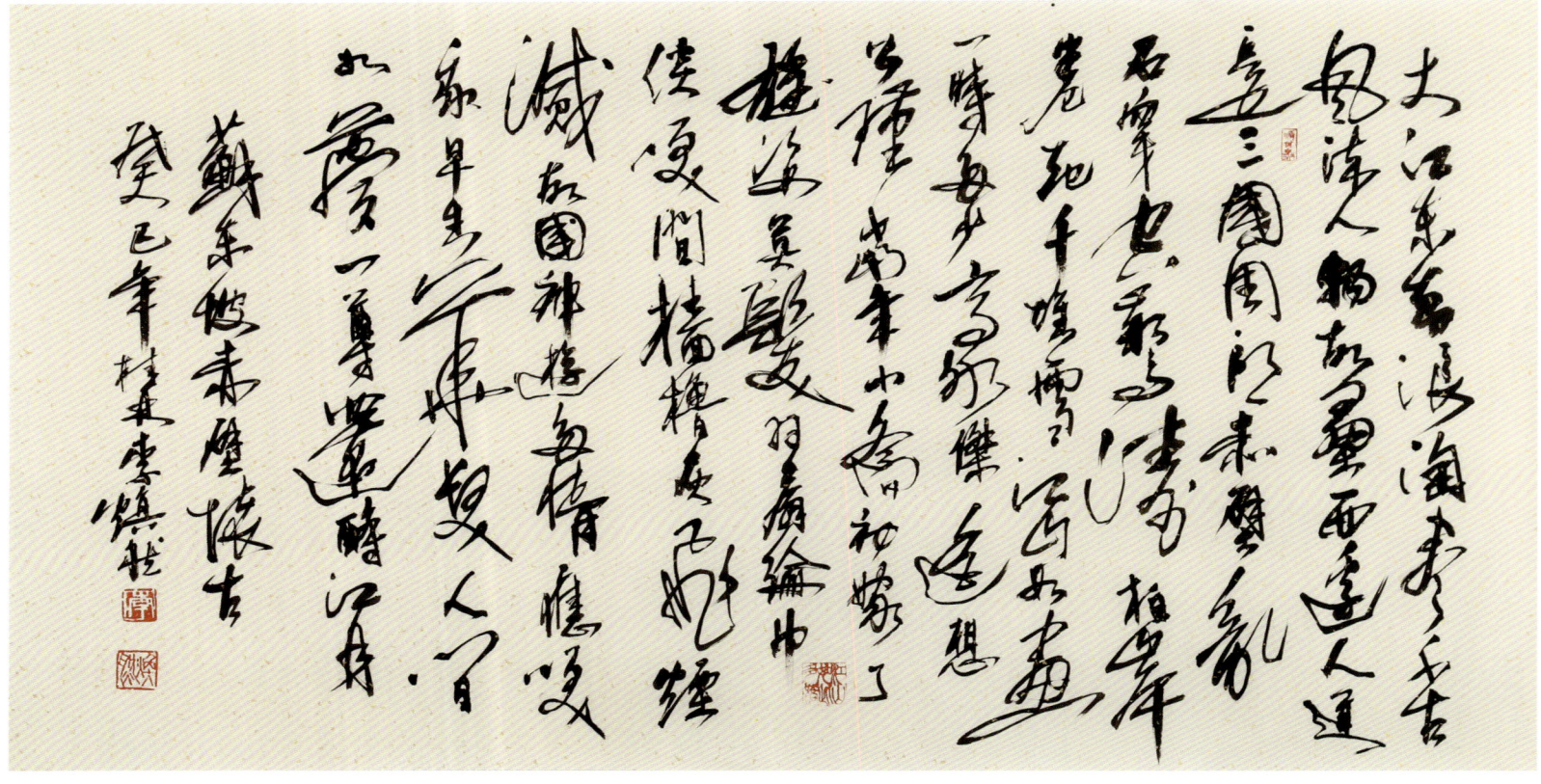

苏轼《赤壁怀古》　　69cm×134cm　　*Su Shi "Chi Bi"*

# 吴长太  *Wu Changtai*

吴长太，男，1935年2月生，黑龙江人，现为中国书画摄影家协会会员，北京华夏国艺书画院院士，高级书画师，中国百杰艺术家。

润笔价格：6,000元/平尺

Wu Changtai, male, born in February 1935, is from Heilongjiang. He is the member of painting Photographers Association, academician of Beijing Huaxia Academy of Arts and Paintings, senior artist, one of the one hundred outstanding artists of China.
*Reference price: 6,000 yuan / square foot*

《嫩江帆影》　　68cm×137cm　　*"Sails on Nen River"*

## 李宝春　*Li Baochun*

李宝春，男，1950年5月生，黑龙江省大庆市人，现为中国艺术名家协会副主席、中华诗书画研究院副院长、中国书画家协会理事、中国书法家协会会员。

润笔价格：5,000元/平尺

Li Baochun, male, born in May 1950, is from Daqing City, Heilongjiang Province. He is the vice chairman of China Art Masters Association, vice president of Chinese Poetry and Calligraphy Research Institute, vice president of Chinese Calligraphers Association, member of the Chinese Calligraphers Association.
*Reference price: 5,000 yuan / square foot*

《三国演义开篇词》　　137cm×65cm　　*"Opening Passage of Three Kingdoms"*

## 彭牧童　*Peng Mutong*

彭牧童，男，1951年生，江西九江人，现为中国企业文化促进会会员、中央民族大学继续教育学院书画院特聘画家、中国中外名人文化研究会书画师。

润笔价格：10,000元/平尺

Peng Mutong, male, born in 1951, is from Jiangxi Jiujiang. He is now the member of China Enterprise Culture Improvement Association, Distinguished Artist of the Continuing Education School of Central Nationalities University, artist of Chinese and foreign celebrities Cultural Studies painting Institute.
*Reference price: 10,000 yuan / square foot*

《吟清风》　69cm×135cm　　*"Sing for Breeze"*

# 韩公修 *Han Gongxiu*

韩公修，男，字石修，号新岱山人，1957年生，山东人，系中国孔子书画研究院理事，北京六艺嘉韵书画艺术院院士。

润笔价格：4,000元/平尺

Han Gongxiu, male, known as Shixiu and Xinyue Dairen, born in 1957, is from Shandong Provinc. He is the director of Chinese Confucius Painting and Calligraphy Research Institute, academician of Beijing Liu Yi Jia Yun Academy of Painting and Calligraphy.
*Reference price: 4,000 yuan / square foot*

欧阳修《竹间亭》　　69cm×137cm　　*Ouyang Xiu " Pavilion in Bamboo "*

# 林桥  *Lin Qiao*

林桥，男，1952年生，四川省人，现为中国中外名人文化研究会、中国书画研究院、中国国画家协会、炎黄书画学会会员，黄河书画院、江南书画院特聘画师。

润笔价格：8,000元/平尺

Lin Qiao, male, born in 1952, is from Sichuan. He is now the member of China and foreign celebrities Cultural Studies, Chinese Painting and Calligraphy Institute, China National Artists Association, Yanhuang painting Institute, guest artist of Yellow River Painting and Calligraphy Institute and Jiangnan painting academy.

*Reference price: 8,000 yuan / square foot*

《春暖》　　70cm×137cm　　　*"Warmth of Spring"*

## 张汉杰  *Zhang Hanjie*

张汉杰，男，笔名介甫，1938年12月生，河南新安县人，中国书画家协会会员，北京长城书画院特约书法家，北京长城书画院洛阳分院副院长。

润笔价格：4,000元/平尺

Zhang Hanjie, male, born in December 1938, with pen name as Jiefu, is from Henan Xin'an County. He is the member of China Calligraphers, distinguished artist of Beijing Great Wall Painting and Calligraphy Institute, vice president of Beijing Great Wall Painting and Calligraphy Institute (Luoyang Branch).

*Reference price: 4,000 yuan / square foot*

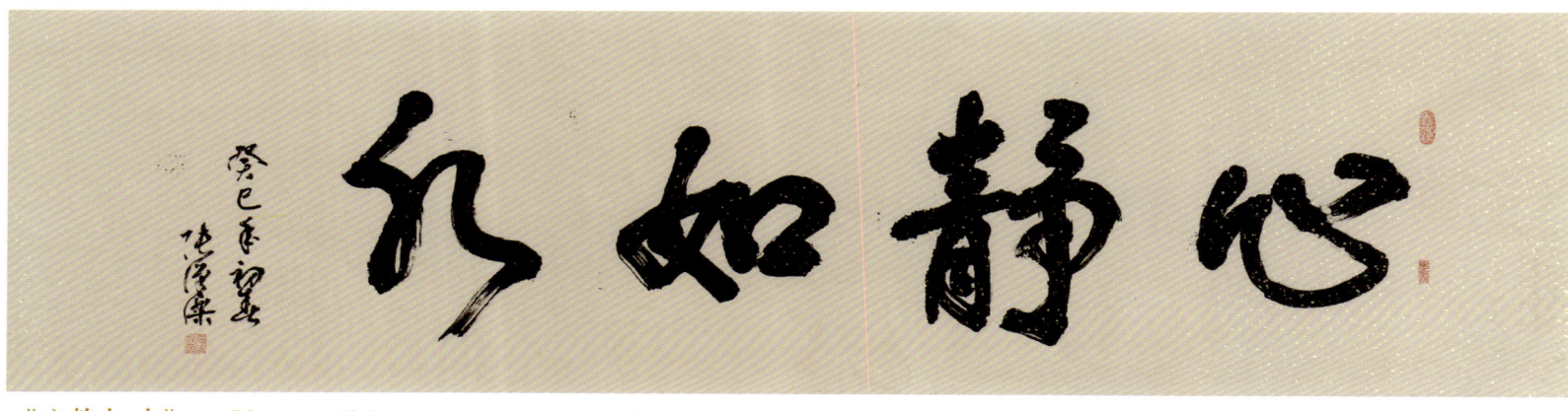

《心静如水》　　50cm×196cm　　"Calm like Water"

# 梁骜 *Liang Ao*

梁骜，号寒石，一级美术师，哈尔滨统战书画院副院长，海峡两岸艺术交流协会副主席，哈尔滨书画研究会艺术顾问，陕西美术馆特聘美术师，黑龙江美术协会会员。

润笔价格：8,000元/平尺

Liang Ao, known as Hanshi, is an A-level artist, vice president of the united painting Institute in Harbin, vice president of artistic exchanges across the Taiwan Strait Association, consultant of Harbin painting art Research Society, distinguished artist of Shaanxi Museum, member of Heilongjiang Fine Arts Association.
*Reference price: 8,000 yuan / square foot*

《盛夏图》　　135cm×70cm　　*"Midsummer Figure"*

## 杨万宝　*Yang Wanbao*

杨万宝，男，1950年11月生，安徽省宣城市人，现为中华书画学会副主席，中国翰林书画艺术院院士，宣城市书法家协会会员。

润笔价格：5,000元/平尺

Yang Wanbao, male, born in November 1950, is from Xuancheng. He is now the vice chairman of Chinese Painting and Calligraphy Institute, academician of Chinese Hanlin Academy of Painting and Calligraphy Art, member of Xuancheng City Calligraphers Association.

*Reference price: 5,000 yuan / square foot*

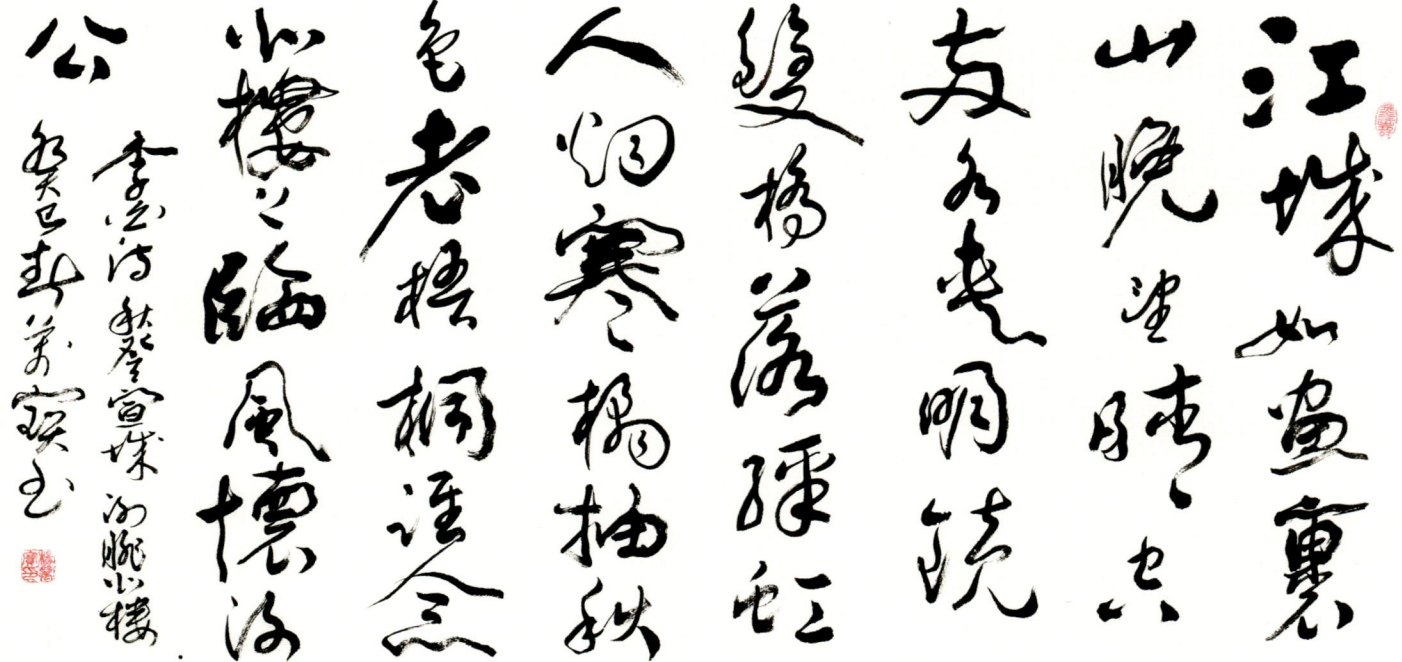

李白《秋登宣城谢朓北楼》　　70cm×137cm　　*Li Bai, "Viewing North Building on Xuancheng Building in Autumn "*

# 杨正温 *Yang Zhengwen*

杨正温，男，笔名洁之，1943年6月生，河南孟州市人，现为河南省书协、美协会员，中国国画家协会理事，中华诗词学会会员，河南省花鸟画研究会会员，河南省华豫书画院院士。

润笔价格：16,000元/平尺

Yang Zhengwen, male, born in June 1943, with a pen name as Jiezhi, is from Henan Mengzhou. He is now the director of Henan Calligraphers, Artists Association, Chinese Painting Association, member of the Institute of Chinese poetry, member of Henan flower and bird Research Association, academician of China Henan Academy of Painting and Calligraphy.
*Reference price: 16,000 yuan / square foot*

《紫气东来燕雀鸣》　　138cm×69cm　　*" The Purple Air comes from the east and birds song"*

# 张弓强 *Zhang Gongqiang*

张弓强，男，原名张天才，笔名弓强，1939年4月生，河南新安县人，现为中国美术家协会会员，中国书画家协会理事，中国国家书画院特约画师，中国书画研究院理事。

润笔价格：4,000元/平尺

Zhang Gongqiang, male, formerly known as Zhang Tiancai, with a pen name as Gongqiang, born in April 1939, is from Henan Xin'an County. He is now the member of Chinese Artists Association, director of China Calligraphers Association, invited artist of China National Painting and Calligraphy Institute, director of Chinese Painting and Calligraphy Institute.

*Reference price: 4,000 yuan / square foot*

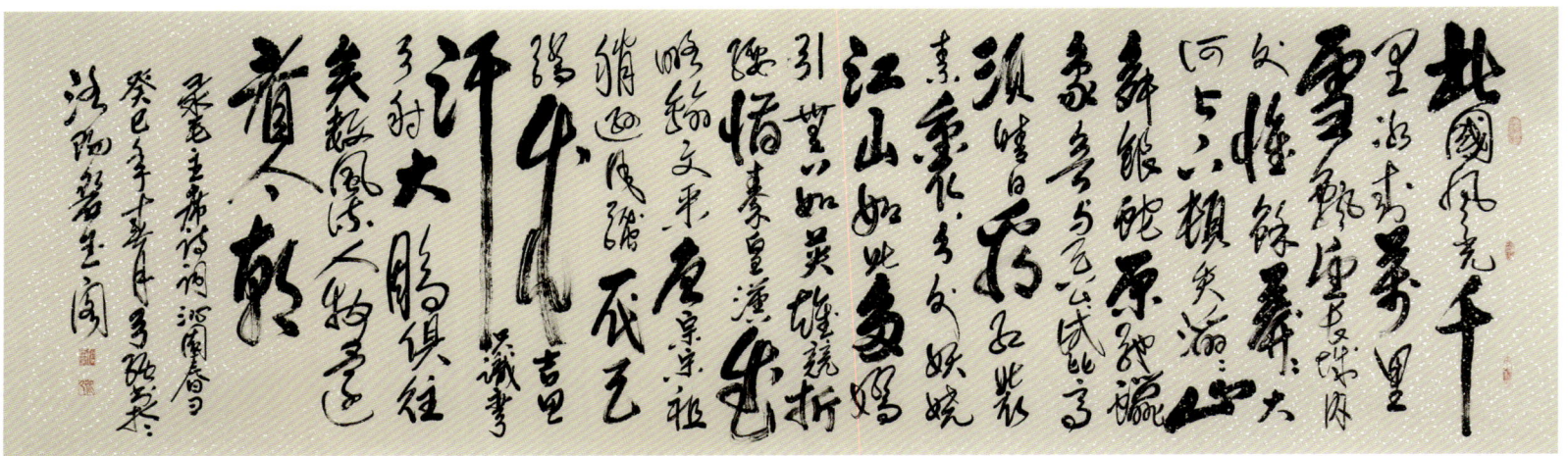

《沁园春·雪》　69cm×242cm　　*"To the Tunes of Qin Yuan Chun-snow"*

# 赵汉忠 *Zhao Hanzhong*

赵汉忠，男，1957年生，陕西省汉中市人，中国书画研究院院士，中国美术家协会山西分会会员，汉中中国画院副院长。

润笔价格：16,000元/平尺

Zhao Hanzhong, male, born in 1957, is from Hanzhong City, Shaanxi Province. He is the academician of China Academy of Painting and Calligraphy Institute, member of Chinese Artists Association of Shanxi branch, vice president of Hanzhong Chinese Painting Institute.

*Reference price: 16,000 yuan / square foot*

《坐在江边看云飞》 137cm×70cm  *"Sitting Beside the Water Watching Cloud"*

## 沈志昂  *Shen Zhi'ang*

沈志昂，男，1952年生，汉族，江苏省苏州人，现任中国翰林书画艺术院副院长、中华书画家协会副主席、中国书画艺术家创作中心理事、中国书画家协会会员、南京市长江书画家协会名誉主席等职。

润笔价格：5,000元/平尺

Shen Zhi'ang, male, born in 1952, Han nationality, is from Suzhou, Jiangsu Province. He is currently the vice president of Chinese Hanlin painting and calligraphy, vice president of China Calligraphers Association, director of Chinese painting and calligraphy artists center, member of Chinese Calligraphers Association, honorary chairman of the Nanjing Yangtze River Calligraphers Association.
*Reference price: 5,000 yuan / square foot*

《物华天宝　集古求真》　　139cm×68cm　　"Treasurs"

# 张友新　*Zhang Youxin*

张友新，男，北京人，1950年生，北京市美术家协会会员，中国文化艺术中心艺委会理事，中国画家协会理事。

润笔价格：12,000元/平尺

Zhang Youxin, male, from Beijing, was born in 1950. He is the member of Beijing Artists Association, director of Arts Council in Chinese Cultural Arts Center, director of Association of Chinese painters.

*Reference price: 12,000 yuan / square foot*

《读》　138cm×70cm　"Read"

## 马海元  *Ma Haiyuan*

马海元，男，1956年11月生，甘肃省人，任中国国画院副院长、中国柳倩艺术研究院书法家、中国收藏家协会会员等职。

润笔价格：6,000元/平尺

Ma Haiyuan, male, born in November 1956, is from Gansu Province, he serves as the vice president of Chinese painting, calligrapher of China Liu Qian Academy of Arts, member of Collectors Association.
*Reference price: 6,000 yuan / square foot*

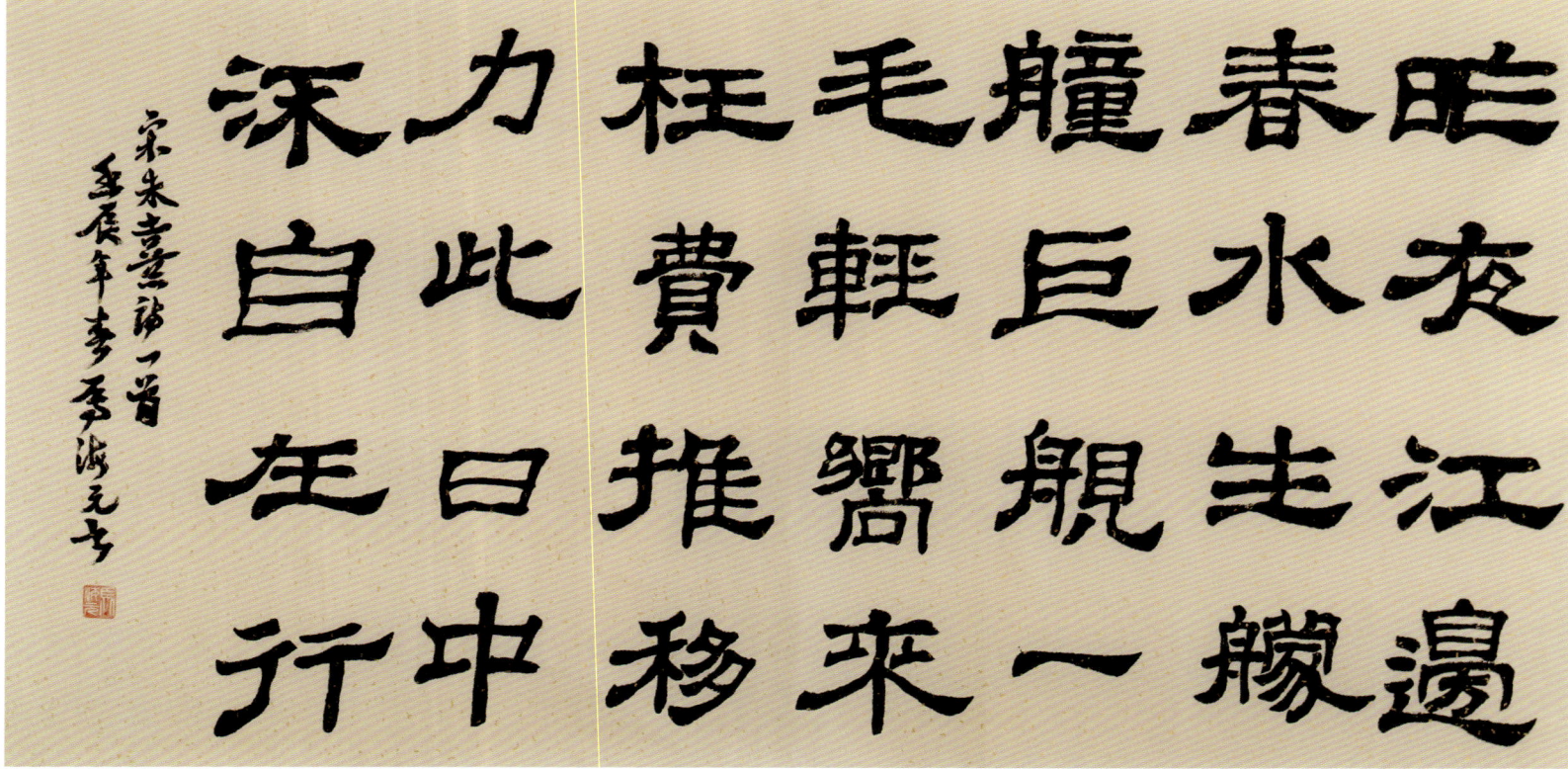

《朱熹诗一首》　　70cm×138cm　　*"Poem of Zhu Xi"*

## 冯萍 *Feng Ping*

冯萍，男，1932年生，中国美协会员，特级教师，擅长花鸟山水人物。
润笔价格：12,000元/平尺

Feng Ping, male, born in 1932, is a member of the Chinese Artists Association, special teacher, and good at painting bird, people and landscapes.
*Reference price: 12,000 yuan / square foot*

《月是故乡明》　83cm×80cm　　"Moon in Hometown is Brighter"

# 林坚  *Lin Jian*

林坚，男，笔名凌凡，1948年生，广东梅州人，现为中国金陵书画院名誉院长、山西省书法家协会会员。

润笔价格：5,000元/平尺

Lin Jian, male, known as Ling Fan, born in 1948, is from Meizhou, Guangdong. He is the honorary president of Jinling Painting and Calligraphy Institute, member of Shanxi Calligraphers Association.
*Reference price: 5,000 yuan / square foot*

李煜《虞美人》　　69cm×136cm　　*Li Yu "The Beauty"*

# 马贵生　*Ma Guisheng*

马贵生，男，1955年10月生，中国书画家联谊会会员，四川省美术家协会会员，四川省美术教育研究会理事，四川省广元市军民艺术团副团长，广元市马氏画院院长。

润笔价格：10,000元/平尺

Ma Guisheng, male, born in October 1955, is a member of Chinese Painting and Calligraphy Association, member of Sichuan Artists Association, director of Sichuan Fine Arts Education Research Association, deputy head of Guangyuan Military Art Troupe, president of Guangyuan Ma's Painting Academy.
*Reference price: 10,000 yuan / square foot*

《江南春韵》　　70cm×137cm　　*"Spring in Jiangnan"*

## 赵润英　Zhao Runying

赵润英，女，中国九华书画院副院长，中国国际书画研究院院士，中国扇子艺术学会常务理事。
润笔价格：4,000元/平尺

Zhao Runying, female, is vice president of the Chinese Jiuhua painting and calligraphy academy, academician of Chinese Academy of International Painting and Calligraphy Institute, executive director of Chinese Fan Art Society.
*Reference price: 4,000 yuan / square foot*

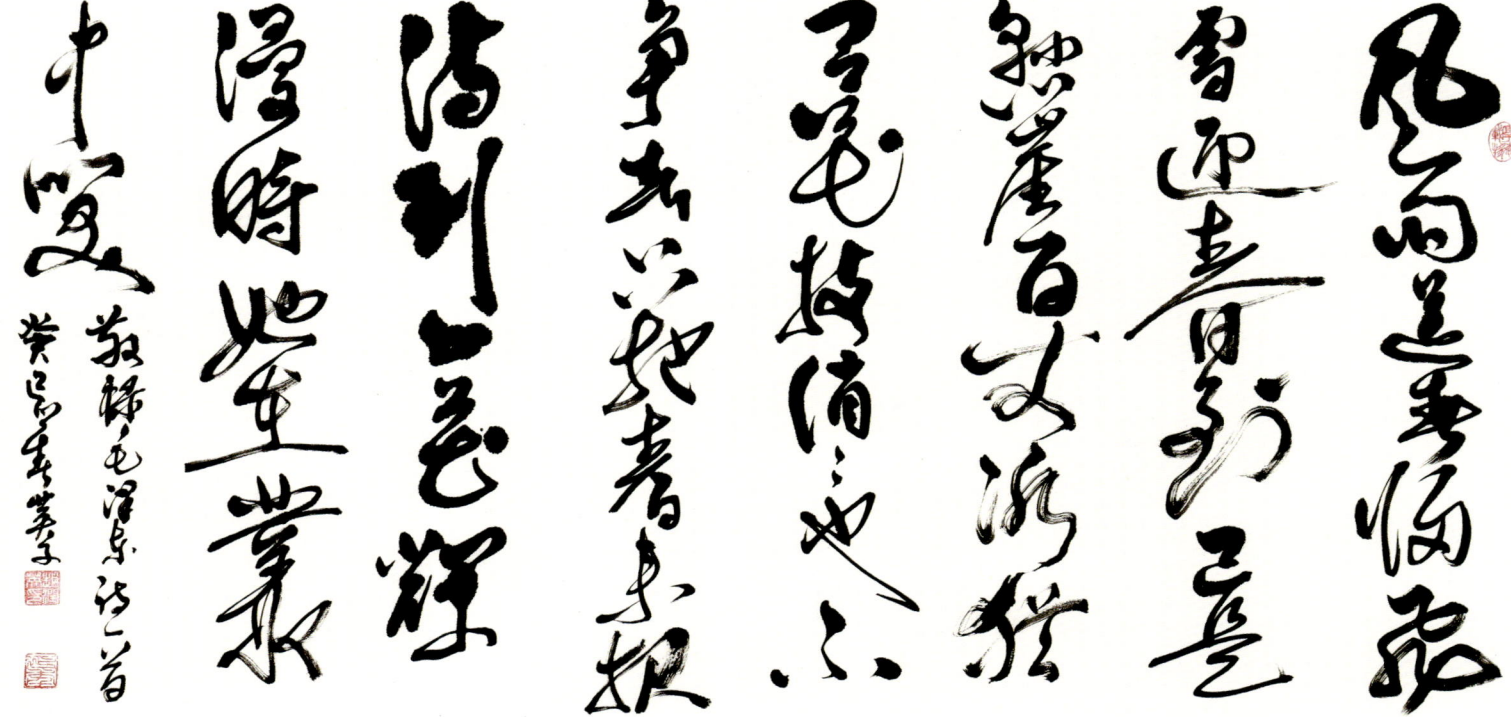

《毛泽东诗一首》　　70cm×137cm　　"Mao Zedong's Poem"

## 谭连华  *Tan Lianhua*

谭连华，男，号松梅客，山东潍坊人，现为中国画院画师、中国书画家协会副会长、齐鲁中国画艺术研究院研究员。

润笔价格：8,000元/平尺

Tan Lianhua, male, known as Songmei Ke, is from Shandong Weifang. He is the artist of China Painting Institute, vice president of Chinese Calligraphers Association, researcher of Chinese Qilu painting art research Institute.

*Reference price: 8,000 yuan / square foot*

《松声》　　137cm×69cm　　　" Sound of Pine"

### 杨道顺  *Yang Daoshun*

杨道顺，男，汉族，山东省德州市人，1951年生，现为国家一级书法师，中国书画艺术促进会常务理事、中国书画家协会理事、山东省书法家协会会员、中国长城诗书画协会名誉主席。

润笔价格：9,000元/平尺

Yang Daoshun, male, Han nationality, from Dezhou City, Shandong Province, was born in 1951. he is a national A-level calligrapher, director of Chinese Painting and Calligraphy Association, executive director of Chinese Calligraphers Association of promotion, member of Shandong Province Calligraphers Association, honorary president of China Great Wall Poetry and Calligraphy Association,.

*Reference price: 9,000 yuan / square foot*

《沁园春·雪》　69cm×137cm　　"To the Tunes of Qin Yuan Chun-snow"

## 刘光政 *Liu Guangzheng*

刘光政，男，1947年生，浙江瑞安人，中国工艺美术家协会会员，浙江省中国画家协会会员，温州市美术家协会会员。
润笔价格：8,000元/平尺

Liu Guangzheng, male, born in 1947, from Ruian, Zhejiang, is the member of China Arts and Crafts Association, member of China Zhejiang Artists Association, member of Wenzhou City Artists Association.
*Reference price: 8,000 yuan / square foot*

《芦塘浴牛》　137cm×70cm　　"Bathing Cow in Lu Tang"

# 朱钢　*Zhu Gang*

朱钢，男，1953年12月生，山东青岛人，中华书画协会会员，青岛书法家协会会员。
润笔价格：4,000元/平尺

Zhu Gang, male, born in December 1953, from Qingdao, Shandong, is the member of China Painting and Calligraphy Association and Qingdao Calligraphers Association.
*Reference price: 4,000 yuan / square foot*

李煜《虞美人》　　137cm×70cm　　*Li Yu "The Beauty"*

# 马秀亮　*Maxiu Liang*

马秀亮，男，1948年2月生，山东省淄博市美术家协会会员，《中国书画报》特聘书画家，中学美术教师。

润笔价格：6,000元/平尺

Maxiu Liang, male, born in February 1948, is the member of Zibo Artists Association, invited artist of "Chinese Painting and Calligraphy", art teacher of middle school.

*Reference price: 6,000 yuan / square foot*

《红梅》　　138cm×70cm　　　"Red Plum"

## 槐芳　*Huai Fang*

槐芳，男，1943年6月生，河北安平县人，现为中国书画家联谊会会员，中国书画家协会会员、理事，中国文人书法家协会理事，洛阳市颜真卿书画院名誉院长。

润笔价格：5,000元/平尺

Huai Fang, male, born in June 1943, is from Hebei Anping. He is the member of Chinese Painting and Calligraphy Association, member and director of Chinese Calligraphy Association, director of Chinese literati Calligraphy Association, honorary president of Luoyang YanZhenQing Painting and Calligraphy Institute.

*Reference price: 5,000 yuan / square foot*

《毛泽东词一首》　138cm×70cm　"Poem of Mao Zedong"

## 陈志春  *Chen Zhichun*

陈志春,男,满族,现为黑龙江省富裕县文化馆党支部书记兼美术辅导员,富裕书画院院长,系中国国画家协会会员、中国美协黑龙江分会会员。

润笔价格:6,000元/平尺

Chen Zhichun, male, Man nationality, is now the Party branch secretary and instructor of Fuyu County cultural centers, president of Fuyu painting academy, member of the Department of Chinese Artists Association, and member of the Chinese Artists Association of Heilongjiang Branch.

*Reference price: 6,000 yuan / square foot*

《黄山云海》　97cm×180cm　"Cloud Sea of Huangshan Mountain"

# 吉师　　*Jishi*

吉师，男，字崇艺，别署四味斋、清风轩，现任山西省新绛县文化体育局副局长，系中国硬笔书协理事、山西省书协会员、运城市书协常务理事、新绛县书协副主席兼秘书长。

润笔价格：7,000元/平尺

JIshi, Male, known as Chongyi and Siwei Zhai, Qingfeng Xuan. He is now the deputy president of Xinjiang County Culture and Sports Department, director of the Chinese Pen Calligraphers Association, member of Shanxi Calligraphers Association, executive director of Yuncheng City Calligraphers Association, vice Chairman and Secretary-general Xinjiang County Calligraphers Association.

*Reference price: 7,000 yuan / square foot*

《岳阳楼记》　　70cm×139cm　　"Yueyang Building"

# 万若愚  *Wan Ruoyu*

万若愚，男，1939年生，四川省成都市人，成都市美协会员。
润笔价格：14,000元/平尺

Wan Ruoyu, male, born in 1939, is from Chengdu City, Sichuan Province, member of Chengdu Artists Association.
*Reference price: 14,000 yuan / square foot*

《青城丹梯近幽意》　　180cm×98cm　　"Qingcheng Ladder"

## 顾建华  *Gu Jianhua*

顾建华，男，1959年生，安徽人，系安徽省书协会员、中国艺术名家协会会员、中国老年书画协会会员。

润笔价格：5,000元/平尺

Gu Jianhua, male, born in 1959, is from Anhui. He is the member of Anhui Department of Calligraphers, member of Chinese art masters Association, member of China paintings Association of the older.
*Reference price: 5,000 yuan / square foot*

《登金陵凤凰台》　　138cm×70cm　　"Phoenix Tower"

# 王志刚　*Wang Zhigang*

王志刚，男，中国书画研究院理事，北京华夏国艺书画院理事，中国书画家协会常务理事，一级美术师。

润笔价格：14,000元/平尺

Wang Zhigang, male, is the director of Chinese Painting and Calligraphy Institut, director of Beijing Huaxia Guo Yi painting and calligraphy academy, executive director of Chinese Calligraphers Association, an A-level artist.
*Reference price: 14,000 yuan / square foot*

《银花飘舞》　　136cm×69cm　　*"Silver Flower Flying"*

## 贺祖荣　*He Zurong*

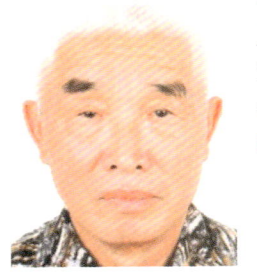

贺祖荣，男，1938年3月生，重庆市奉节县人，中国书画家协会会员，中国书画研究院艺术委员会会员，山东省书法家协会会员。

润笔价格：8,000元/平尺

He Zurong, male, born in March 1938, is from Fengjie County of Chongqing. He is the member of China Calligraphy Association, member of Chinese Painting and Calligraphy Institute art committee, member of Shandong Province Calligraphers Association.

*Reference price: 8,000 yuan / square foot*

《将进酒》　138cm×70cm　"Bring the Wine"

# 徐如彬  *Xu Rubin*

徐如彬，男，1936年生，作品入选《中国书画名家大辞典》，作品在海外交流展、在全国画展中多次获奖。

润笔价格：6,000元/平尺

Xu Rubin, male, was born in 1936. His works have been selected into" Chinese painting and calligraphy dictionary", and are displayed in overseas exchange exhibition. He has won numerous awards in domestic exhibitions.
*Reference price: 6,000 yuan / square foot*

《椒陵人家》　138cm×70cm　"People in Jiaoling"

### 张春水　　*Zhang Chunshui*

张春水，男，1940年生，北京人，作品参加全国大型书画展并多次获奖，北京电视台多次采访。
润笔价格：5,000元/平尺

Zhang Chunshui, male, born in 1940, is from Beijing. His works have participated in numerous national large-scale painting and calligraphy exhibition and won numerous awards. He was interviewed by Beijing TV station several times.
*Reference price: 5,000 yuan / square foot*

岳飞《满江红》　　138cm×70cm　　"Azolla"

# 罗孟基 *Luo Mengji*

罗孟基,男,1947年3月生,广东省阳西县人,中国高级美术教师,作品《山水图》被辽宁省锦州博物馆收藏。

润笔价格:14,000元/平尺

Luo Mengji, male, born in March 1947, is from Guangdong Yangxi. He is a Chinese senior art teacher. His work "Landscape" is kept by Jinzhou, Liaoning Province Museum.

*Reference price: 14,000 yuan / square foot*

《红叶催春》　　138cm×70cm　　"Red Leaves Represents Spring"

## 叶升夫  *Ye Shengfu*

叶升夫，男，号子辅，浙江乐清人，1967年4月27日生，中国硬笔书法协会会员，中国书画名家协会理事，中国书画创作院教授。

润笔价格：6,000元/平尺

Ye Shengfu, male, with a pen name of Zifu, from Yueqing, Zhejiang, was born on April 27, 1967. he is a member of Chinese Pen Calligraphy Association, director of Chinese calligraphy celebrity Association, professor of Chinese painting and calligraphy.

*Reference price: 6,000 yuan / square foot*

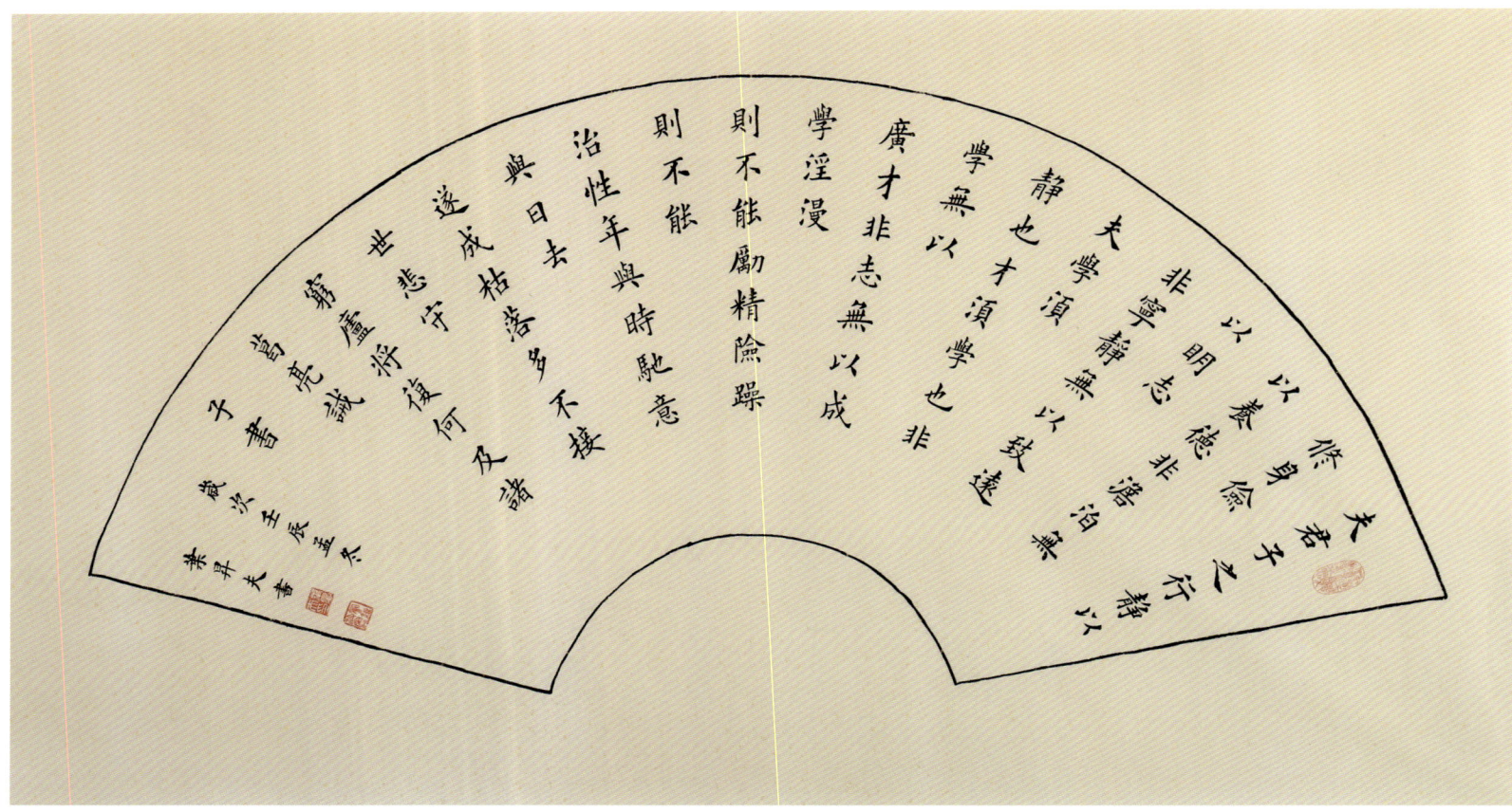

《扇面》　　68cm×126cm　　"Fan"

## 尹晓彦  *Yin Xiaoyan*

尹晓彦，男，1960年生，黑龙江人，现为中国美术家协会会员，国家一级美术师，中国艺术学院教授、博士生导师，中华文化书画院常务理事。

润笔价格：12,000元/平尺

Yin Xiaoyan, male, born in 1960, is from Heilongjiang. He is the member of China Artists Association, national A-level artist, Chinese Arts professor, doctoral tutor, executive director of Chinese Culture Painting and Calligraphy Institute.

*Reference price: 12,000 yuan / square foot*

《农家日子火炭红》　　70cm×137cm　　"Lives of Farmer are Booming"

# 周建华  *Zhou Jianhua*

周建华，男，清江上人，1963年生，河南人，现供职于国务院国资委，作品多次参加全国及全军画展，中国书法家协会会员。

润笔价格：7,000元/平尺

Zhou Jianhua, male, with a pen name of Qingjiang Master, born in 1963, is from Henan Province, He is now working at the State Council, the SASAC and is the member of Chinese Calligraphers Association. His works participated in numerous national and army exhibition.

*Reference price: 7,000 yuan / square foot*

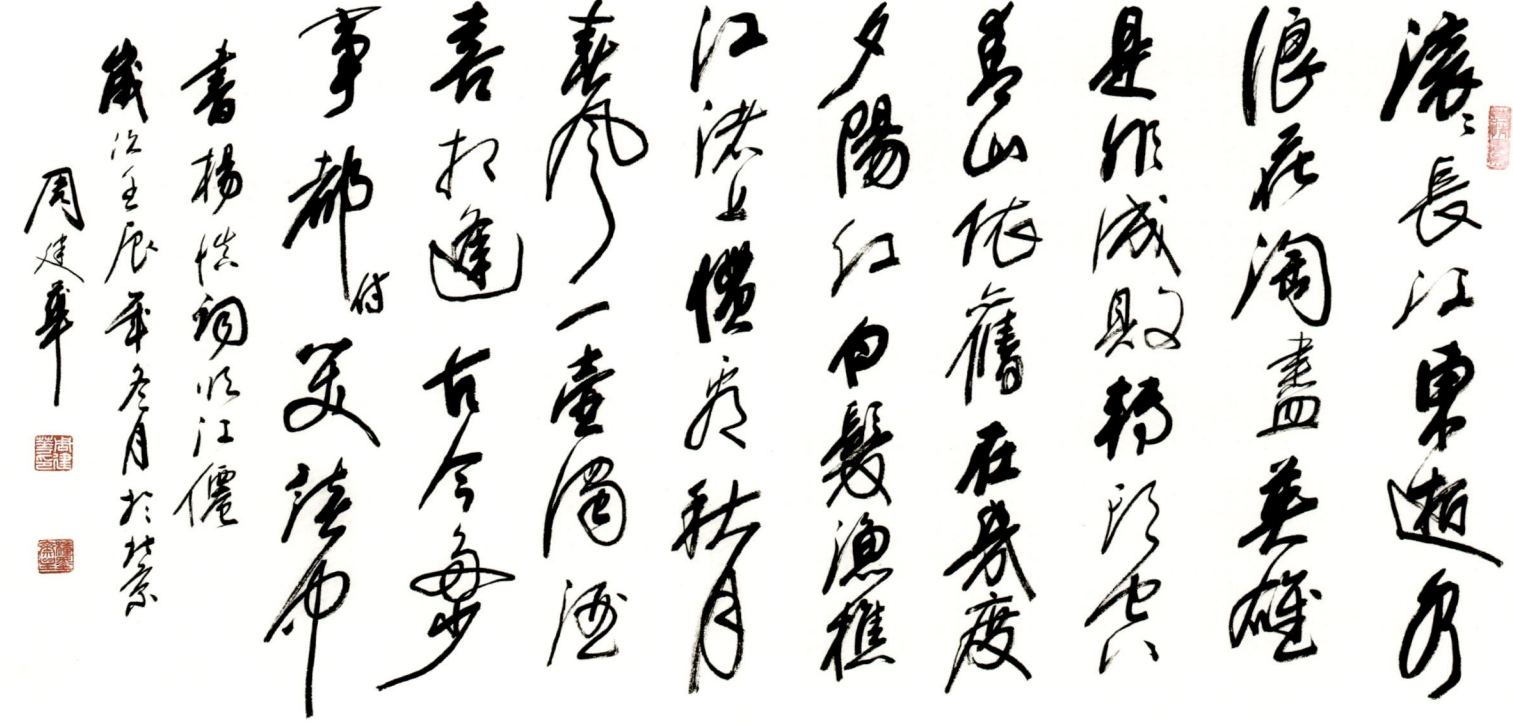

《三国演义开篇词》　　69cm×138cm　　*"Opening Passage of the Three Kingdoms"*

## 陈艳  *Chen Yan*

陈艳，女，1966年生，山东潍坊临朐人，中国书画家协会会员，酷爱文学绘画，荣宝斋画院范扬工作室画家。

润笔价格：10,000元/平尺

Chen Yan, female, born in 1966, is from Shandong Weifang Linqu. He is the member of China Calligraphers Association, painter of Painting Fan Yang studio of Rong Bao Zhai Academy. She is fond of literature painting.

*Reference price: 10,000 yuan / square foot*

《溪山秋雨图》　　137cm×70cm　　"Mountains in Autumn"

## 贺勤江　　*HE Qin Jiang*

贺勤江，男，汉族，1954年2月生，河北邢台人，现为中国老年书画研究会会员。
润笔价格：4,000元/平尺

HE Qin Jiang, male, Han nationality, born in February 1954, is from Hebei Xingtai. He is the member of the elderly Painting Research Association.
*Reference price: 4,000 yuan / square foot*

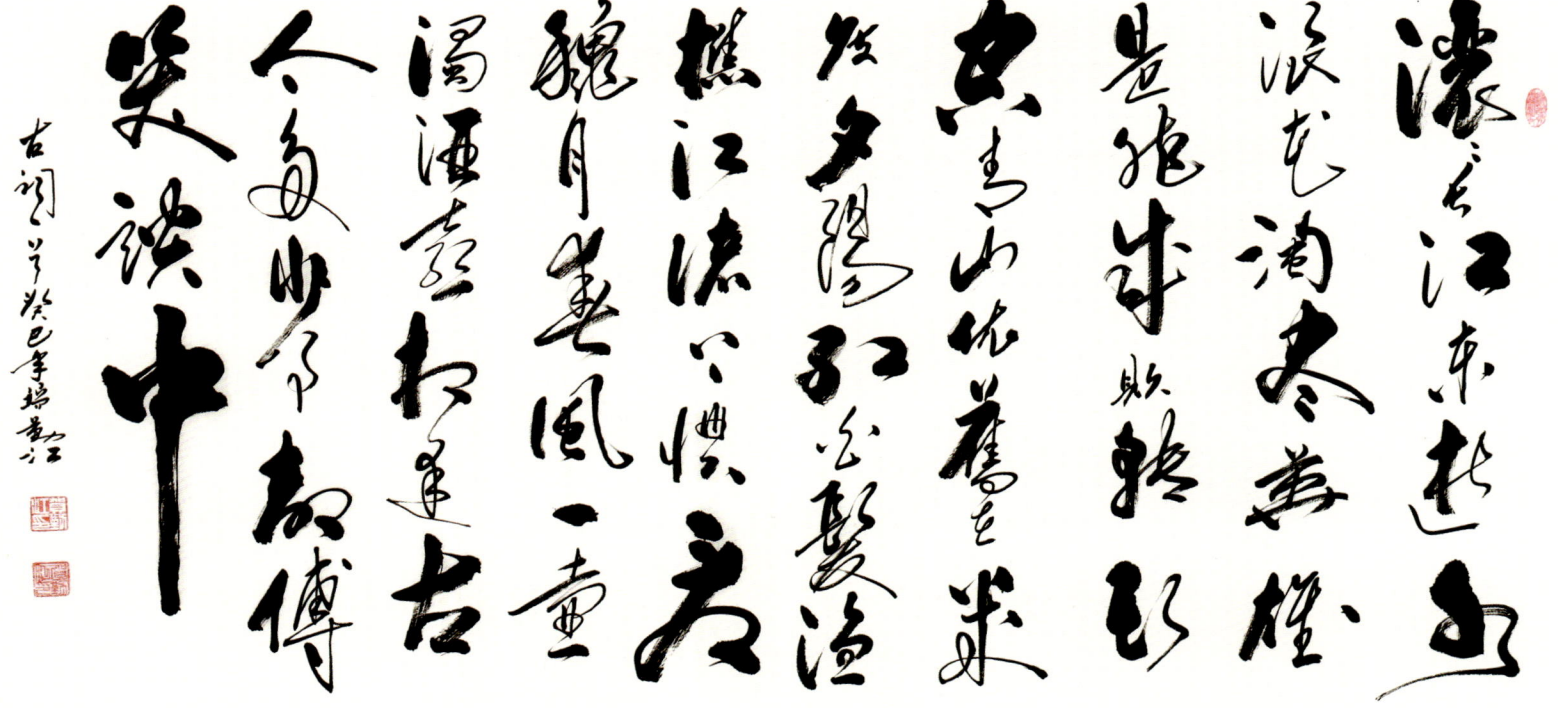

《三国演义开篇词》　　70cm×137cm　　*" Opening Passage of the Three Kingdoms "*

# 李羿　*Li Yi*

李羿，名晓燕，字羿，1975年生于山东高密，师从当代大家霍春阳先生，现为北京荣宝斋画院画家、霍春阳工作室画家、中国书画家协会会员。

润笔价格：6,000元/平尺

Li Yi, known as Xiaoyan, and Yi, born in 1975 in Shandong Gaomi, is the disciple of Mr. Huo Chunyang. He is now painter of Beijing Rong Bao Zhai Painting academy, painter of Huo Chunyang studio, member of Chinese Calligraphers Association.

*Reference price: 6,000 yuan / square foot*

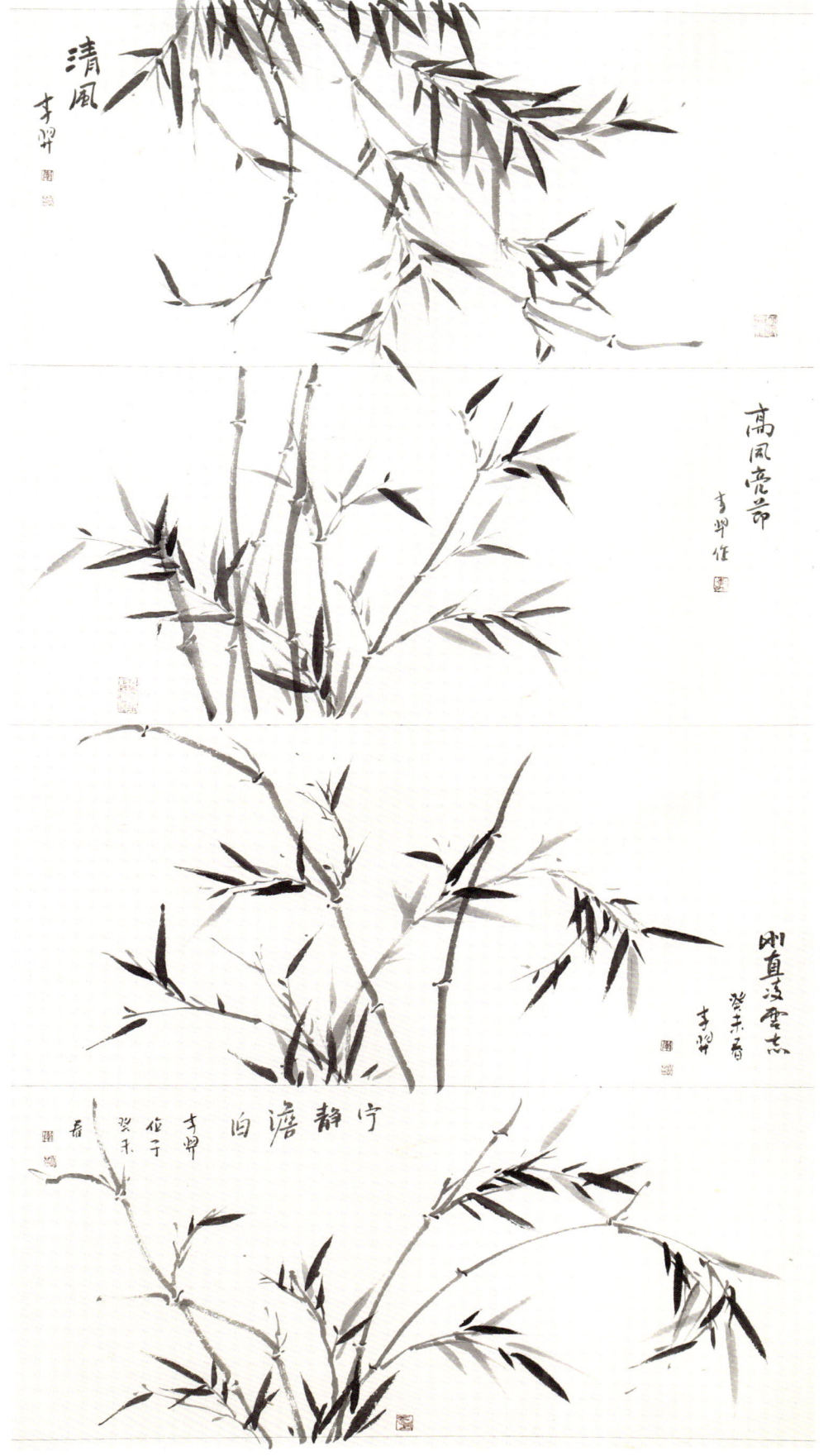

《竹子》　145cm×76cm　　"Bamboo"

# 张怡 *Zhang Yi*

张怡，男，汉族，1940年11月生，现为保定市老年书画研究会会员，中国当代艺术家协会理事，东坡书画艺术研究院院士。

润笔价格：5,000元/平尺

Zhang Yi, male, Han nationality, born in November 1940, is now Baoding painting Research Association for the old, director of China Association for Contemporary Art, academician of Dongpo Academy of Painting and Calligraphy Art Academy.
*Reference price: 5,000 yuan / square foot*

苏轼《念奴娇》　　137cm×70cm　　*Su Shi "To The Tunes of Nian Nu Jiao"*

# 赵志金 *Zhao Zhijin*

赵志金，1950年生于陕西省宝鸡市，陕西省美术家协会会员，陕西省工艺美术家协会会员。主攻人物肖像、山水、书法，画风采取"中西合璧"、"古今结合"的写实手法。

润笔价格：6,000元/平尺

Zhao Zhijin, 1950 Born in Baoji City, is the member of Shaanxi Province Artists Association, member of the Shaanxi Provincial Arts and Crafts Association. He is majoring in portraits, landscapes, calligraphy, with a style of "East meets West", "combining ancient and modern".

*Reference price: 6,000 yuan / square foot*

《山河正气 大地生辉》 70cm×137cm  *" Brilliance Land of Mountains and Rivers "*

# 王立民　*Wang Limin*

王立民，男，号醉墨雕虫，河北省承德市人，中国诗书画协会会员，承德市国学研究会成员。

润笔价格：4,000元/平尺

Wang Limin, Male, known as Modiaochong, is from Chengde City, Hebei Province. He is the member of Chinese Poetry and Calligraphy Association, a member of Chengde City Sinology research Institution.

*Reference price: 4,000 yuan / square foot*

《精气神》　　59cm×138cm　　*"Spirit"*

## 佟起来　*Tong Qilai*

佟起来，男，1950年生，河南省开封市人，中国民间文艺家协会会员，开封市美协会员。2012年作品《腾派蝶画》被列入河南省省级非物质文化遗产名录。

润笔价格：10,000元/平尺

Tong Qilai, male, born in 1950, is from Kaifeng City, Henan Province. He is the member of Chinese Folk Literature and Art Association, member of Kaifeng City Artists Association. His "Butterfly of Teng style" was included in Henan provincial intangible cultural heritage in 2012.

*Reference price: 10,000 yuan / square foot*

《牡丹》　138cm×69cm　"Peony"

# 王绍文　Wang Shaowen

王绍文，男，汉族，1941年生，山西省人，参加过全国教职工书法家大赛，获奖。

润笔价格：4,000元/平尺

Wang Shaowen, male, Han nationality, born in 1941, is from Shanxi Province. He participated in the national faculty calligrapher contest and wined.
*Reference price: 4,000 yuan / square foot*

《沁园春·雪》　　68cm135cm　　*"To the Tunes of Qin Yuan Chun-snow"*

# 徐声才　*XU Shengcai*

徐声才，男，1944年10月生，广西容县人，现任国际名家书画院副院长、客座教授、中国文人美术家协会理事，北京华夏国艺书画院高级画师，中国书画名家协会会员。

润笔价格：8,000元/平尺

XU Shengcai, male, born in October 1944, is from Guangxi Rong. He is currently vice president and visiting professor of international famous paintings, director of Chinese literati Artists Association, senior artist of Beijing Huaxia Guo Arts Academy, member of Chinese painting and calligraphy Association.

*Reference price: 8,000 yuan / square foot*

《祥和图》　　136cm×68cm　　*"Auspicious"*

# 曾繁堪 *Zeng Fankan*

曾繁堪，男，1934年12月生，福建省平和县人，中国书画艺术促进会常务理事，曾经受"海峡卫视"专访并在该台播出。

润笔价格：4,000元/平尺

Zeng Fankan, male, born in December 1934, is from Fujian Pinghe. He is the director executive of Chinese painting and calligraphy Association, has been interviewed by "Haixia Channel".
*Reference price: 4,000 yuan / square foot*

《观沧海》　　138cm×69cm　　*"Viewing the Sea"*

## 苏望秦  *Su Wangqin*

苏望秦，男，山西运城人，现为中国石齐艺术研究会画家，2009年作品《祖父祖母》参加人民日报新闻信息中心举办的纪念改革开放30周年全国书画展。作品《主席来到咱家中》参加中央文史举办的伟人画展。

润笔价格：16,000元/平尺

Sue Wangqin, male, from Shanxi Yuncheng, is painter of China Shi Qi Art Research Association. His work "grandparents" participated in the national painting and calligraphy exhibition to commemorate the 30th anniversary of reform and opening up organized by People's Daily News and Information Center. The work "president came to our house" participated in the exhibition held by the Central Cultural and History.

*Reference price: 16,000 yuan / square foot*

《偶然值隣叟》　　70cm×137cm　　*"Accidentally Met Lin"*

### 侯培强  *Hou Peiqiang*

侯培强，男，汉族，1959年生，内蒙古人，内蒙古书协会员，草原书画院理事。

润笔价格：4,000元/平尺

Houn Peiqiang, male, Han nationality, born in 1959, is from Inner Mongolia. He is the member of Inner Mongolia Calligraphers, director of grasslands Painting and Calligraphy Institute.

*Reference price: 4,000 yuan / square foot*

《观海听涛》　　50cm×200cm　　*"Watch the Sea"*

# 张洪彬 *Zhang Hongbin*

张洪彬，男，1948年12月生，承德市美协会员，华夏张氏书画院副院长，承德武阳书画院画师，中国诗书画协会理事。

润笔价格：14,000元/平尺

Zhang Hongbin, male, born in December 1948, is the member of Chengde City Artists Association, vice president of China Zhang Shi painting Institute, painter of Chengde Wu Yang calligraphy and painting academy, director of Chinese Poetry and Calligraphy Association.

*Reference price: 14,000 yuan / square foot*

《泉由白云起》　　138cm×70cm　　"Spring from the Clouds"

# 吴广华 *Wu Guanghua*

吴广华,男,中华书画学会副主席,中国书画家协会理事,中国书画艺术研究会理事。

润笔价格:6,000元/平尺

Wu Guanghua, male, is the vice president of Chinese Calligraphy and Painting Society, director of Chinese Calligraphy Association, director of Chinese Painting and Calligraphy Art Research Association.
*Reference price: 6,000 yuan / square foot*

毛泽东《钟山风雨》　69cm×138cm　　*Mao Zedong's "Zhongshan Rain"*

# 樊长金  *Fan Changjin*

樊长金，男，号陋室居士，1972年生，广西人，中国国画院副院长，北京京华兰亭书画院名誉院长，东方美术馆艺术顾问。

润笔价格：6,000元/平尺

Fan Changjin, Male, known as Lay Buddhist of Loushi, born in 1972, is from Guangxi. He is the vice president of Chinese painting, honorary president of Beijing Jing Hua Lanting calligraphy and painting academy, art consultant of the Oriental Art Museum.
*Reference price: 6,000 yuan / square foot*

《硕果累累》　　138cm×68cm　　"Fruitful"

## 张茂华  *Zhang Maohua*

张茂华，男，1949年生，开封人，中国书法家协会会员，中国书法研究院副院长兼评审主任，中国书画名家联合会一级书法师。
润笔价格：6,000元/平尺

Zhang Maohua, male, born in 1949, is from Kaifeng. He is the member of China Calligraphers Association, vice president and research director of accreditation of Chinese calligraphy research Institute, an A-level calligrapher of Chinese painting and calligraphy Federation.
*Reference price: 6,000 yuan / square foot*

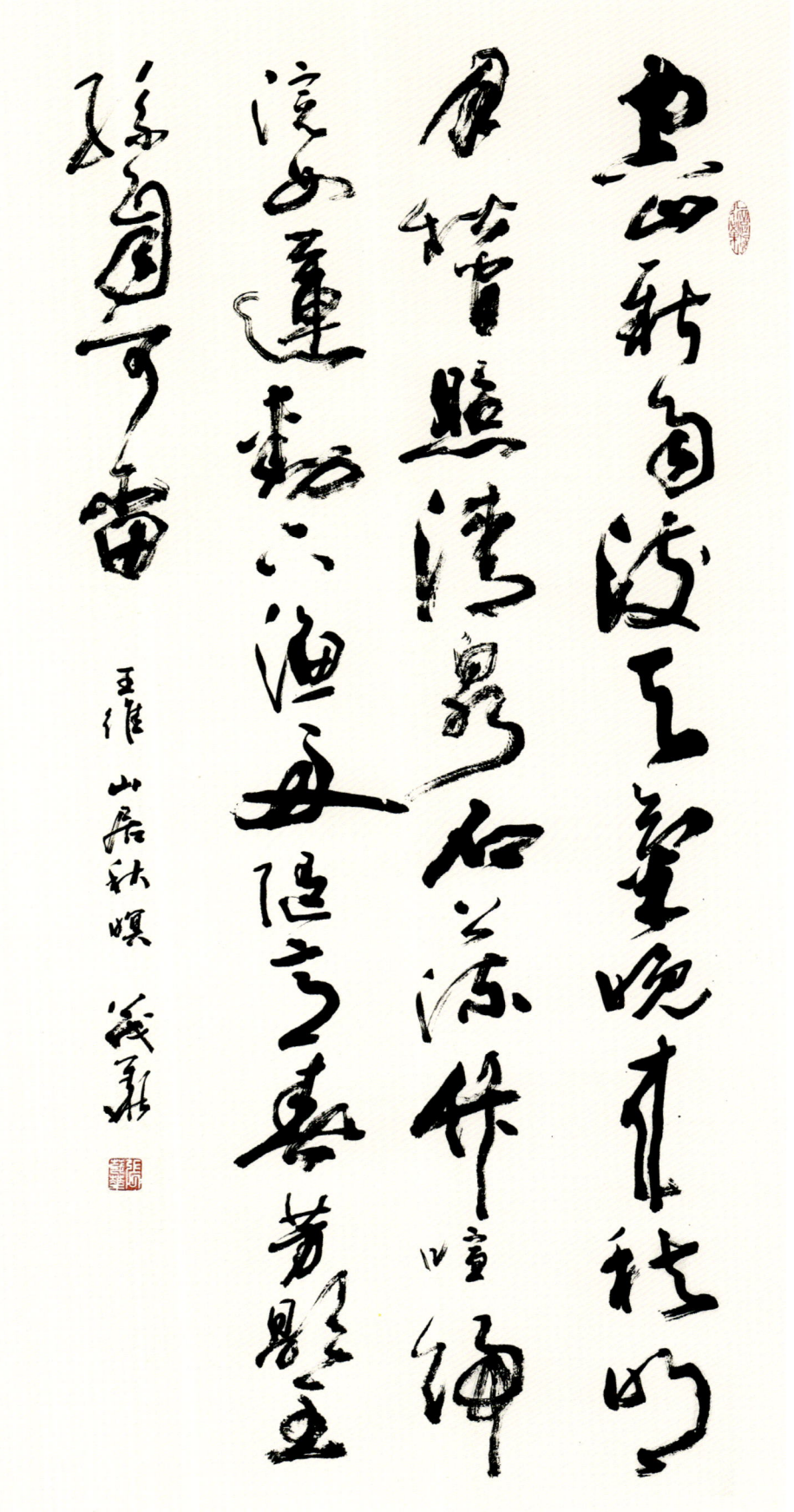

王维《山居秋暝》　　137cm×70cm　　Wang Wei, "Mountain Evening in Autumn"

## 罗士捷　袁人秋　　*Luo Shijie , Yuan Renqiu*

罗士捷，号苦耕颠人，1961年生于沈阳，自幼酷爱绘画，后得曹勇老师启蒙，力功画业，不囿于成法。

袁人秋，1966年生于沈阳，自幼耳濡目染，对中国书画艺术至爱有佳，孩提时曲尽涂鸦之作，蒙羞不知所以然，时至豆冠，得王文和老师引入门径。

润笔价格：8,000元/平尺

Luo Shijie, known as Kugneg Dianren, was born in 1966 in Shenyang. He was fond of painting in childhood and made good efforts on painting after learning from Cao Yong. He has a creative mind.

Yuan Renqiu was born in 1966 in Shenyang. She had a passion for Chinese painting from childhood and was instructed by Wang Wenhe at the age of 13.

*Reference price: 8,000 yuan / square foot*

《万里一击中》　　97cm×178cm　　"Hit Miles Away"

### 谭克成　Tan Kecheng

谭克成，男，1941年生，青岛人，汉族，中国书画研究院艺术委员会委员，中国著名书画家协会名誉主席，中国摄影家协会理事，青岛市书法家协会会员。

润笔价格：5,000元/平尺

Tan Kecheng, male, Han nationality, born in 1941, is from Qingdao. He is the commissary of Chinese Painting and Calligraphy Institute Art Committee, honorary chairman of a famous Chinese Calligraphers Association, director of the China Photography Association, member of Qingdao City Calligraphers Association.
*Reference price: 5,000 yuan / square foot*

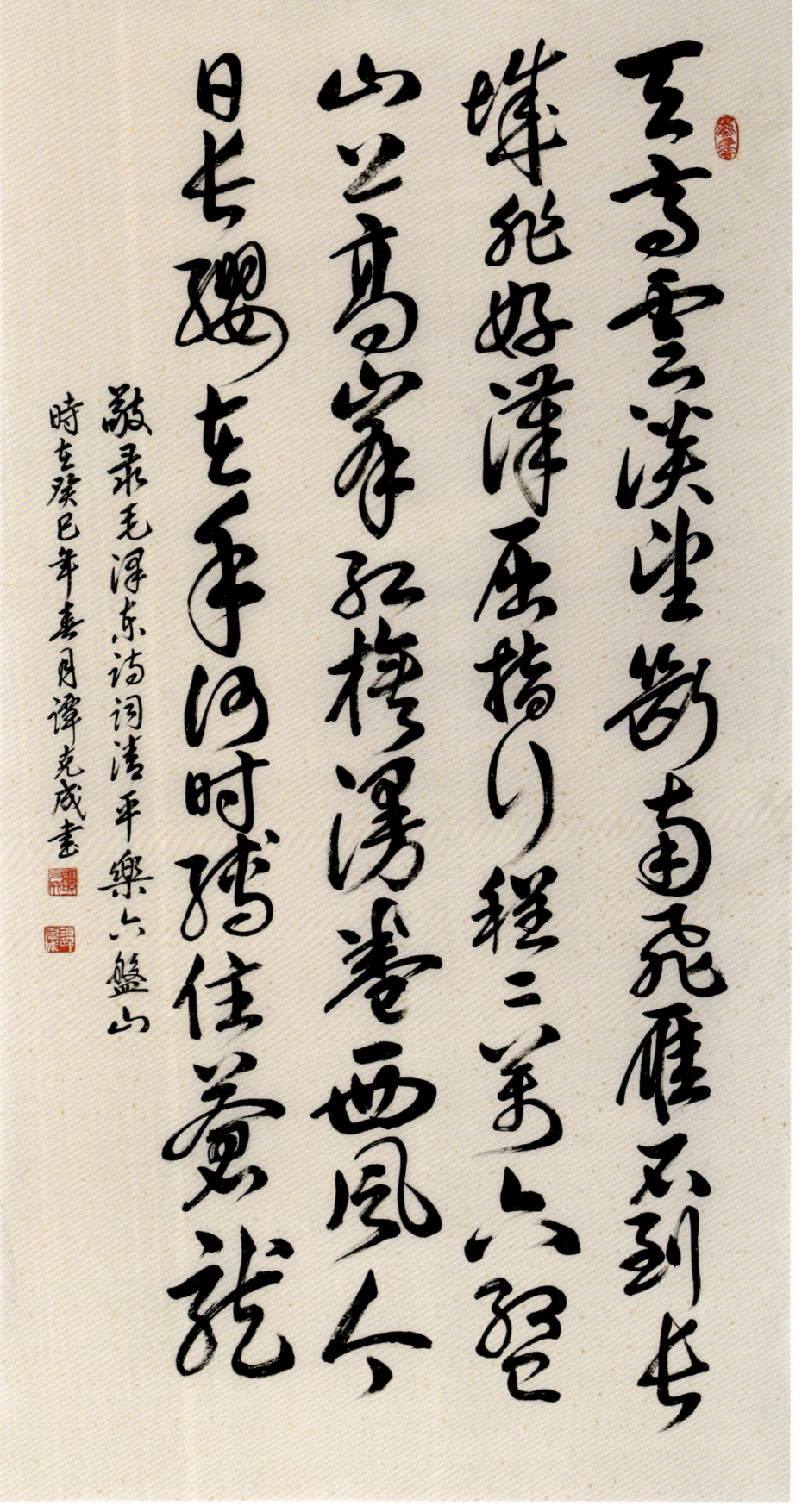

毛泽东《清平乐·六盘山》　　136cm×68cm　　Mao Zedong's "To the Tunes of Qin Ping Yue – Liupan Mountain"

## 张志远 *Zhang Zhiyuan*

张志远，1955年12月生，黑龙江海林市人，现任深圳市南国书画院院士，从事书画研究20多年，多次参加海内外大展并获得大奖，作品多次被国内外收藏家收藏。

润笔价格：6,000元/平尺

Zhang Zhiyuan, born in December 1955, is from Heilongjiang Hailin. He is currently the academician of Shenzhen North Country Academy of Painting and Calligraphy. He has participated in many exhibitions and wined awards for 20 years after he became an artist and his works are collected in domestic and abroad.

*Reference price: 6,000 yuan / square foot*

《雨过荷花香》　　98cm×180cm　　*"Fragrant Lotus after Rain"*

## 郗士贞  *Xi Shizhen*

郗士贞，男，1938年4月生，现为中国书法研究院艺术委员会会员，中国文化艺术协会副会长，中国书画家联谊会百名中国书画名家，中国书画研究院院士。

润笔价格：6,000元/平尺

Xi Shizhen, male, born in April 1938, is currently a member of the Committee of Chinese Calligraphy Institute of Arts, vice president of Chinese Culture and Arts Association, one of the one hundred masters of the Federation of Artists of Chinese Painting and Calligraphy Association, academician of Chinese painting and calligraphy research Institution.
*Reference price: 6,000 yuan / square foot*

**苏轼《水调歌头》**　　70cm×138cm　　*Su Shi's " Prelude to Water Melody "*

# 陈秀兰　*Chen Xiulan*

陈秀兰，女，现为兰州职业技术学院副教授，甘肃画院"张建中工作室"画家。
润笔价格：12,000元/平尺

Chen Xiulan, female, is now an associate professor of Lanzhou Vocational and Technical College, painter of Gansu Zhang Jianzhong studio.
*Reference price: 12,000 yuan / square foot*

《争香斗艳》　48cm×138cm　　"Blooming"

# 常厚仁　*Chang Houren*

常厚仁，男，汉族，1950年生，河北省永清县人，中国刑警学院客座教授，中国吴道子画院理事，中国传统书画院理事，一级书画师，中国国画院理事。

润笔价格：5,000元/平尺

Often Houren, male, Han nationality, born in 1950, is from Yongqing. He is the invited professor of Chinese Criminal Police College, director of China Wu Daozi academy, director of traditional Chinese calligraphy and painting Institute, an A-level painter, director of China calligraphy painting academy.

*Reference price: 5,000 yuan / square foot*

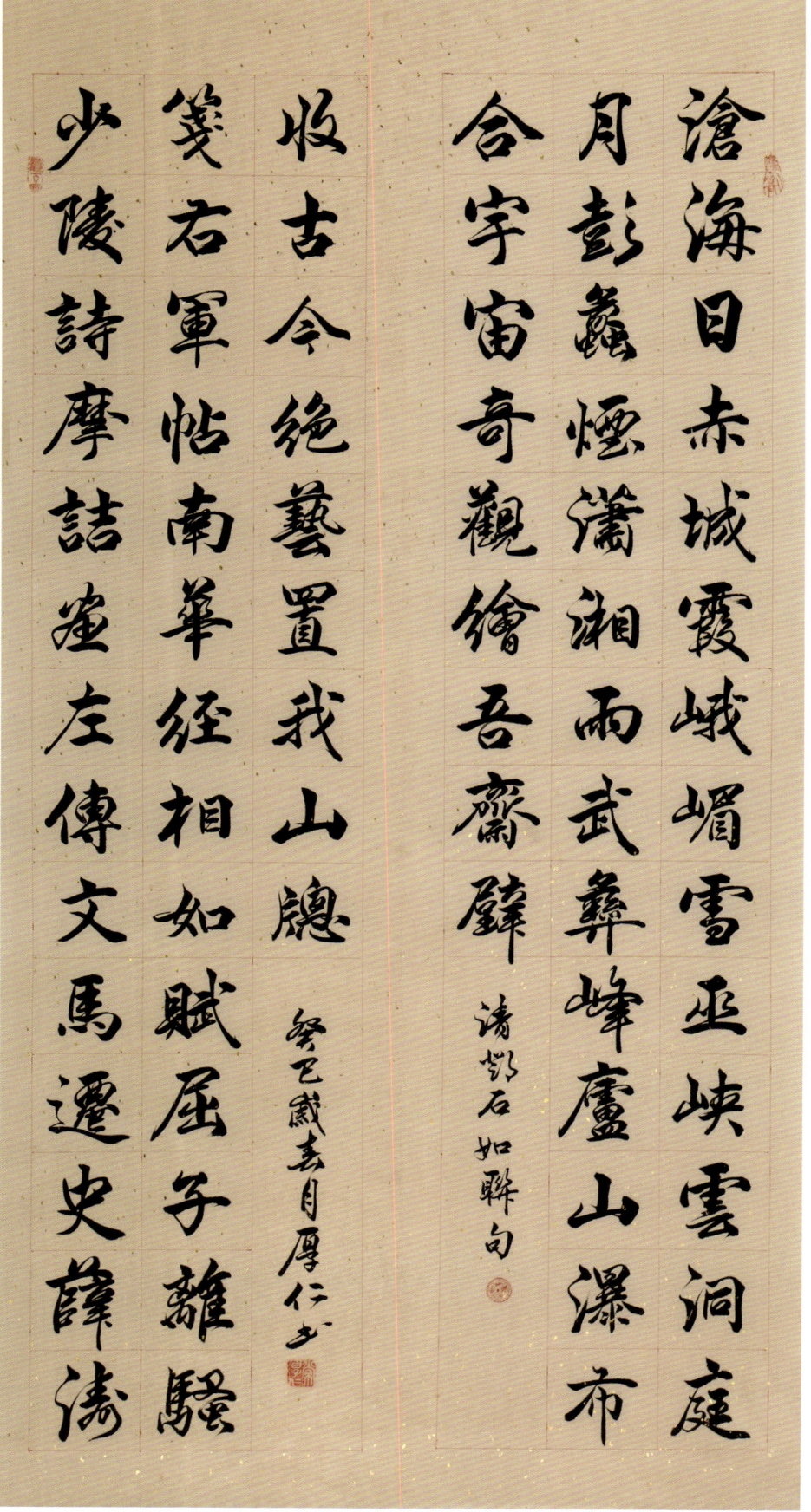

清　邓石如《联句》　　132cm×67cm　　*Deng Shiru of Qing Dynasty "Sentences"*

## 刘西秦  *Liu Xiqin*

刘西秦，男，1956年生，现为中国工艺美术学会会员、宝鸡美术家协会会员、红旗书画院院士。

润笔价格：6,000元/平尺

Liu Xiqin, male, born in 1956, is now member of China Arts and Crafts Association, member of Baoji Artists Association, academician of Hongqi Academy painting and callegraphy.
*Reference price: 6,000 yuan / square foot*

《春韵》　　138cm×68cm　　"Chun Yun"

# 王自强　*Wang Ziqiang*

王自强，男，笔名：老丑，山西人，中国书画名家协会会员，万荣县书画会常务理事。

润笔价格：4,000元/平尺

Wang Ziqiang, male, pen, known as Laochou, is from Shanxi. He is the member of Chinese painting and calligraphy Association, executive director of Wanrong County painting and calligraphy Association.
*Reference price: 4,000 yuan / square foot*

《家》　46cm×180cm　"Home"

# 段惠娟　*Duan Huijuan*

段惠娟，笔名山美主人，1947年生，山东人，现任中国书画家协会会员、国家一级书画师、北京尔康画院国际艺术大师和特级书画师。

润笔价格：6,000元/平尺

Duan Huijuan, known as Holder of Shanmei, born in 1947, is from Shandong Province. She is the member of Chinese Calligraphers Association, an A-level painter, International Art Painting Master and Special grade calligrapher of Beijing Erkang painting academy.

*Reference price: 6,000 yuan / square foot*

《清和不染》　138cm×68cm　　"Pure"

# 党正　*Dang Zheng*

党正，男，1956年生，北京市沙河飞机场任放映员，薛镇书法协会会长，富平县书法协会会员。

润笔价格：5,000元/平尺

Dang Zheng, male, was born in 1956. He is the projectionist of Beijing Shahe Airport, member of Fuping County Calligraphy Association.

*Reference price: 5,000 yuan / square foot*

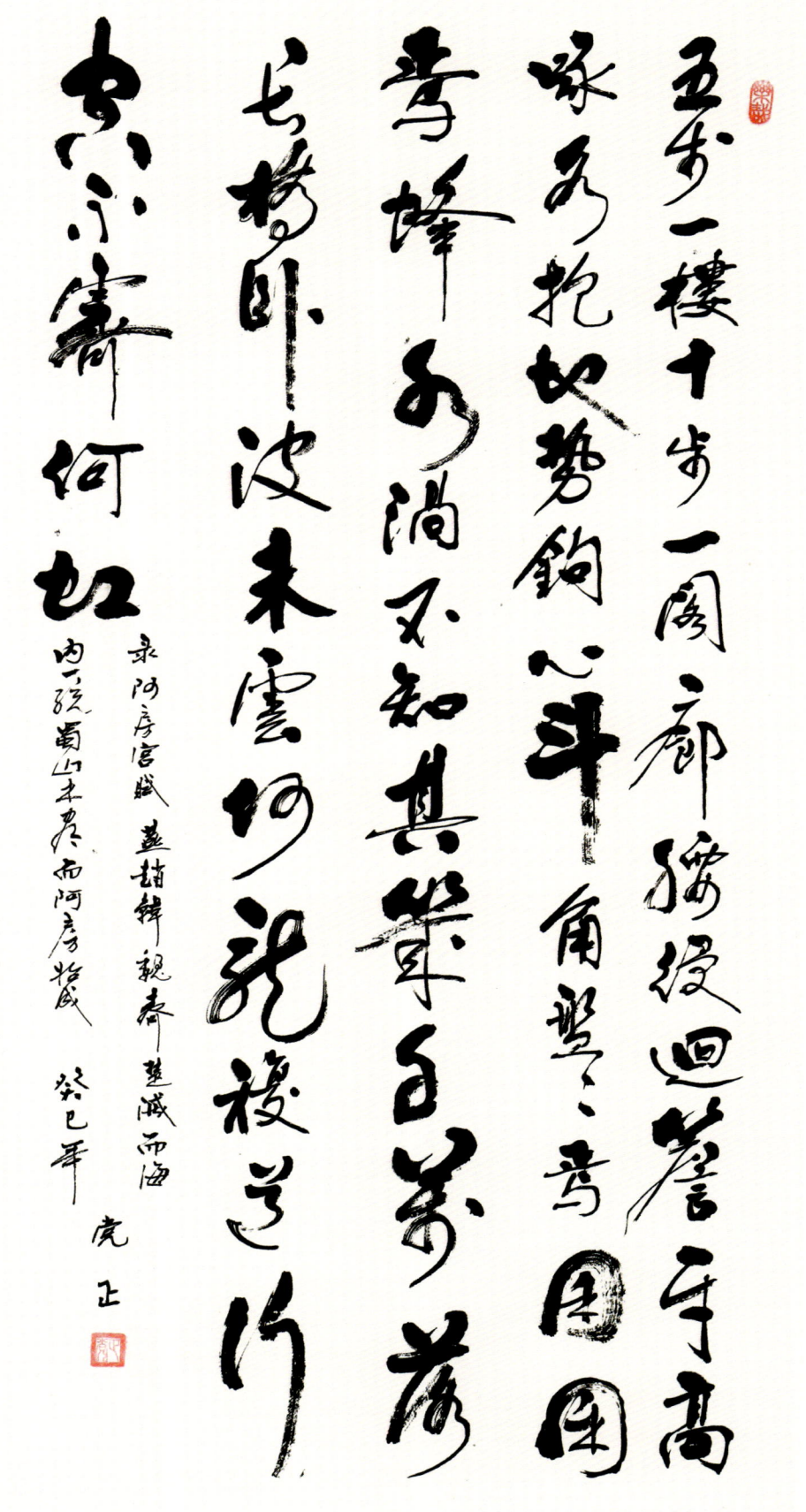

《阿房宫赋》　　138cm×68cm　　Recorded "Compose of E Pang Palace"

# 梁伟仪　*Liang Weiyi*

梁伟仪，男，笔名梁光辉，1967年生，广州人，中国青年美术家协会理事，广州美术家协会会员。
润笔价格：6,000元/平尺

Liang Weiyi, male, known as Liang Guanghui, born in 1967, is from Guangzhou. He is the director of China Youth Art Association, member of Guangzhou Artists Association.
*Reference price: 6,000 yuan / square foot*

《荷风》　　68cm×138cm　　"Style of Lotus"

## 唐永葆　*Tang Yongbao*

唐永葆，男，号忘言斋主，安徽省书法协会会员，中国书画名家研究会客座教授。

润笔价格：5,000元/平尺

Tang Yongbao, male, known as Holder of Wangyan Building, is the member of Anhui Calligraphy Association, visiting professor of Chinese painting and calligraphy research Institution.

*Reference price: 5,000 yuan / square foot*

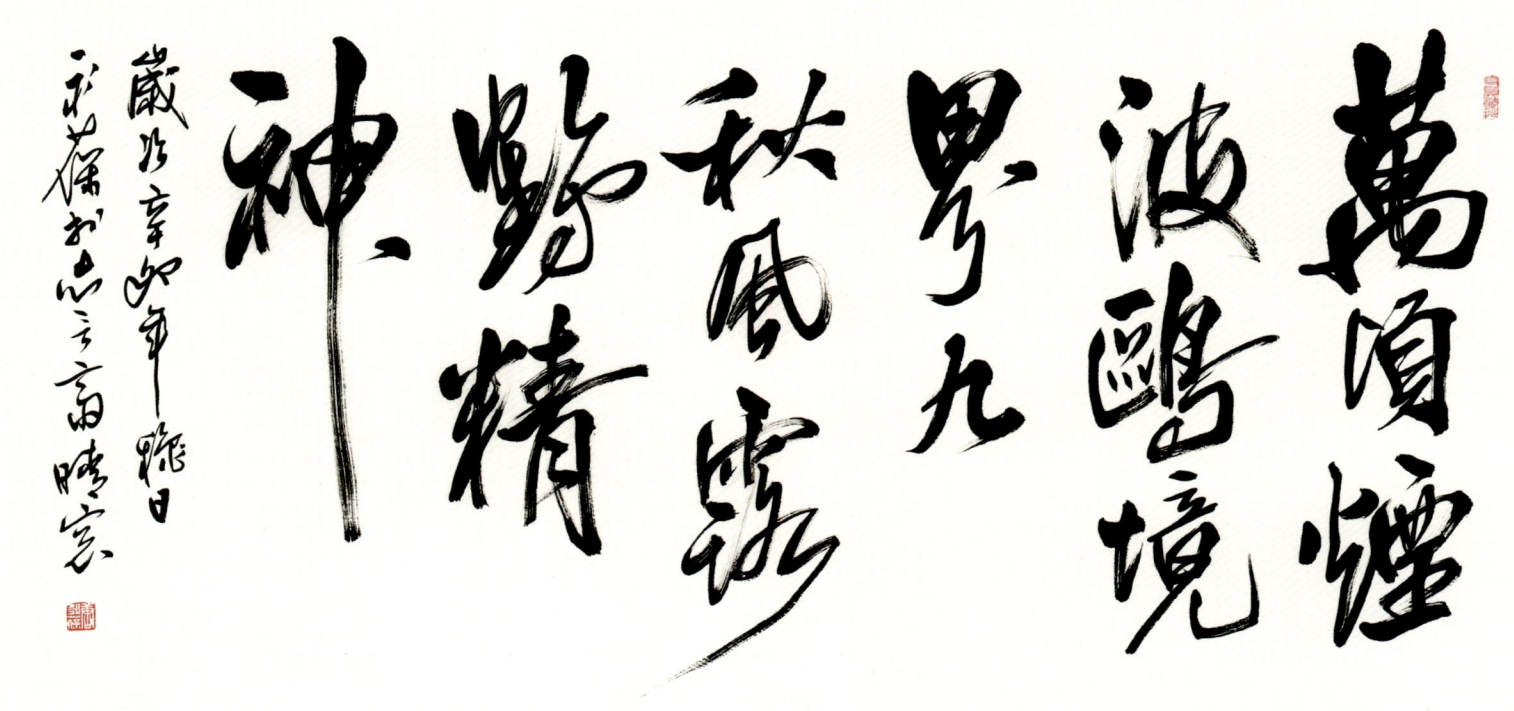

《万顷九秋联》　68cm×138cm　　*"Couplet of Permanent"*

# 陈福圣  *Chen Fusheng*

陈福圣，男，1957年3月生，重庆人，九洲枫林国际书画艺术院院士，被多家书画艺术研究院聘为研究员、院士、终身高级书画师。

润笔价格：8,000元/平尺

Chen Fu-sheng, male, born in March 1957, is from Chongqing. He is the academician of Jiuzhou Fenglin International Fine Arts Academy of Painting and Calligraphy Institute, and is hired as researchers, academicians, lifelong senior artist by many painting and calligraphy research Institute.

*Reference price: 8,000 yuan / square foot*

《千里远航图》　68cm×138cm　*"Oceangoing Voyage"*

# 万长发　*Wan Changfa*

万长发，男，1945年生，贵州江口人，中国书法家协会理事，中国书画摄影家协会理事，中国文人书法家协会理事，江苏省唐伯虎书画研究院副院长。

润笔价格：6,000元/平尺

Wan Changfa, male, born in 1945, is from Guizhou Jiangkou. He is the director of Chinese Calligraphy Association, director of Chinese Calligraphy Photography Association, director of Chinese literati Calligraphy Association, vice president of Jiangsu Tang Bohu Painting Research Institute.

*Reference price: 6,000 yuan / square foot*

古人學問無遺力　少壯工夫老始成　紙上得來終覺淺　絕知此事要躬行

陸游詩一首　萬長發書

《陆游诗一首》　138cm×68cm　"A Poem of Lu You"

# 魏习武  *Wei Xiwu*

魏习武，男，1964年生，甘肃榆中县人，现为甘肃画院张建中工作室画家，人物、山水、花鸟兼习，尤其擅长山水画。

润笔价格：12,000元/平尺

Wei Xiwu, male, born in 1964, is from Yuzhong County, Gansu. He is now the painter of Zhang Jianzhong studio of Gansu Painting academy. He has learnt figures of landscapes, flowers and birds, especially good at landscape painting.

*Reference price: 12,000 yuan / square foot*

《幽居图》　　138cm×68cm　　"Living Remotely"

## 季佩芳　*Ji Peifang*

季佩芳，男，北京东方名家书画院高级专业书画家，大河书画院名誉院长，东坡书画艺术研究院客座教授。

润笔价格：4,000元/平尺

Ji Peifang, male, is the senior professional painter of Beijing Oriental Painting and Calligraphy Institute, honorary president of Dahe painting and calligraphy academy, invited professor of Dongpo Calligraphy and Painting Institute.
*Reference price: 4,000 yuan / square foot*

李白《早发白帝城》　　138cm×68cm　　*Li Bai, "Leaving Baidi City in an Early Time"*

# 曾光艺　*Zeng Guangyi*

曾光艺，中国工艺美术家协会会员，福建美术协会会员，国际名家画院副院长、客座教授，中国书画名家协会会员。

润笔价格：14,000元/平尺

Zeng Guangyi is the member of China Arts and Crafts Association, member of Fujian Artists Association, vice president and visiting professor of international famous painters Institution, , member of Chinese painting and calligraphy Association.

*Reference price: 14,000 yuan / square foot*

《奇石无言情更韵》　97cm×180cm　"Speachless Stone, Dense Affection"

## 李文志  *Li Wenzhi*

李文志，男，字博友，汉族，1964年生，河北沧州人，中国国际艺术家协会会员，中国工艺美术家协会会员。

润笔价格：4,000元/平尺

Li Wenzhi, male, known as Boyou, Han nationality, born in 1964, is from Cangzhou, Hebei. He is the member of China International Artists Association, member of China Arts and Crafts Association.
*Reference price: 4,000 yuan / square foot*

《赤壁怀古》　68cm×138cm　　"Chi Bi"

# 韩凤山 *Han Fengshan*

韩凤山，男，1962年出生，河北省兴隆县国税局干部，河北省美术家协会会员，雾灵书画交流会副会长，承德美术家协会会员，兴隆县美术家协会秘书长。主攻山水、花鸟画创作。

润笔价格：8,000元/平尺

Han Fengshan, male, born in 1962, is the cadres of IRS in Xinglong County, member of Hebei Province Artists Association, vice president of Wuling painting and calligraphy exchange meeting, member of Chengde Artists Association, Secretary General of Xinglong County Artists Association. He Majors in creating paintings on landscape and bird.
*Reference price: 8,000 yuan / square foot*

《大地回春》　138cm×68cm　　"Earth Rejuvenation"

## 刘士毅　*Liu Shiyi*

刘士毅，男，汉族，1939年3月生，河南省尉氏县人，中国书法学会会员，北京宝延轩书画院高级理事。

润笔价格：5,000元/平尺

Liu Shiyi, male, Han nationality, born in March 1939, is from Weishi County, Henan Province. He is the member of Chinese Calligraphy Society, senior director of Beijing Baoyan Xuan Painting and Calligraphy Institute.
*Reference price: 5,000 yuan / square foot*

《空谈误国　实干兴邦》　　138cm×68cm　　"Empty Talk Decays a Nation Whereas Hard-work thrives a nation"

# 钱飞龙 *Qian Feilong*

钱飞龙，男，1968年生，河北省人，中国雾灵书画摄影艺术社社长，兼京东雾灵书画院院长。

润笔价格：10,000元/平尺

Qian Feilong, male, born in 1968 in Hebei Province, is the president of China Wuling painting and photography art club and president of Jingdong Wuling painting and calligraphy academy.

*Reference price: 10,000 yuan / square foot*

《掌上明珠》　68cm×138cm　　"A Pearl in the Palm"

# 孙振山 *Sun Zhenshan*

孙振山，男，笔名松石，中国经济报协会新闻信息部部长，《农民日报》主编，大地书画院副院长兼秘书长。

润笔价格：4,000元/平尺

Sun Zhenshan, male, known as Songshi, is the Minister of the Department of News Information of China Economic News Association, editor of "Farmer's Daily", vice president and secretary-general of Dadi painting and calligraphy academy.
*Reference price: 4,000 yuan / square foot*

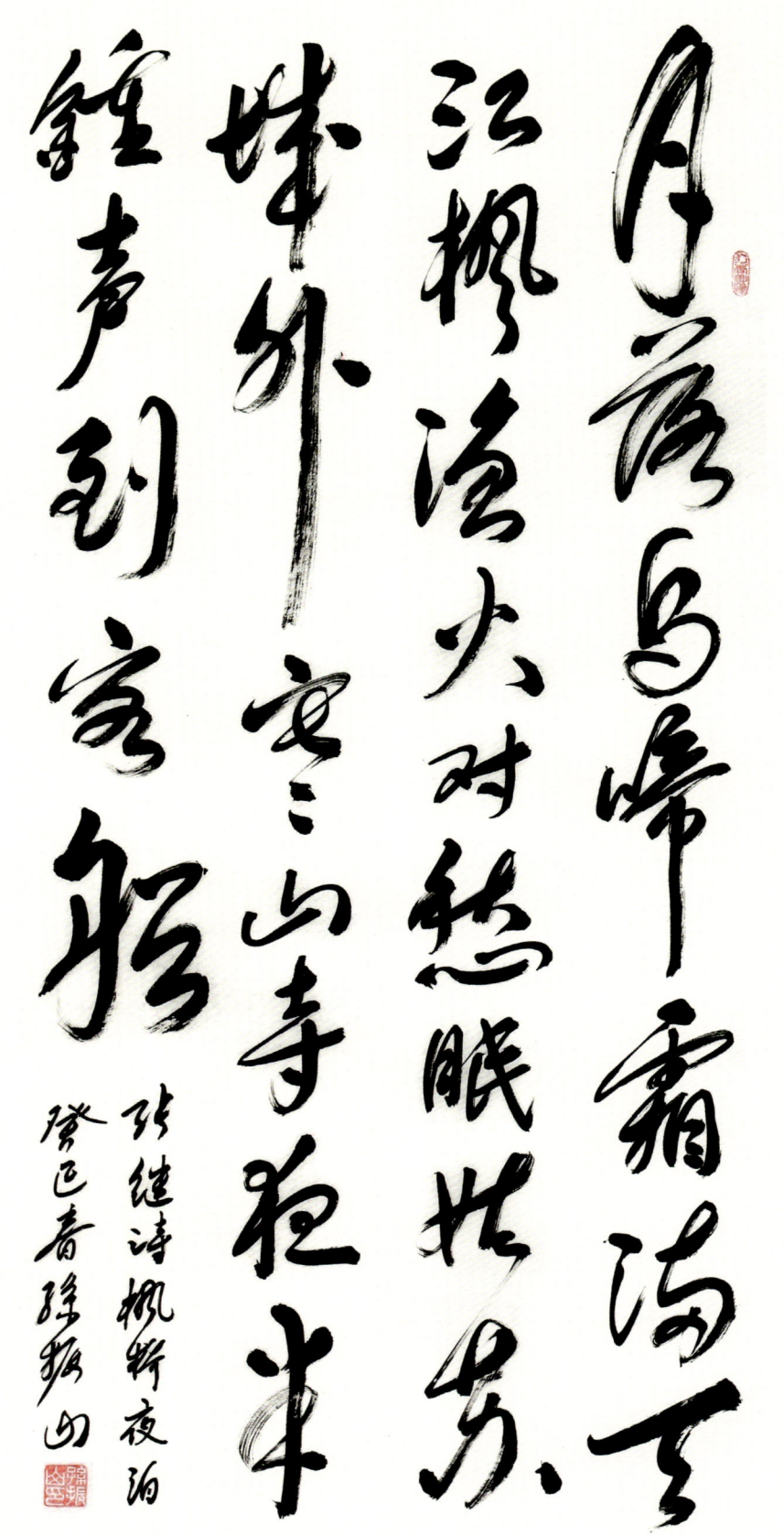

《枫桥夜泊》　　138cm×68cm　　"Stop by Feng Bridge"

# 于春雨　*Yu Chunyu*

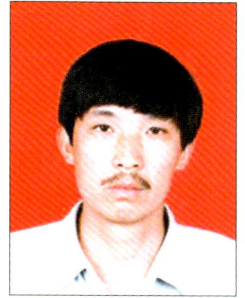

于春雨，1966年7月生，河北省兴隆县人，河北省美术家协会会员，作品多次参加全国省、市美展并获奖。

润笔价格：8,000元/平尺

Yu Chunyu, born in July 1966, is from Xinglong County, Hebei Province. He is the member of Artists Association. His works participated in many provincial and municipal art exhibition and won awards.
*Reference price: 8,000 yuan / square foot*

《秋山云雨图》　　66cm×137cm　　*"Raining in Qiu Mountain"*

## 梁青山 *Liang Qingshan*

梁青山，男，1934年生，黑龙江省文学学会萧军研究会副会长，黑龙江中外书画交流促进会副秘书长，黑龙江省毛泽东书法研究会主席。

润笔价格：4,000元/平尺

Liang Qingshan, male, born in 1934, is the vice president of Xiaojun research Association of Heilongjiang Literature Society, deputy Secretary-General of Heilongjiang Chinese painting and calligraphy Exchange Association, president of Heilongjiang Chairman Mao calligraphy research Institute.
*Reference price: 4,000 yuan / square foot*

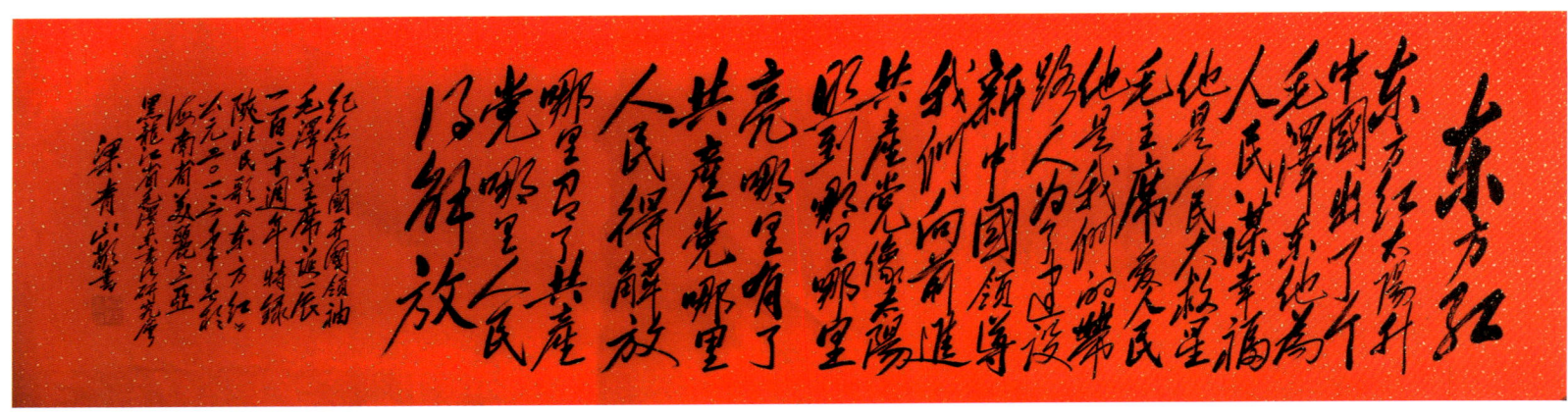

《东方红》　68cm×270cm　" Red East "

# 赵锡武  *Zhao Xiwu*

赵锡武，男，1962年生，河北廊坊人，现任中国书画艺术研究会理事，河北美协会员，北京华夏书画院高级画师。

润笔价格：12,000元/平尺

Zhao Xiwu, male, born in 1962, is from Langfang. He is the director of Chinese Painting and Calligraphy Art Research Association, member of Hebei Province Artists Association, senior artist of Beijing China Painting and Calligraphy Institute.
*Reference price: 12,000 yuan / square foot*

《春运奇似雨》　　138cm×68cm　　"Spring is Like Rain"

## 古建雄  *Gu Jianxiong*

古建雄，男，1962年6月生，广东省吴川市人，吴川市书法家协会会员，湛江市书法家协会会员，中国书画摄影家协会理事，中国书画研究院院士。

润笔价格：4,000元/平尺

Gu Jianxiong, male, born in June 1962, is from Wuchuan City, Guangdong Province. He is the member of Wuchuan City Calligraphers Association, member of Zhanjiang City Calligraphers Association, director of Chinese Calligraphy Photography Association, academician of Chinese Painting and Calligraphy Institute.
*Reference price: 4,000 yuan / square foot*

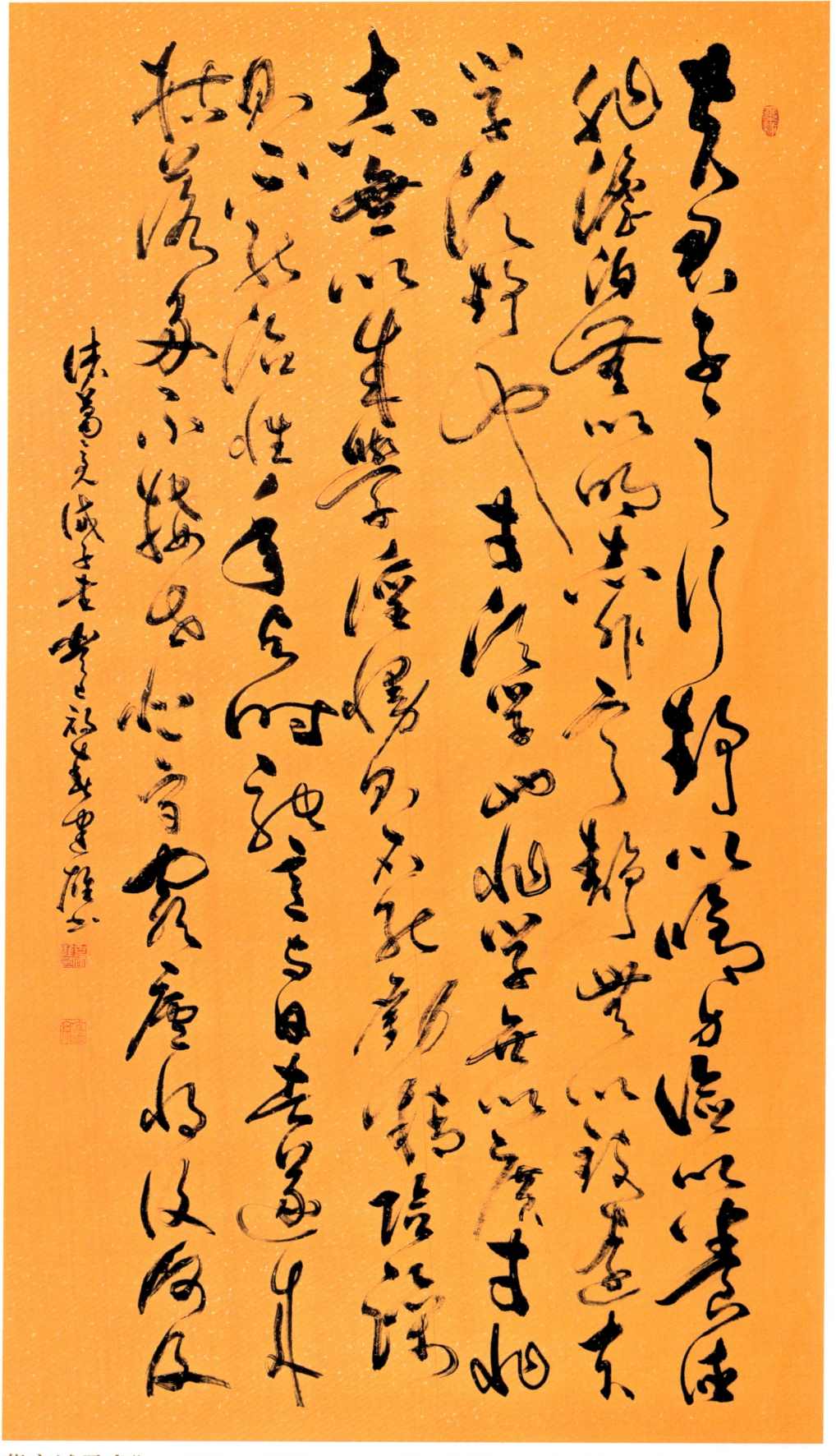

《诸葛亮诫子书》　　180cm×98cm　　"Book Written by Zhuge Liang to Warn Child"

# 方东霖　Fang Donglin

方东霖，男，1968年生，云南腾冲人，中国美术家协会楚雄分会会员，被桂林炎黄书画艺术研究院聘为院士。

润笔价格：8,000元/平尺

Fang Donglin, male, born in 1968, is from Yunnan Tengchong. He is the member of China Artists Association, Chuxiong branch, and was hired as academician of Guilin Yan Huang Art and Painting Academy.
*Reference price: 8,000 yuan / square foot*

《傲骨凝香》　　138cm×68cm　　"Proud Fragrant"

# 王忠民 *Wang Zhongmin*

王忠民，男，开封市宋都书画研究院会员，开封市文联书法家协会会员。

润笔价格：6,000元／平尺

Wang Zhongmin, male, is the member of Kaifeng Song Du Painting and Calligraphy Institute, member of Kaifeng Literary Federation Calligraphers Association.
*Reference price: 6,000 yuan / square foot*

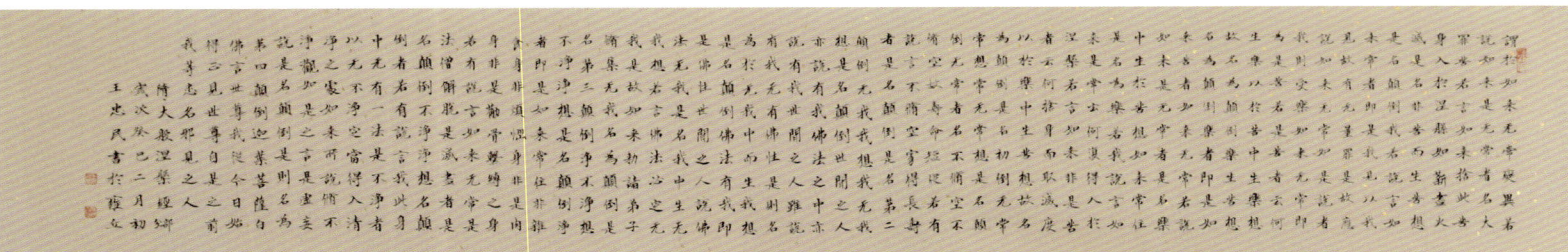

《隋大般涅槃经》　22cm×132cm×2　　*"Sui Lection"*

《隋大般涅槃经》局部　　*Partly "Sui Lection"*

## 谢从荣 *Xie Congrong*

谢从荣，男，笔名从容，1944年生于福建霞浦。现为中国美术家协会会员、编审、高级摄影师、福州林则徐画院副院长、浙江三味书画院名誉院长、南京徐悲鸿画院顾问、北京东方书画院理事等。

润笔价格：8,000元/平尺

Xie Congrong, male, known as Congrong, was Born in 1944 in Fujian Xiapu. He is currently a member, senior editor and senior photographer of the Chinese Artists Association, vice president of Fuzhou Lin Zexu painting academy, honorary president of Zhejiang Sanwei Painting and Calligraphy Institute, adviser Nanjing Xu Beihong Painting Academy, director of Beijing Oriental Painting and Calligraphy Institute.

*Reference price: 8,000 yuan / square foot*

《百雀竿头》　68cm×138cm　*"One Hundred Birds on Rod Head"*

## 蔡喜明 *Cai Ximing*

蔡喜明，男，1965年12月生，现为中国青年书法家协会会员、中国书法研究院艺术委员会委员、汕头市书法家协会会员。

润笔价格：6,000元/平尺

Cai Ximing, male, born in December 1965, is now the member of ChinaYouth Calligraphers Association, commissary of Art Committee of Chinese Calligraphy Institute, member of Shantou City Calligraphers Association.
*Reference price: 6,000 yuan / square foot*

《物华天宝》　　50cm×140cm　　"Treasures"

## 赵志祥　*Zhao Zhixiang*

赵志祥，男，汉族，1943年6月生，河北宁河县人，现为北京美术家协会会员、中国教育电视台艺术顾问、北京九州书画院高级美术师。

润笔价格：6,000元/平尺

Zhao Zhixiang, male, Han nationality, born in June 1943, is from Hebei Ninghe. He is the member of Beijing Artists Association, Consultant of China Education Channel, senior artist of Beijing Jiuzhou Painting and Calligraphy Institute.
*Reference price: 6,000 yuan / square foot*

《骏业宏图》　138cm×68cm　　*"Grand Prospect"*

## 方永柏　*Fang Yongbo*

方永柏，男，笔名方柏，1940年12月生，江苏无锡人，江苏省书法家协会会员，江苏省国画院特聘书法家，中国书画家协会终身理事。

润笔价格：6,000元/平尺

Fang Yongbo, male, known as Fangbai, born in December 1940, is from Jiangsu Wuxi. He is the member of Jiangsu Province Calligraphers Association, distinguished calligrapher of Jiangsu Province calligraphy painting academy, lifelong-director of Chinese Calligraphers assciation.
*Reference price: 6,000 yuan / square foot*

《云鹤游天》　　138cm×48cm　　*"Flying Cranes"*

# 梁冠英　*Liang Guanying*

梁冠英，女，广西人，桂林美协会员，中国书画研究会理事，华夏东方杰书画院理事。

润笔价格：12,000元/平尺

Liang Guanying, female, from Guangxi, is the member of Guilin Artists Association, director of Chinese Painting Research Association, director of China Oriental Jie Painting and Calligraphy Institute.

*Reference price: 12,000 yuan / square foot*

《幽居鸣泉》　69cm×180cm　　*"Living Remotely beside a Spring"*

## 裴敦安　*Pei Dunan*

裴敦安，男，1954年生，中国书法家协会会员，山东省书法家协会会员，国家二级美术师。

润笔价格：4,000元/平尺

Pei Dunan, male, born in 1954, is the member of Chinese Calligraphers Association, member of Shandong Province Calligraphers Association, National B-level artist.

*Reference price: 4,000 yuan / square foot*

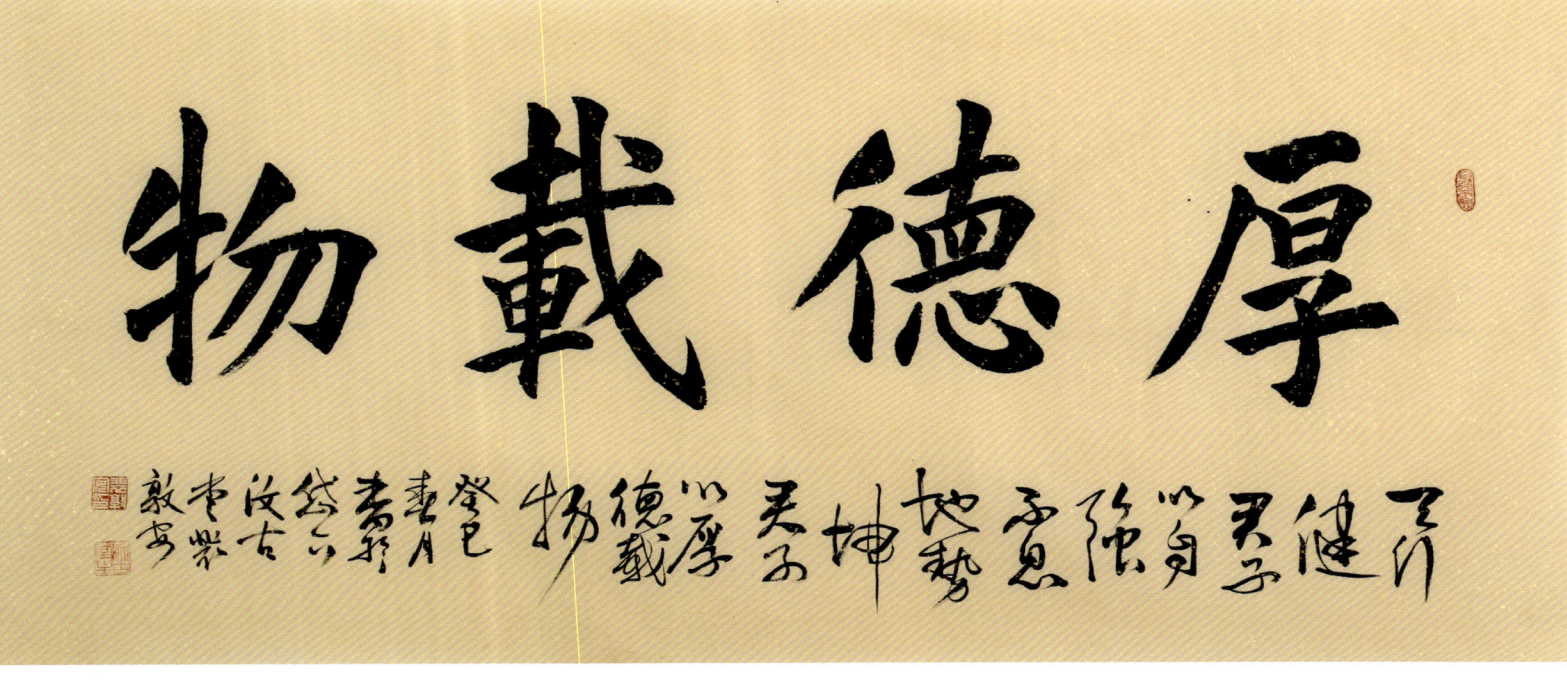

《厚德载物》　　59cm×135cm　　　"Morality Bears Anything"

# 孙其彬  *Sunqi Bin*

孙其彬，男，中国美术家协会会员，中国书画家协会理事，北京长城画院院长，北京国际精典画院客座教授。

润笔价格：6,000元/平尺

Sunqi Bin, male, is the member of Chinese Artists Association, director of the Chinese Calligraphers Association, president of Beijing Great Wall Painting Academy, visiting professor of Beijing International classical painting academy.
*Reference price: 6,000 yuan / square foot*

《春报吉祥》　　138cm×68cm　　"Spring Represents Good Luck"

# 王文其 *Wang Wenqi*

王文其，男，1945年生，无锡人，南京市书法家协会会员，中国书画艺术家协会会员。

润笔价格：5,000元/平尺

Wang Wenqi, male, born in 1945, is from Wuxi. He is the member of Nanjing Calligraphers Association, member of Chinese Painting and Calligraphy Artists Association.

*Reference price: 5,000 yuan / square foot*

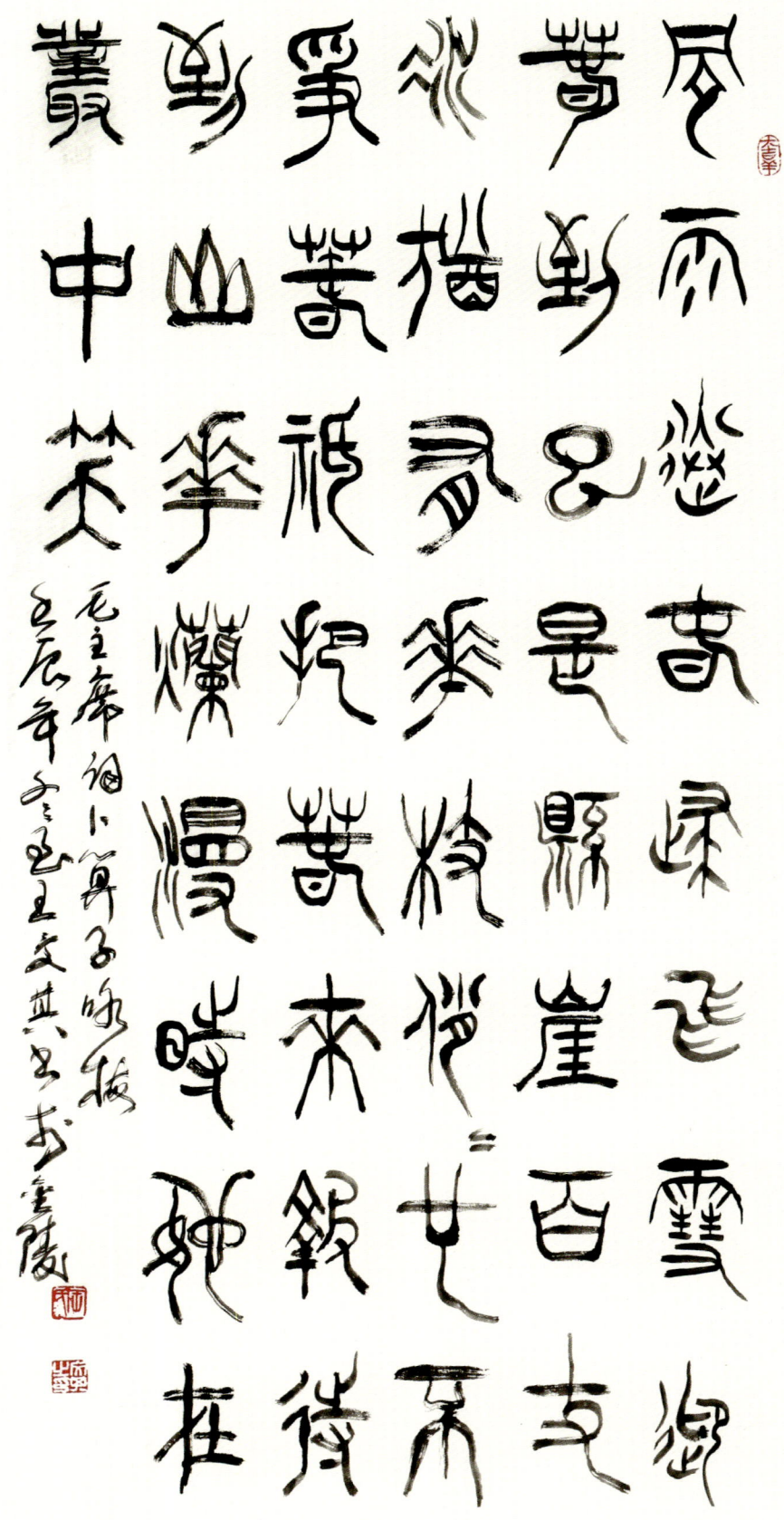

毛泽东《卜算子·咏梅》　138cm×68cm　　*Mao Zedong's "To the Tunes of Pu Suan Zi - plum"*

# 潘星儒  *Pan Xingru*

潘星儒，字墨空，1961年生于河北永清，自幼喜爱书画艺术，近年来多次参加全国省市大展，成绩喜人。被中华全国总工会、中国文联授予"慈善大使"称号。现为河北美协会员，任古燕画院院长、廊坊市公共关系协会副秘书长等职。

润笔价格：12,000元/平尺

Pan Xingru, known as Mokong, born in 1961 in Hebei Yongqing, has been fond of painting and calligraphy since early age. He has participated in national and provincial exhibitions in recent years and got gratifying results. He was awarded the "Goodwill Ambassador" title By ACFTU and China Culture Federation. He is currently a member of the Artist Association of Hebei, the president of Gu Yan Painting Academy, deputy Secretary-General of Langfang City Public Relations Association.

*Reference price: 12,000 yuan / square foot*

《牡丹》　　138cm×68cm　　"Peony"

## 释宏正　*Shi Hongzheng*

释宏正，男，国家著名书法大家，现任嵩山少林寺住院文僧住持、全国残疾人书法绘画评委艺术顾问、北京浩天国展书画院禅学艺术部住持。

润笔价格：4,000元/平尺

Shi Hongzheng, male, famous national calligraphy, is currently the abbot of The Shaolin Monastery, art consultant and rater of National Disability calligraphy and painting Institute, abbot of Zen art department of Beijing Haotian Guozhan painting and calligraphy academy.
*Reference price: 4,000 yuan / square foot*

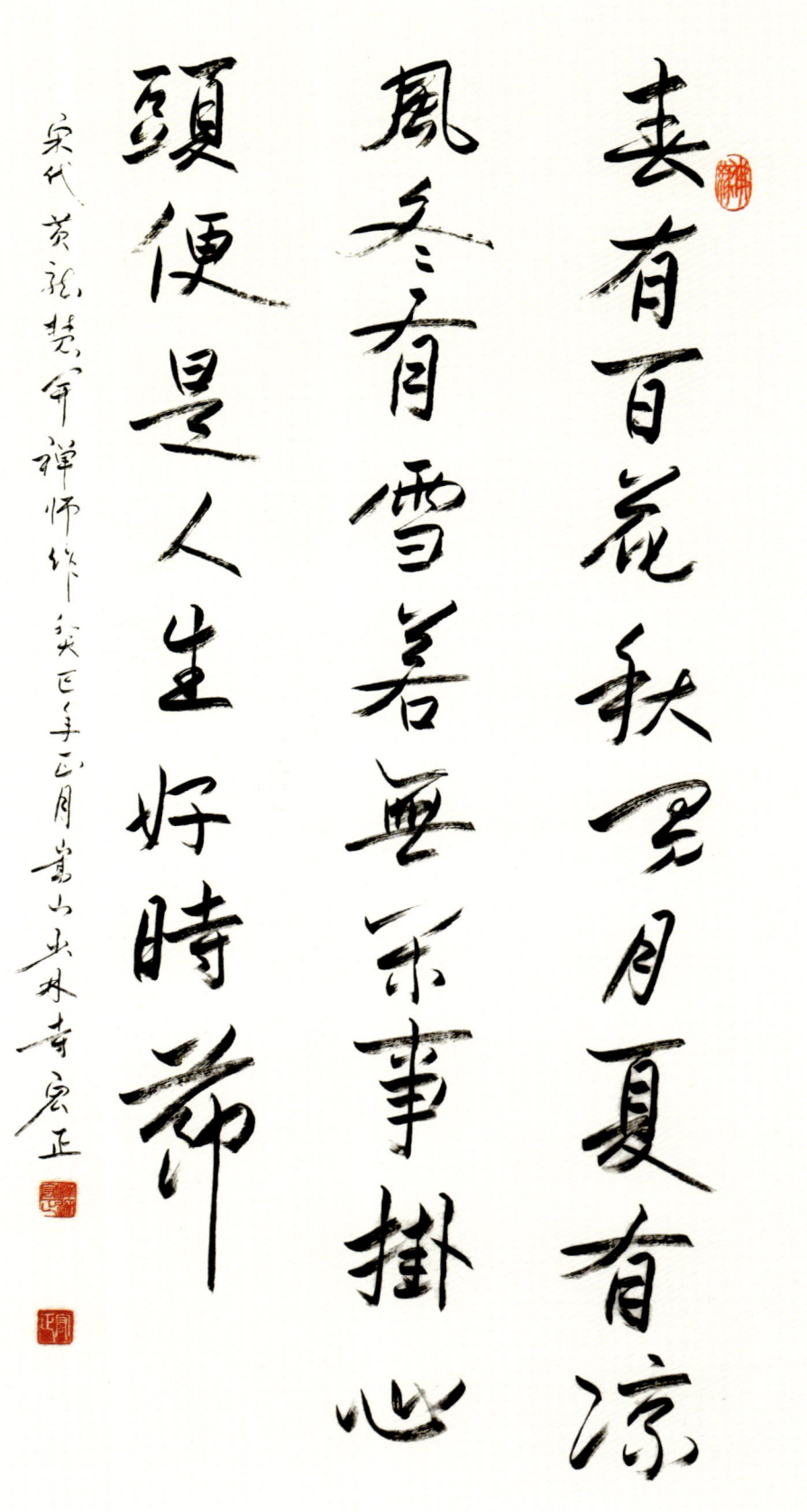

《春有百花秋有月》　138cm×68cm　"Flowers in Spring and Moon in Autumn"

# 高志水  *Gao Zhishui*

高志水，1965年出生于河北廊坊市。香港美术家协会理事，河北省美术家协会会员，中国书画家协会会员，中国书画家研究会会员，中国"五老"书画院院士，中美画院副院长，北京金辉鸿书画院院委，河北省公安文联会员，香港画院画家。师承原廊坊市美协主席、著名画家雷金池先生，主修中国画山水。作品被众多机关、企事业单位和个人收藏。

润笔价格：12,000元/平尺

Gao Zhishui, born in 1965 in Langfang City, is from Hebei. He is now the director of Hong Kong Artists Association, member of Hebei Province Artists Association, member ofChinese Calligraphy Association, member of Chinese painting and calligraphy Research Association, academician of China "five old" fine art academy, vice president of Artist painting academy, commissary of Beijing Jinhui Hong painting committee, member of Hebei Province Public Security Culture Association, painter of the Hong Kong Painting Academy. He is the disciple of Lei Jinchi, the former president of Langfang City Artists Association, majoring in Chinese landscape painting. His works are collected by many organs, enterprises, institutions and individuals.

*Reference price: 12,000 yuan / square foot*

《听水韵与琴》　68cm×68cm　　*"Listen to Water and Zither"*

# 江金明　*Jiang Jinming*

江金明，男，中国书画名家研究会副会长，中国艺术学会常务委员会常务委员。
润笔价格：7,000元/平尺

Jiang Jinming, male, is the vice president of Chinese painting and calligraphy research, executive commissary of the Standing Committee of China Society of Arts.
*Reference price: 7,000 yuan / square foot*

柳宗元《溪居》　　137cm×67cm　　*Liu Zongyuan, "Living beside River"*

# 刘桓麟 *Liu Huanlin*

刘桓麟，原名广来，师竹堂主，出生于1970年，河北廊坊人，自幼喜爱绘画、书法艺术，有扎实的基本功。河北美术家协会会员，中国美术家协会培训中心创作室特聘画师，中国国画家协会会员、北京金辉鸿书画院高级画师。出版有《刘桓麟黑竹画集》。

润笔价格：6,000元/平尺

Liu Huanlin, formerly known as Guanglai and Holder of Shizhu Hall, was born in 1970. He was fond in painting and calligraphy and possesses solid basic skills. Now he is the member of Hebei Fine Arts Association, guest artist of training center creation room of China Artists Association, member of Chinese National Association, senior artist of Beijing Jinhui Hong Calligraphy Institute. He has the publication of "Black Bamboo Painting of Liu Huanlin"

*Reference price: 6,000 yuan / square foot*

《素花多蒙》　68cm×139cm　　*"Pure Flowers"*

# 吕慧泉  *Lv Huiquan*

吕慧泉，1935年生，中国道家书画院院士，京都华夏书画艺术研究院副院长、教授，中国书协会员，中国政协榜书协会会员。

润笔价格：4,000元/平尺

Lv Huiquan, born in 1935, is the director of Chinese Taoist Academy of painting, vice president and professor of Jingdu Huxia Painting and Calligraphy Art Research Institute, member of Chinese Calligraphers Association, member of China Calligraphy Association of CPPCC.
*Reference price: 4,000 yuan / square foot*

《沁园春·雪》　　69cm×138cm　　*"Patio Spring Snow"*

# 肖志敏　*Xiao Zhimin*

肖志敏，字碧霄，号荷香斋主，重庆人，现为新燕都画院常务副院长兼秘书长、重庆美协会员、中国美协高研班特聘画师。

润笔价格：10,000元/平尺

Xiao Zhimin, with pen names as Bixiao and Moderator of Hexiang Building, from Chongqing, is now the vice president and secretary-general of Xinyan Du Painting Academy, member of Chongqing Artists Association, guest artist of the research classes in Chinese Artists Association.

*Reference price: 10,000 yuan / square foot*

《紫藤》　　138cm×68cm　　" Wisteria "

## 谢庆会　*Xie Qinghui*

谢庆会，号淡泊楼主人，1944年7月生，河北省雄县人，现为楹联学会会员、中国楹联学会书法艺术委员会委员、河北书法协会会员、河北楹联学会会员。

润笔价格：4,000元/平尺

Xie Qinghui, known as Holder of Danbo Building, born in July 1944, is from Hebei Province, Xiong. He is now the member of couplets Society, commissary of calligraphy art committee of Chinese couplets Society, member of Hebei Calligraphy Association, member of Hebei couplets Society.
*Reference price: 4,000 yuan / square foot*

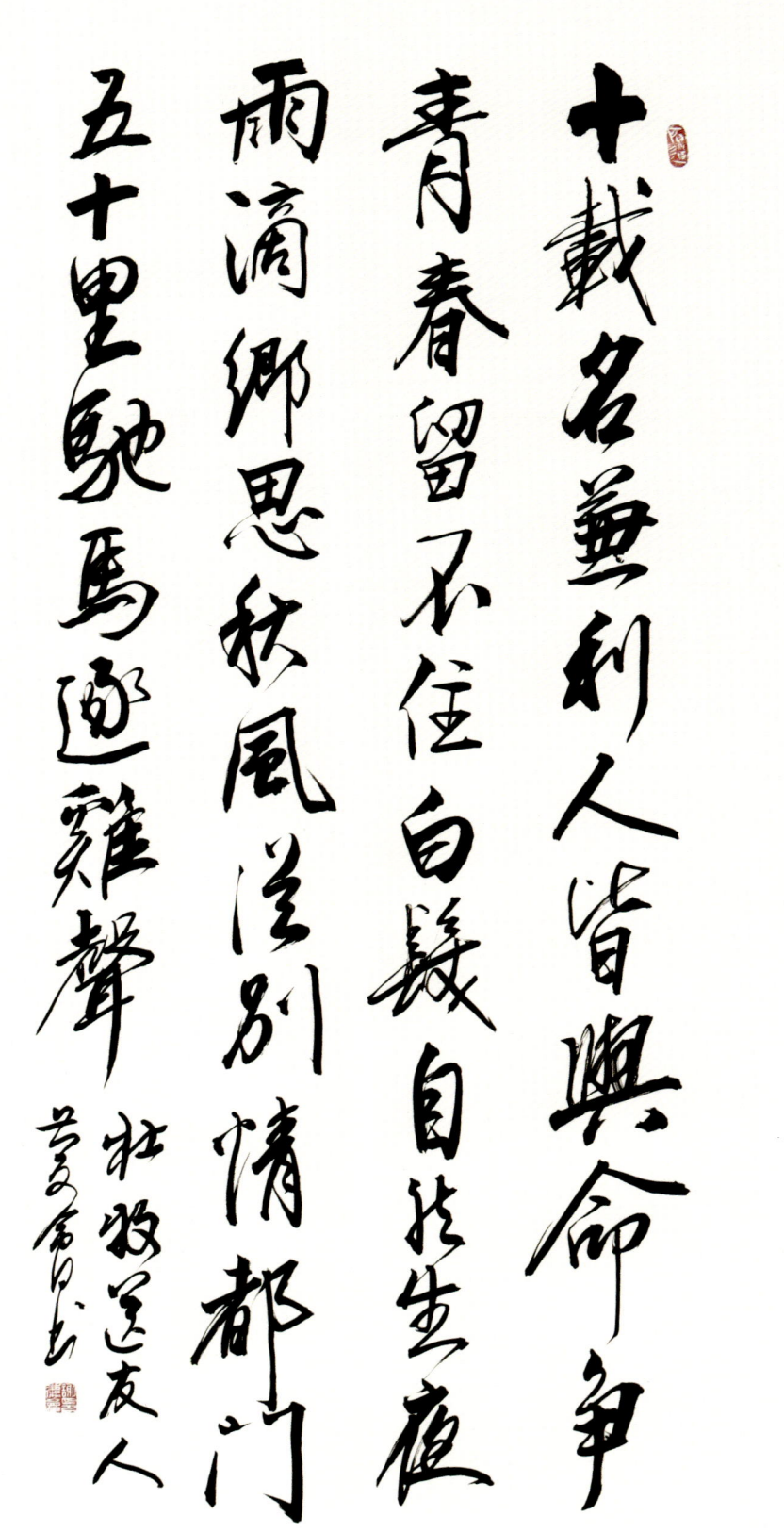

杜牧《送友人》　　138cm×67cm　　*Mu "Farewell to a Friend"*

## 安震　*An Zhen*

安震，又名安文浩，1953年生，中国诗书画研究会研究员，中国书画艺术促进会理事，被中国诗书画艺术促进会中国紫光阁国礼艺术中心授予"国礼艺术家"荣誉称号。

润笔价格：6,000元/平尺

An Zhen, also known as An Wenhao, born in 1953, is a researcher of Chinese Poetry and Calligraphy Research, director of Chinese painting and calligraphy Promotion Association, and was awarded the "national ceremony artist" honorary title by the Ziguangge Guoli Arts Center of China Association of Chinese painting, calligraphy and poem.

*Reference price: 6,000 yuan / square foot*

《荷花》　　138cm×68cm　　"Lotus"

# 张福增　Zhang Fuzeng

张福增，男，字府曾，河北雄县人，1964年生，河北书法家协会会员，中华诗词学会会员。
润笔价格：6,000元/平尺

Zhang Fuzeng, male, known as Fuzeng, from Hebei, was born in 1964. H member of e is now the Hebei Calligraphers Association, member of the Institute of Chinese poetry.
*Reference price: 6,000 yuan / square foot*

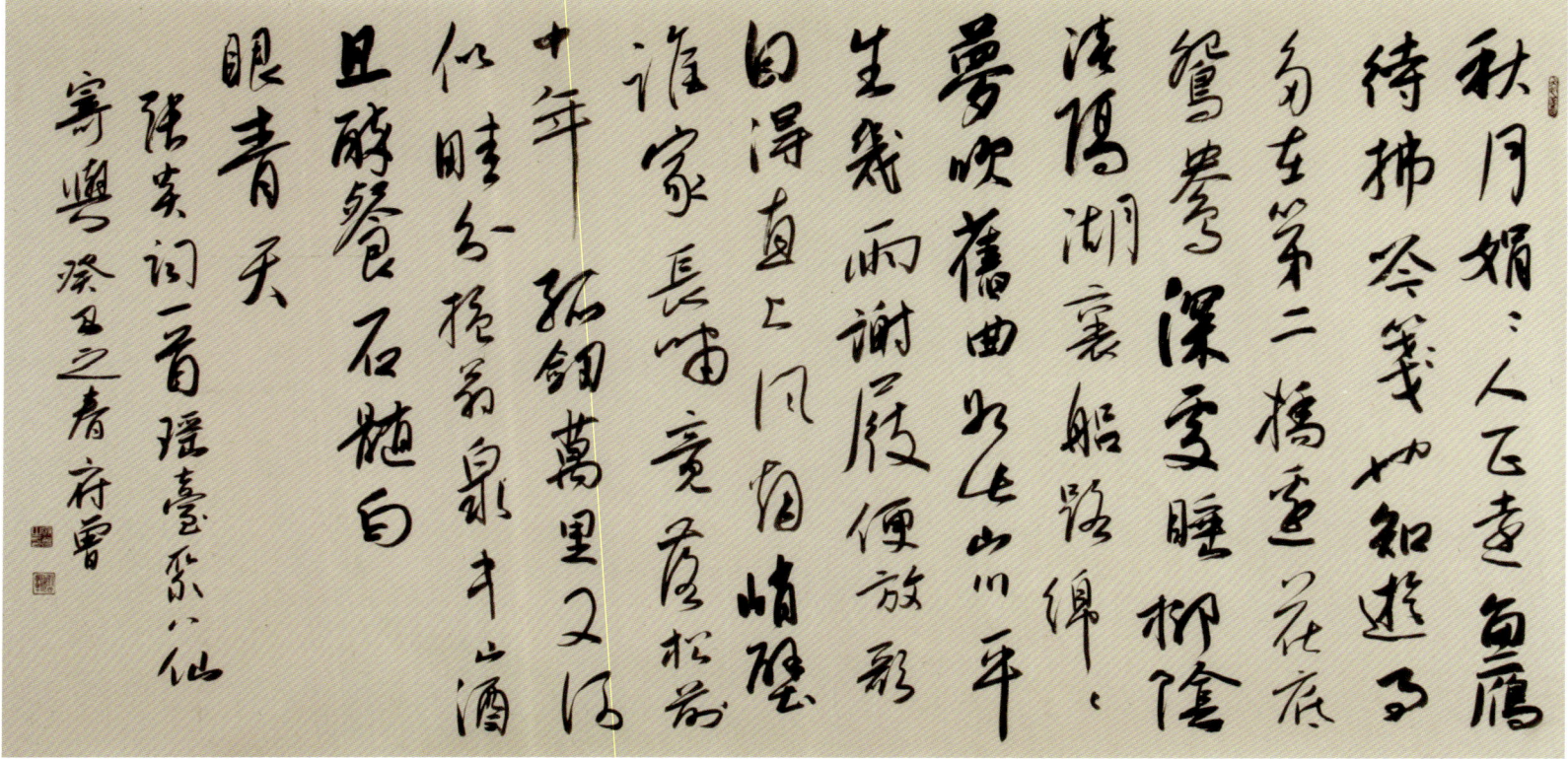

《张炎词一首》　68cm×138cm　　"One Poem of Zhang Yan "

# 任国政　Ren Guozheng

任国政，男，1947年生，河北省黄骅市人，行政干部，作品曾在省市多次获奖，并被全国各地友人收藏。

润笔价格：6,000元/平尺

Ren Guozheng, male, born in 1947, is from Hebei Huanghua. He is an administrative cadre and his works has won numerous awards in the provinces and are kept by many people.

*Reference price: 6,000 yuan / square foot*

《花开富贵》　138cm×69cm　"Blossoming"

# 孙法先  *Sun Faxian*

孙法先，男，汉族，古池墨人，1950年12月生，山东省莘县古云镇东池村人，现为中国书画家协会会员，被聘为台北故宫书画院院长。

润笔价格：5,000元/平尺

Sun Faxian, male, Han nationality, known as Guchi Moren, born in December 1950, is from Dongchi Village, Guyun Town, Xin Country. He is now the member of Chinese Calligraphers Association member, and was appointed as the president of the Painting and Calligraphy Institute of Taipei Palace Museum.
*Reference price: 5,000 yuan / square foot*

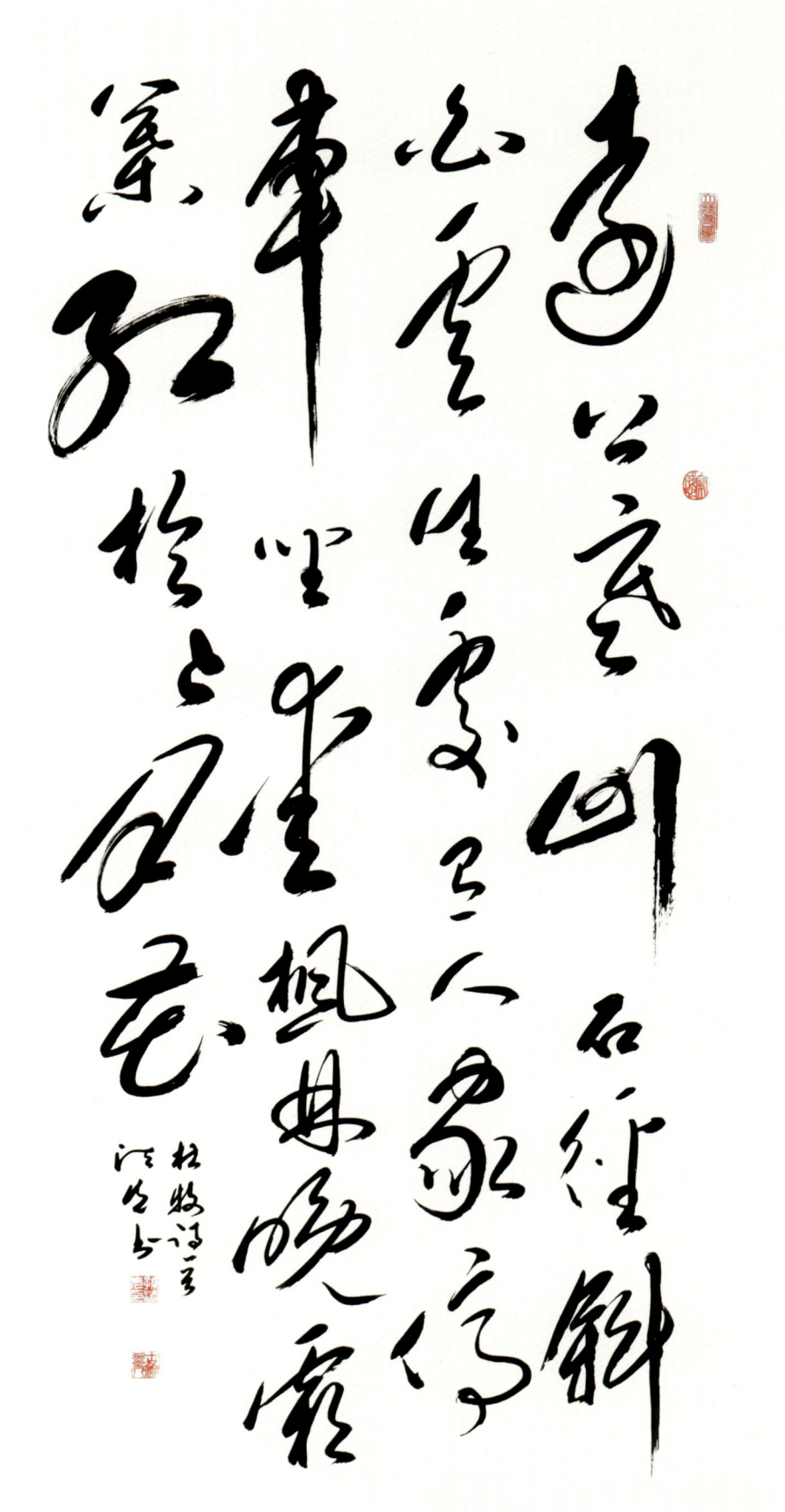

《杜牧诗一首》　　138cm×68cm　　"One Poem of Du Mu"

## 权万通  Quan Wantong

权万通，男，1940年生，河南洛阳人，中国书画艺术家协会会员，中国画家协会会员，北京长城书画院特聘画家，北京长城书画院洛阳分院副院长，洛阳中山书画院艺术顾问。

润笔价格：6,000元/平尺

Quan Wantong, male, born in 1940, is from Henan Luoyang. He is the member of China Painting and Calligraphy Artists Association, member of China Artists Association, distinguished painter of Beijing Great Wall Painting and Calligraphy Institute, vice president of Beijing Great Wall Painting and Calligraphy Institute in Luoyang Branch, art consultant of Zhongshan Calligraphy Institute in Luoyang.

*Reference price: 6,000 yuan / square foot*

《马到成功》　85cm×85cm　　*"Instant Success"*

# 吴晓懿  *Wu Xiaoyi*

吴晓懿，男，1971年生，广东湛江人，广东高校书法学术委员会秘书长，中国书画等级考试广东专家委员会委员。

润笔价格：7,000元/平尺

Wu Xiaoyi, male, born in 1971, is from Guangdong Zhanjiang. He is the Secretary-genaeral of calligraphy Academic Committee in Guangdong University, commissary of Guangdong Expert Committee of Chinese painting and calligraphy grade examination.

*Reference price: 7,000 yuan / square foot*

《半亩方塘一鉴开》　　100cm×50cm　　"Half an Acre Pool is Open"

## 刘萍　　*Liu Ping*

刘萍，北京人，中国美术家协会北京分会会员，北京教育研究会会员，毕业于北京教育学院美术系，进修于中央美院国画研究班。

润笔价格：8,000元/平尺

Liu Ping, from Beijing, is the member of China Artists Association, Beijing Branch, member of Beijing Educational Research Association. She was graduated from the Beijing Institute of Education Department of Fine Arts, studied at the Central Academy of Fine Arts painting seminars.

*Reference price: 8,000 yuan / square foot*

《一堂和气图》　　69cm×138cm　　"Harmonious"

# 袁展泉 *Yuan Zhanquan*

袁展泉，男，1961年生，江西永修人，现为江西省书法家协会会员。
润笔价格：5,000元/平尺

Yuan Zhanquan, male, born in 1961, from Jiangxi Yongxiu, is now member of Jiangxi Calligraphers Association.
*Reference price: 5,000 yuan / square foot*

《千字文》　　35cm×280cm　　"Thousand Characters Passsage"

# 陶光辉　*Tao Guanghui*

陶光辉，字吉卿，1978年生于山东烟台，自幼酷爱书画艺术，1996~2009年在中央警卫局工作，经常得到刘大为、吴悦石、李小可、龙瑞、任惠中等诸先生教诲。

润笔价格：8,000元/平尺

Tao Guanghui, known as Jiqing, was born in 1978 in Yantai, Shandong Province. He was fond of painting from an early age. He worked at the Central Guard Bureau from 1996 to 2009, and learnt from Liu Dawei, Wu Yueshi, Li Xiaoke, Long Rui, and Ren Huizhong, etc.

*Reference price: 8,000 yuan / square foot*

《横空过雨》　138cm×69cm　"Raining in the Sky"

## 刘德生  *Liu Desheng*

刘德生，字近仁，1958年生于北京。书法本科，中国民主建国会会员，中国硬笔书法协会会员，北京书法家协会会员，民建中央画院院士。

润笔价格：4,000元/平尺

Liu Desheng, known as Jinrn, was born in 1958 in Beijing. He possesses a bachelor degree majoring in Calligraphy, and is the member of China Democratic National Construction Association, member of China Pen Calligraphy Association, member of Beijing Calligraphers Association, academician of Central Art Academy of Democratic National Construction Association.
*Reference price: 4,000 yuan / square foot*

《草书》    100cm×50cm    *"Cursive"*

# 王世元  *Wang Shiyuan*

王世元，1944年4月生于北京，自幼酷爱丹青，少时自修，后师承著名山水画家周汝谦和花鸟画家刘冠廷，现为北京美术家协会会员、中国少数民族美术促进会会员、中国三峡画院一级画师、微州书画院副院长、中国工艺美术协会会员。

润笔价格：10,000元/平尺

Wang Shiyuan, born in Beijing in April 1944, with passion for calligraphy from childhood, taught himself in an early age. He is the disciple of Landscape Master Zhou Ruqian and Bird and flower Master Liu Guanting. He is now the member of Beijing Artists Association, member of China minorities Artists promotion Association, an A-level painter of China Sanxia Painting Academy, vice president of Weizhou Painting and Calligraphy Institute, member of China Arts and Crafts Association.

*Reference price: 10,000 yuan / square foot*

《富贵吉祥》　　138cm×68cm　　*" Wealth and Good Fortune "*

## 苏世忠  *Su Shizhong*

苏世忠，男，56岁，内蒙古赤峰人，内蒙古自治区书法家协会会员，赤峰市书法家协会会员，赤峰巴林印社社员。赤峰市委政研室副主任。市政协委员。

润笔价格：5,000元/平尺

Su Shizhong, male, 56 years old, is from Inner Mongolia Chifeng. He is the member of Inner Mongolia Calligraphers Association, member of Chifeng City Calligraphers Association, member of Chifeng Bahrain Seal community, vice president of Chifeng Municipal Committee, commissary of Municipal CPPCC.

*Reference price: 5,000 yuan / square foot*

《驾龙观海》　　69cm×138cm　　"Viewing the Sea on Dragon"

# 后 记

文化产业是市场经济条件下繁荣发展社会主义文化的重要载体，党中央、国务院高度重视发展这一产业，为此采取了一系列政策措施，深入推进文化体制改革，加快推动文化产业发展。2009年7月22日，国务院总理温家宝主持召开国务院常务会议，讨论并原则通过了《文化产业振兴规划》。中国书画是我国传统文化的重要组成部分，是我们的国粹，书画产业是我国文化产业的一个重要方面。在当前国内外的新形势下，书画市场的繁荣对于满足人民群众多样化、多层次、多方面精神文化需求，以及扩大内需、推动经济结构调整，都具有十分重要的意义。

总的来看，目前我国的书画产业呈现出健康向上、蓬勃发展的良好态势，正在成为推动社会主义文化大发展、大繁荣的重要引擎和经济发展新的增长点。但同时要看到，我国书画产业的发展水平还不高、书画市场还不太规范，这不但与人民群众日益增长的精神文化需求、日趋完善的社会主义市场经济体制不相适应，而且与我国对外开放不断扩大的新形势也不和谐。

为了适应当前国内外文化市场的新形势，由东方水墨文化有限公司和中央编译出版社联合出版发行的《中国当代书画名家作品收藏指南》系列丛书与大家见面了。编者本着艺术、学术至上的原则来选择书画家和作品，力争把本丛书打造成书画收藏界的经典之作，给广大的书画研究和创作者以及投资者、收藏者以参考借鉴。同时，我们还会给该书所收录的有实力、有潜力的书画家提供一系列的书画经纪服务。我们坚信，通过不懈地努力，本丛书的问世将会为书画市场科学良性产业链的形成大有裨益。

本书的出版发行得到社会各界的帮助和支持，在此一并感谢。囿于各种条件，书中纰漏及不足之处在所难免，恳请读者不吝赐教，以便我们在以后工作中及时改正。

# Epilogue

Cultural industry is one of the important carriers of the prosperous development of culture in the socialist market economy; consequently, the CPC Central Committee and State Council have attached great importance to its development, and a series of policy measures have been taken to further promote the reform of cultural system so as to accelerate the development of cultural industries. Premier Wen Jiabao chaired a meeting of standing committee of the State Council on July 22nd, 2009, discussed and approved in principle Promotion Plan of Cultural Industry. Chinese painting and calligraphy is a critical constituent part of our traditional culture, and as one of the most esteemed art, calligraphy and painting industry is an important aspect of China's cultural industry. In the current new situation at home and abroad, the prosperous development of painting and calligraphy market plays an indispensible and important role in satisfying the diverse, multi-level and multi-faceted spiritual and cultural needs of the people, which is also critical in expanding the domestic demand and in the readjustment of economic structure as well.

The painting and calligraphy industry in China appears progressive and flourishing as a whole, which is becoming a major engine to promote the vigorous development and prosperity of socialist culture and a new growth point in economic development as well; however, the development level of Chinese painting and calligraphy is not high and its market management lacks standardization, which is not only incompatible with people's growing spiritual and cultural needs and with the gradually perfecting economic system of socialist market, but also inharmonious with the new stage of our expanding opening-up.

In order to adapt to the new situation of the current domestic and international cultural market, Orient Wash-Painting Art Center in collaboration with Central Compilation & Translation Press issued and published Collection Guide to Contemporary Chinese Painting and Calligraphy Works. Our editors, following the principle of "Art and Academic First", chose some great painting and calligraphy works, so that this book would be classic in painting and calligraphy art, which is bound to benefit most art enthusiasts and creators, and serve for the value reference of investors and collectors. Meanwhile, we also provide a series of painting and calligraphy brokerage services for the talented and promising artists. We firmly believe that through our tireless efforts, the advent of this series of books will be of great benefit for the forming of good industrial chain in art market.

We have received a great deal of assistance and support from various circles in the publishing and distribution of the book. However, owing to a variety of limited conditions, there are flaws and inadequacies in the book, and we appreciate your valuable suggestion for further improvement so that we can promptly improve them.

*Yunfei Meng*

图书在版编目（CIP）数据

中国当代书画名家作品收藏指南：第三辑/孟云飞主编．
—北京：中央编译出版社，2013.8
ISBN 978-7-5117-1745-0

Ⅰ.①中…

Ⅱ.①孟…

Ⅲ.①中国画–收藏–中国–现代–指南
②汉字–法书–收藏–中国–现代–指南

Ⅳ.①G894-62

中国版本图书馆CIP数据核字（2013）第186178号

## 中国当代书画名家作品收藏指南（第三辑）

| | |
|---|---|
| 出 版 人 | 刘明清 |
| 出版统筹 | 谭　洁 |
| 责任编辑 | 杜永明 |
| 责任印制 | 尹　珺 |
| 出版发行 | 中央编译出版社 |
| 地　　址 | 北京西城区车公庄大街乙5号鸿儒大厦B座（100044） |
| 电　　话 | （010）52612345（总编室）　（010）52612341（编辑室）<br>（010）66161011（团购部）　（010）52612332（网络销售）<br>（010）66130345（发行部）　（010）66509618（读者服务部） |
| 网　　址 | www.cctpbook.com |
| 经　　销 | 全国新华书店 |
| 印　　刷 | 廊坊市飞腾彩印制版有限公司 |
| 开　　本 | 787毫米×1092毫米　1/8 |
| 字　　数 | 114千字 |
| 印　　张 | 38.5 |
| 版　　次 | 2013年8月第2版第1次印刷 |
| 定　　价 | 380.00元 |

本社常年法律顾问：北京市吴栾赵阎律师事务所律师　　闫军　梁勤
凡有印装质量问题，本社负责调换，电话：（010）66509618